Leaders from the Barracks

Attention Authors

'We Convert Fighters into Writers'. That has been the motto of Manas Publications, since more than four decades. Our message to the world is that India can win the battle, not only by the bullet but also by the pen. There is no dearth of intellectuals in our country, but their knowledge is confined to them only. No sincere effort has been made by any other publisher to channelise their knowledge in national interest. That is why the talent of a large number of intellectuals, remains latent. An author transforms his knowledge, into a manuscript, and it is our job to spread his/her knowledge by converting it into a beautiful book.

For over four decades, Manas has been motivating the intellectuals by publishing their manuscripts and would like to publish your manuscript too. If you or your colleagues have any manuscript, ready for publication or are working on it, kindly contact us with detailed synopsis and the list of contents. We would transform your work, into a valuable publication. If you wish, we can also suggest you, the suitable subjects for writing books, related to your area of expertise. Manas is known for its publishing quality and commitments. We take utmost care in production and give wide publicity to the book, as well as its author, through our national and international distribution network.

Leaders from the Barracks

Brigadier AK Ganguly, SM, VSM (Retd)

Manas Publications
(We Convert Fighters into Writers)
New Delhi-110002 (INDIA)

MANAS PUBLICATIONS
(We Convert Fighters into Writers)

(Publishers, Distributors, Importers & Exporters)
4402/5-A, Ansari Road (Opp. HDFC Bank)
Darya Ganj, New Delhi-110 002 (India)
Off. 23260783, 23265523, Res. 23842660
Fax: 011-23272766
E-mail: manaspublications@gmail.com
manaspublications@yahoo.com
Website: www.manaspublications.in

ISBN 978-81-7049-518-5
₹ 795/-

Designed at Innovative Processors

Printed in India at
R.K. Print Services, Delhi and
Published by Mrs Suman Lata for
Manas Publications, 4402/5-A, Ansari Road (Opp. HDFC Bank),
Darya Ganj, New Delhi-110 002 (INDIA)

"I dedicate this book to my son Trideeb Ganguly. He was the one who had mooted the idea. It was his conviction and faith in the Indian Armed Forces, which inspired me to take this attempt"

Contents

Preface

I found that leadership as practiced in Indian corporate and Indian Armed Forces are unique and different in their own ways. It was on joining the Indian corporate sector and seeing the functioning of the managerial cadre I realized that Armed Forces can offer some good leadership practices which can benefit the corporate leadership concepts and techniques. The variations in application of leadership technique in their respective distinctive domain and environment are very different, however the literary concepts as in the books of management are very similar. I am of the opinion that the corporate considers leadership as practice. In Armed Forces the same leadership is considered as an art of leading the troops. Pragmatically in both Armed Forces and Corporate, it is 'practicing the art of leadership' which I feel is an appropriate way of describing the concept. Thus, it dawned upon me to take an attempt to highlight certain very rudimentary issues of combat leadership which can help the corporate employees at managerial level to develop their leadership instincts.

The endeavor which I am attempting is not to compare the concept and theories of management as applicable in Armed Forces and the corporate or amplify the jargons and technique of management. What I am endeavoring is, to highlight the uniqueness of leadership and management of human resources in Armed Forces (in context of Armed Forces I am referring to Indian Armed Forces in general and Indian Army in particular).

The military leadership technique of handling human resource is unique in certain ways; the factors which have direct bearing on the uniqueness are - uncertainty and fluidity in combat situations, constantly changing functional environment and frequent changes in human behavior under combat stress. It is a challenge to leadership under such circumstances and especially when it comes to synchronizing human resources prerequisites and initiatives with the tasks or the objectives. The organizational ethos, values, traditions and time tested operational procedures are the additional aspects, which are predominant in bringing uniqueness in the approach towards the concept of leadership. Handling of trained and disciplined combat forces gives exclusivity and a separate distinctiveness. Leadership in Armed Forces needs multi-dimensional and well-integrated sets of competencies to excel in a battlefield environment or in the conflict situations. The evolving and changing character of conflict have made the role of military leaders even more complex and demanding. In peace time and no conflict environment, the leadership is equally demanding, it is during this period that the military is forged as instrument of national power.

The views expressed in the chapters are totally personal. Chapters have been designed not in a text book fashion or in a sequence of importance. It is basically an attempt to highlight the experience of leadership behaviors' both during command of troops, during conduct of actions in combat and non-combat environment. Leadership attributes in command of troops have some relevance in outside world concept of leadership and I believe industries and corporate can derive some benefits in developing their leadership cadres. The topics are general in nature and will be useful to both people in uniform and those who are outside the uniform. The complete endeavor is totally my personal views and observations, in no way any of the issues discussed is official or part of any official manual or literature of any Armed Forces. The observations are based on personal experiences of human behaviors under varied combat situation or otherwise, during my career in the Indian Army and after superannuation from forces during my innings in the Indian Corporate Sector.

Brig. AK Ganguly

Introduction

> *"Human-being is a complex entity and in combat situation its complexity increases mani–fold. It is the testing ground of leaders to carry the force willingly into the realm of uncertainty and risk."*
>
> —Sun Tzu

The leadership is a bestowed appointment of officers in Indian Armed Forces, who are responsible to lead the troops into battle. The process of leadership development is progressive during the course of career progression and through experience of leading troops/units under combat/non-combat environment. Leadership and management are also based on time tested operating procedures, values handed over through generations, ethos, customs, traditions and military grooming into the system. There are defined principles and procedures which make practice of leadership and management confined to military dictums and this gives the uniqueness. Individual personality and proclivity are important proponents which have direct bearing on the style of leadership, it is for this very reason we find variety in military leadership styles each having certain specific attributes which are distinctive and personality specific. The environment of risk, uncertainty and frequently transforming/changing military wherewithal and concepts of warfare, also makes leadership a challenge in Armed Forces.

In the world outside uniform, leadership and management is taken as practice, whereas in Forces it is considered as an art. The art of leadership have number of variants depending on the veracity of the situation, use of 'out of book' techniques and venturing into the known/unknown domain of human behavior under stress and strain of uncertainty and risk. There cannot be any leadership matrix in such an environment. The techniques will be very fluid and the factor of consistency in approach will keep varying based on the task and the prevailing military/combat environment. Thus leadership is more prone towards individualistic handling with no fixed cut-out models. The complexity increases as the troops especially in the Indian context are region and caste based, which in itself gives the Indian Army its inherent uniqueness of diversity of a larger order, an interesting point to note is that the composition of forces is heterogeneous by nature in units and formations but homogeneous structure is maintained in the professional front. The homogeneity factor is achieved through 'FARZ' - the duty towards the unit and 'IZZAT' - the honour of serving the forces and the nation. Therefore, leadership and management have more variables, making practicing of leadership an art which is definably challenging.

By no means are the leadership and human resources management in Armed Forces is not based on scientific methods or on the principle of management techniques as being taught in B schools. It also does not mean that Armed Forces management techniques are in extreme variance to the books of management or might not be that well defined. The concepts are workable in their unique way in the forces. The difference from the corporate sector is only in the 'military ways of addressing' the concept of leadership and management which is different.

Today's Armed Forces are highly specialized, technologically advanced and yet manpower intensive. Human resource management is an important aspect of command; it involves maintaining a level of operational integrity beyond reproach, addressing frequently changing warfare philosophy, continuous up-gradation of technologies and functioning under varied conditions of geo-political and socio-economic environmental challenges.

In the Indian Armed Forces, spectrum of management is spread over a very large area in terms of geographical sphere, fighting and support echelons and heterogeneity of composition of troops. It is not possible to have qualified and trained managers at each level of the spectrum, therefore cadets have to be developed into a manager/officer. Management of human resources in Armed Forces is thus a process of 'operational orientation' followed by 'operational application'. The importance of management of human resources as taught in management school and the corporate cannot be totally relegated, the Armed Forces understands its importance and it is to this end most of the officers who plan to join corporate after a career in forces are given an opportunity to undertake courses in management institutions across the country before hanging their uniform. The basics of corporate management, techniques and methods thus have its own importance as being practiced and applicability depending on the business parameters and dynamics specific to the industry.

It is the uniqueness of Armed Forces system of management which every officer is expected to embark upon, for being a successful leader. A successful leaders as per military norms is exceptional, General Douglas McArthur of US Army very aptly described it as *"A true leader have the confidence to stand alone, the courage to make tough decisions, and the compassion to listen to the needs of others. He does not set out to be a leader, but becomes one by the equality of his actions and the integrity of his intent"* and he further reiterated *"Duty, Honour, Country. Those three hallowed will be"* and this is what is expected from any military leader.

I would be dwelling on the basic proponent of expected leadership qualities and try to bring out certain essentials and traits which I have observed during my career and command of troops both in combat and non-combat environments. Certain unique leadership qualities of military commanders at various levels of command, which left lasting impression and made me improve my command techniques, I have incorporated these in various chapters.

That 'something more' in a military officer will be my focus and answer to the often asked question by my corporate colleagues 'what makes a solider put his life at risk'. I am a firm believer of the fact that there has to be an X Factor in any leader i.e. something that makes for star quality to lead or carry the team into combat. The endeavour therefore, is not to teach about leadership. What I have experienced during my innings outside uniform I can say with conviction that leadership practice in corporate or other agencies is very sound and based on well researched/tried out techniques. Forces have lot to learn from the corporate world. The only variation which I found in the Indian Corporate context is in terms of approach to leadership and leadership support.

What I have tried to pen down are certain ways, means, methods, ingenuity and uniqueness of command used by officers at various levels when leading troops in combat/battle and resultant leadership success or failures thereof. I am of the view that a leader must have an identifiable self entity with ability to lead and demand obedience and that is what matters the most, this makes the men under command to follow the leader. Armed Forces uniqueness in leadership techniques and certain leadership ethos is what I want to project, which I am sure will make some difference to both the men in uniform and people outside uniform.

> *"Leadership is seeing the possibilities in a situation while others are seeing the limitations".*
>
> —John C. Maxwell

1 Grooming of a Leader

"If a drop of water falls in a lake there is no identity, but if it falls on a leaf of lotus it shines like a pearl."

—Kautalya

When young men/women don's the military uniform, their very first day begins with establishing their identity with that of the institution which they have joined, living up to its ethos, respecting the values and traditions, living up to its standards and maintaining its honour. It is these very military fundamentals which are the bedrock of foundation of grooming or moulding in the Indian Armed Forces. Field Marshal Chetwode's aphorism *"The safety, honour and welfare of your country comes first, always and every time. The honour, welfare and comfort of the men you command come next. Your own ease, comfort and safety comes last, always and every time"* is the norm of life in Indian Armed Forces and basic grooming dictum.

'Leaders are not born but they are nurtured' this expression is very much a synonym to the concept of leadership development in Armed Forces. The potential leaders are made to develop all those qualities of leadership required in leading the troops. The complete process is progressive in nature and developed through the stages of service training, service exposure and combat experience. It is the transition through the phases of military service and exposure to varied conditions during these phases which help in developing the leadership traits, what matters is the individual's discernment in building the personality to meet the leadership requisites. Other aspects which have equal importance in building the leadership qualities during grooming is awareness of the environment, ethos, values, traditions and the retrospective study of military history/campaigns and biographies of great military leaders.

Leadership qualities and traits are not tangible at all times and during personality projection by an officer, these get displayed when handling situation and is reaction dependent. Leaders can be extrovert, introvert, combination of both or thespian persona, each or all will be having traits in varying degree. The kind of the leadership which is to be developed will depend on the personal traits, trade/field requirement, type of unit/work platform, type of work environment, exposures and professional skills of superiors/team and the organizational principles. The quality in leadership being a human factor is never a constant factor and is very subjective thus grooming must cater for coverage of all areas of leadership application, this is to give a level of consistency and facilitate in deciding what is actually expected from the leader. Grooming of a leader is thus based on the introspective adaption of military tradition, values and ethos. In Indian Armed Forces quotient of leadership development depends on three factors, firstly Field Marshal Chetwode's maxim, secondly 'follow me' i.e. leading by example and from the front and lastly, but most important is 'FARZ' the duty towards the Unit/Regiment and 'IZZAT' the honour of the Forces and the Nation. Based on these primary factors the basic grooming of the leader is planned. The challenges which are predominantly unique are:

- The cadet is selected as potential leader not specialized or trained in human resource (HR) management.
- Moulding comprises of making a perfect 'leaders' who should be a professional, a manager, an administrator and a role model.

- Have to work in isolation and take independent decision. When leading the battle team or a group should be leading from the front.
- The spread of the areas of the operations are large both in geographical terms and dynamically in functional ambit of task and objectives. Astute supervision is always not possible. Leader has to be responsible for own action and must be answerable to the men under command.
- Get identified as an officer/leader, capable of acting without orders and/or in anticipation of orders and/ or without waiting for approval, yet always within the overall intention of the superior commander.

The grooming of leaders commences from the day a cadet joins the training academy. The initial phase is to build up the physical and mental robustness with the aim to make them sustain prolonged stress and strain in uncertain conditions and under adverse situations. This is followed by skill acquisition of a combatant, awareness of military ethos and values. The day cadets' passes out from the academy they are appointed as commissioned officers and thus 'the leader' is born. In the non-commission grade, the leader is selected from the rank and file, the process is combination of competency and merit. The authority is bestowed by assigning rank and appointment, in true sense from here onwards starts the development process and grooming of an officer into true leader. In the present state, the officer is raw, not fully trained and skills are inferior from the men whom they are going to command.

It is this initial team of individuals who are mentors and who are going to groom their worthy leaders. There is this age old concept in Forces, where one is made to live with the men (troops) to understand the environment, establish identity, build the sense of belongingness, get recognized and accepted in the unit/team and be an effective member of the team. The development of traits, personalities and quality of leadership are progressive incorporation alongside professional enhancement and during this process each member of the team contributes. The first and foremost aspect in grooming a leader is conditioning of the individual in the unit, once this aspect is achieved then development process commences. The initial grooming is based on its basic ethos of 'service to the nation' in other words it is the maxim 'service before self' which is a recognized factor and one has to live up to the expected expectations.

The aim of grooming, therefore, is to bring stability and consistency to the human variables, which have direct implication on behavioural spectrum of a leader. At the initial stage of grooming three aspects are stressed upon - professionalism, bonding with the unit and interactive relationship with the sub unit i.e. the team - these are basic groundwork which makes the leader relate with the team and the unit.

To be recognized as leaders is the most difficult aspect of grooming. My first Company Commander on my joining the unit, said, "*Within the existing requirement of job/task and goal each person involved in the said task possesses some leadership qualities and traits in varying degree and proportion. When one among them who is capable to reason out and make such group to mobilize towards the set goal is said to be the true leader, rests are followers. But you are a nominated leader by virtue of your rank and appointment, so you have to first prove yourself and establish your acceptance as their leader*". To establish the authority, the leaders first have to understand the team's dynamics, capabilities and then work towards getting the same compatibility and match the level of performance/expertise. Therefore, in order to gain acceptance with/within the team three C's are a must in a leader, these are credibility, courage and competence. To prove, the leaders have to establish the professional competence, awareness and physical and mental robustness standards above the level of the group/team or at the same level.

In the processes of grooming, the subordinates have an important role to play in making of the leader; this is an accepted norm in all the armies. Certain values in the personality development which are expected out of the leaders are inculcated through the group exchange and participation. Endowment by each member of the group irrespective of the position plays an important role in grooming of the officer.

Before initiation into the realm of command of body of troops, the officer is made to spend the initial days in barracks with the men. It is here that leader's appropriate grooming starts. In Indian Army as the troops are from varied regions, cast, language and customs, it is a tradition in some of the units to make newly commissioned officers to stay with troops in barracks. The basic logic is that the leaders must understand their unit and the men before they start commanding them into the battle. On being commissioned to my unit (Infantry Battalion) had to spend an eight month stint in the men barracks before moving to officers' billet. Some of the very catchy phrases which I now recollect was often quoted by my subordinate mentors at various levels during the barrack days and had substantial impact during the grooming phase. I am sharing some of them with my understanding of their relevance:

- ***"Hard work is not an end, but a means. It is not a product, but a process. Like other valuables, it has its counterfeits which one must guard i.e., temptation to give up".*** Resolve in leaders is 'must have' character, the work output and consequent accomplishments are dependent on this character. Resolve is relative in nature and is situation dependent. It is proportionate to the capability of the leader and the team, to meet the desired goal. Doggedness towards the given task and determination are two important elements which is expected by the team from the leader and builds resolve to achieve the set target or goal. Persistency makes persuasion worthwhile when resolve exists.
- ***"Don't count every hour in the day, make every hour count for the day"*** A rudimentary quote often repeated. Time is

not a one sided issue, it is applicable to all the participating elements of the task, the leader and the team. Time management is the foremost thing which a leader needs to master during grooming phase, initially to start with the time slot matrix method and subsequently on Time - Work analysis method. Time being a critical element of operations, is given lot of importance during grooming phase. VALUE OF TIME and VALUE FOR TIME during grooming predominantly takes a special place, punctuality is considered as part of professional ethics. Who can better understand the value of time than a soldier, where every minute of his existence counts in a combat? Use of time to advantage is another important requisite of a successful leader; this aspect is therefore given lot of importance during this stage. Management of time during any given situation depends on taking advantage of the windows of opportunity which the situation presents. All actions are time governed and one has to master the time management to control the situations. Time also have negativity which one has to guard - too less and too much can be costly. Rightful use of time is what actually matters.

- ***"Have guts to accept"***. Decisiveness and courage of conviction are two primary traits which the subordinates look for in their leaders, in the initial interaction and participation in group actions these aspects are very much commented upon. It is the ability to make up your mind to make decision and accept full responsibility for that decision is what leadership is about. The ability of decision making and taking accountability of the outcome is watched very intimately. During the grooming stage this aspect is given credence, the aim is to makes the leader improve the ability of making judgment and appreciate the situation before arriving at a decision.
- ***"Always be what you are and trust yourself"*** A very common phrase which the sergeant major keeps repeating, he might not be aware of the wisdom of these words or

its valued application in leadership qualities. Being your true self is the most vital of all military virtues and this is possible only when a leader has self confidence, is able to garner courage for righteousness, catalyst by nature to make a difference and identify weakness to take corrective measures or work a way out through difficult situations.

- ***"No one can play your role better than you. You will be the best when 'you are you' ".*** Originality is one aspect which gets relegated when 'matrix' concept based leadership get predominance. The human factor of a leader cannot be replicated or controlled, behavioural matrix of each individual have variables and are not identical. Any pseudoisom in behavioural matrix will make the reliability factor of the leader questionable to the men under command. Originality with ingenuity is most desirable; this increases the acceptability of the leader and gives impetus to self belief.

Another important link between the officers and their development as leaders are senior officers. Mentoring by seniors is essential during the initial phase of grooming and it is a command responsibility of the senior to ensure. Company and Battalion/Regimental Commanders are the first mentors of a newly commissioned officer, some of the leadership traits and qualities of these mentors become part of one's personality. Some of my seniors sermons which I want to share which I feel deserves mention in this chapter are:

- Striving for excellence and self introspection are continuous process. Standards have to be set, reviewed, upgraded and new ones incorporated to break the patterns and give impetus to achievement. Stagnation in standards leads to complacency. In grooming, the said aspect must be stressed upon and made into a habit. These recompenses in making the leader mature and develop the self belief. *"One has to be passionate with his profession and the position bestowed upon"*, often emphasized by the seniors during the grooming days. Basically, the idea behind this is to make a youngster aware of the value of professionalism and excellence.

- ***"You are not beaten until you admit it."*** The leader's drive, determination, will power, foresight and prudency are ingredients of success. To achieve, is an art of employing these ingredients of success. In taking the best out of the team, two important facets which the young leaders must inculcate as a part of their character, these are honesty of purpose and persistency. To 'take on the enemy' what actually matters, is to get into this attitude and there are certain attributes which are must i.e. positivity in the approach of the leader, leader's commitment and personal involvement, courage, the survival instinct and firmness. To build the survival instinct leader has to develop his/her self belief and this in turn will build the spirit of resoluteness in execution of orders. The desire to achieve is one of the attributes in the leader which motivates the team and is an important feature in confidence building. During the initial grooming days it is ensured that the young leaders are in maximum contact with the troops and are made to break the inhibition factors. Development of the spirit of participation and involvement is an essential part of grooming and this facilitates in providing impetus to the team psychosis 'to achieve'. The determination of 'making up to the standards' must gets factored in the officer character during the grooming, this builds the self belief.
- ***"The life is like a football play field, see the goal post strike hard at it and score, resume the play after each goal with a kick off from centre line till the game runs."*** To maintain consistency with achievements, momentums have to be ensured by series of successes. Follow up events are never similar, therefore, all starts are afresh. Past laurels are booster to new approach; too much dependency on

'the past' brings stagnation in process of planning. Ability of forecasting and planning of contingencies are two important aspect of leadership which has direct bearing on planning of each fresh task.

- ***"Unit is a value based organization. Value is build over ages. Each individual of the unit must exemplify the established values by his deeds and back it up with total commitment."*** Each unit since its raising imbibes certain time tested working models and ethos of functioning which is unique to its existence, honour and standing .These are acquired after front line experiences and sacrifices in the combat zone. Such values are the guiding principles and foundation for grooming the officers into the organization. Duty (FARZ) and pride (IZZAT) are the two components of character which makes a leader committed to the values of the organization. The most important aspect is the feelings and belongingness for the organization.
- ***"Casualness and non-committal of purpose leads to complacency. Complacency gives impetus to mistakes."*** This, young officers often hear from their seniors. This is a caution at each stepping stone for an officer during his/her career progression. What is important is to create habits for efficiency, thus what matters is proficiency, in case there are proficiency gaps in the initial stage of the career between the team and the leader the level of efficiency will get adversely affected, to make this into a apt work culture, it is necessary to professionally develop the leader. Another aspect is seriousness in approach; leaders must be serious and professional when at work. Complacency is contagious by its very nature; a little bit of it in the leader will affect the performance level of the team.
- ***"To err is human, but also doing it very frequently is not human, 'first' mistake should be the last, for the 'next', you might not be there,"*** and ***"Genuine and unintentional mistakes are acceptable but ignorance is never."*** These are

very common phrases in Armed Forces which youngster have to encounter many a times during their grooming period. In variable working environment, prudency in approach and decision making is based on minimum mistake frequency. What one has to guard are two syndromes, firstly, factors of no risk and secondly, no work, no mistake and these are detrimental to the output. Capabilities of retrospection of a mistake and derivation of lesson learnt to minimize the scope of repetition are two imperatives which are part of moulding an officer. It is said that with experience the mistakes become negligible, the more one ventures more one will learn through mistakes. Here I would like to quote Dr APJ Abdul Kalam, (11th President of India) *"Your best teacher is your last mistake"*.

- ***"Authority of leader exists only when the officers demonstrates it by better competency."*** Young officer is expected to hone onto the selected trade and master it in the process of initial grooming; even though during his/her career varied disciplines are addressed to bring in higher grade of competency as the job spectrum width keeps enlarging. It is often said that a true leader is more competent than the troops under command. Competency must not be restrictive or be centric specific; it should be spread over the complete spectrum of the task to cover the working field of the team/group. Alongside the degree of competency are personal and professional ethics which must be looked into during the grooming phase. As per the military ethos, professionalism in all sphere of command is expected out of a leader thus competency is not restricted to a particular field but the complete spectrum of command of troops.
- ***"Honesty and courage of conviction are two very important pillars; it establishes the leaders among the men."*** Transparency is an important factor which has direct and proportionate influence to any working relationship. The aim, purpose and intention of the leader get reflected in

the degree of honesty and courage of conviction. Honesty is understood as being true and correct, whereas courage of conviction is calling 'spade a spade' and righteousness. The values and ethos of the organization in the grooming days bear a strong influence on honesty and courage of conviction. Sincerity and commitment are very closely linked to this very aspect of foundation and character building.

- ***"In order to win, your desire for victory should be greater than your fear of failure".*** An important aspect of grooming is to inculcate a spirit of shrewdness and will to win. What matters is determination to succeed, taking calculated risk and exploiting opportunity. The degree and balances of these proponents determine the ratio of success as against failure? Fear of failure is always detrimental to success, but some element of fear has to be there in a person to succeed otherwise there will be no good sense in undertaking risk and striving for success. *"You have to risk going too far to discover just how far you can really go"* and *"a pessimist sees the difficulty in every opportunity; an optimist sees the opportunity in every difficulty"* these two idioms are very frequently quoted by the seniors and rightly so. Hope and risk are the two factors which balances the leaders' attitude towards accomplishment.
- ***"Reason why."*** Leaders have to be trained in arriving at a right decision. During my grooming days I was made to make check lists of all activities, these were scrutinized in detail by my company commander, the list is to have very absurd remarks and number of question marks, at times I used is to feel disgusted. The idea was to make you realize that without reasoning and that too sequential reasoning, it is not possible to come to conclusive decision. Reasoning clarifies doubts and provides answer to indecisions. The purpose must always be clear and this is possible when leader is able to get the answer of why? The aspect of

taking feedback and retrospection is made into a habit by exposures to briefing and debriefing. I remember my company commander who after training exercises use to make me to conduct the debriefing, feedbacks were always great learning experience.

- ***"Better than banging your head on the wall, try to climb it, if you can't then go around it."*** Use of time has two outcomes, too long or too short of either or both leads to inconsistency and indecisiveness. Taking too much time is not being patience and taking attempts after attempts is not persistence. As time is an important element, it has to be judiciously exploited and no window of opportunities can be left going especially in a combat situation. Basically, what matters is the sense of observation, analysis, appreciating the situation, this helps in taking decision at the right point of time and seeking alternatives to come to a successful conclusion of the assigned task. The grooming of the leaders in utilization of maximum potential of time and resources is ensured by giving independent tasks with proper briefings followed by detailed debriefing after the task.

By quoting the phrases/idioms usually said in the barracks I tried to bring out the issues which are stressed upon during the basic grooming days of an officer, there might be many variants and many more but ultimately the contents mostly hovers around the crux issues of :

- Being mentally and physically strong.
- Control over emotions and self discipline.
- Wise management of time.
- Drive to fulfill the objectives.
- Seek to grow stronger and more competent.
- Take challenges as opportunity.
- Problem solving and setting example.
- Being realistic and honest.
- Responsibility and accountability.

Trait Development

The trait oriented approach of development of leaders is restricted to the understanding of each aspect of latent trait in an individual during moulding and grooming phase. The applicability of each trait within the realm of the functional environment is dependent on inter-se relation between the team, task and the leader; here professional accreditation and acceptability of leadership are simultaneous. Certain identified and specific traits which are required in the initial stages of command of troops are emphasized and developed, these have direct bearing on the character building of the young leaders:

- *Adaptability* – Flexibility based on ground situation and demand of the mission.
- *Compatibility* – Participative leadership, inter personal relationship and understanding the dynamics of the team/group.
- *Courage of conviction* – Down to earth approach, taking rightful stand, truthful reporting and having moral fiber of high order.
- *Dexterity* – Speed in decision making.
- *Endurance* – Physical and psychological robustness.
- *Mental mobility* – Ability to transit through various situations and associated stress. Capable of taking independent decision.
- *Resoluteness* – Deftness in accomplishment of task, sense of purpose and steadfastness.
- *Tenacity* – Persistence and perseverance in pursuance.

In actual, traits which are highlighted above are the crux of grooming and will be handy during command of troops especially in combat environment. Leadership traits have been well defined in the manuals of management. Certain specific traits and attributes which one must possess in Armed Forces - we call it as OLQ i.e. officer like qualities, which is expected out of a leader. I still remember a Brigade Commander commenting during a lecture on leadership *"from A to Z as much qualities, you can phrase out of a single alphabet - are the traits which you have to develop to lead your men, for example Z .... Zealous, Zest, Zippy......Zing are also traits, each human-being have some iota of every variety of traits any English Alphabet can throw out".*

There is no set course to develop the traits; it is either inborn or imbibed from the environment. Giving a value to a trait and its development is dependent on identification of the environmental requirement, its importance, and legitimacy of application and/or objective to be achieved. Self introspection and self development are the process which a leader must adopt to develop traits and associate the same with the personality requirements. It is an obligation on the part of the leaders to develop the traits which they require to manage the men under command. During grooming usually I was quoted "To get the best out of your men, they must feel that you are their real leader and must know that they can depend upon you", this can best be achieved when a leader knows what is required out of him.

Personality gets determined through compulsive attributes of traits of an individual and this is environment dependent. One must guard against forced personality; it gives a false illusion and is misleading. The 'Trait suitability' of the personality must be in consonance and with matching frequency of functional attributes of the group/teams operability.

Soft Skill Development

Another important factor in grooming in Armed Forces is to develop the soft skill, an important ingredient of personality development. In the management schools, there are contrary views with respect to development of soft skill, one school is of the opinion that soft skill cannot be developed but is acquired by experience and is inborn quality; on the other hand the other schools have opined that these can be taught and developed. "Soft skills" is seen as the behavioural ways in which people go about their occupational tasks. Leadership has its own set of occupational skills, such as the ability to synthesise data; the clarity of vision, to make timely decisions; the capability to define priorities and goals; and ability to rally resources and the manpower to meet the desired goal. Leader has to develop the aptitude to understand the ground realities and the organisational perspective of the assigned task. On the behavioural side, the leader should understand the team and its dynamics and posses the ability to marshal the team's potential to meet the assigned target. Making the team to follow the leader into the combat, soft skills have a great say and is considered as one of the predominant factor of leadership behaviour. The development of soft skill has been made an integral part of curriculum of the training academy and on posting to unit it is part of moulding and grooming.

The soft skills are categorized in two parts interpersonal and intrapersonal skills which require fine tuning during the grooming days. *Interpersonal skills* are predominantly developed during induction and environmental adaption phase which is part of the initial years of training. The manners, etiquettes and community behaviours is given importance and as a drill interposed in the code of conduct of the officer. *Intrapersonal skills* gets developed during the course of exposure during the command of troops, a young leader is made to establish a social and functional relationship and in doing so the commanders ensure that regimental ethos and the institutional values are not compromised. The applicability of intrapersonal skills is for development of social personality, makeover from civilian life style/behavior to military way of life and development of self confidence to meet the requirement of the functional/operational tasks. In both, the interpersonal and intrapersonal skills the group/team has a big role to play in grooming the leader.

The important facet of leadership is ability to visualize and carry out pragmatic retrospection and these two are important elements of grooming of the leader, it develops the ability to analyze, ability to fine tune the behavioural parameters and take corrective measures. Visualization and retrospection is considered a necessity as it applicability is predominantly important in decision making, planning and execution of the plans. This is best achieved when independent responsibility is entrusted to the young officer and he/she is made answerable and accountable. Introspection on the other hand helps in developing the self belief and provides impetus to the confidence level. Visualization, retrospection and introspection thus are very important aspect of soft skill in Armed Forces; this is built partially during the induction phase of the officer after passing out. In actuality this phase begins when the officer faces the reality of leading men into combat.

In personality, traits and style, changes do take place during the grooming phase when the cadet/newly commissioned officer experiments with the leadership qualities. The question is how much is the change and quantum which a leader can accommodate to meet the requirement of the task, dynamics of the operational requirement and interpersonal and/or intrapersonal skills. To give an authenticity to the behaviour and interaction potential the aspect of adaptability and change must be instilled in the officer's way of thinking as these reinforces the soft skills. One of my General Officer during his visit to young officer training, in his talk made a very apt remark towards self improvement and change, he said, *"Change is an important ingredient, if there are no changes tediousness will set in and quickly adapting to change is also necessary otherwise you will be left out of the race. Changes pay handsome dividends but are difficult to make and adaption is held back if the will to accept change is not there. 'CHANGE' is fixed by mindset and fixations. Officers must get into the habit to think and accept change and to make the change; first you must change before expecting your command to accept the change".* Actually, adaptability to change and intention of making a change, both are relevant in development of interpersonal and intrapersonal soft skills. A good leader will have to adapt his/her personality to the demand of functional environment and social considerations, thus matching soft skills have to be developed and here the ethos and the values of the organization count.

Character Building

Character building is an important aspect of grooming; every human-being is born with certain characters which are personal. The characters get governed by the environment, society and functional relationship and some get induced in the process of vocation. In human-beings some characters are latent and some are open, each individual will be having varying degree of intensity of both types of characters. Grooming in Armed Forces develops both open and latent characters including acquired and in-born ones. Character building basic aim is, to build the confidence level in the leaders to handle situations under adverse conditions. There are certain latent characters which get reflected during the conduct of leadership, as these have direct influence on the group and the assigned task especially under combat environment. There are certain other characters which are open by nature and which makes the group react favourably as these are visible. The productive characters which one must have are:

- *Authenticity:* Authenticity encompasses the quality of genuineness, transparency and dependability in conduct and handling of affairs as a leader, the most important aspect of this quality is to develop confidence and faith among the team members. It gives legitimacy to command, respect and men without hesitation following orders. This quality must be part of the repertoire of characters of the leader as it is essential in command of troops. This particular character is developed through sustained exposure to independent decision making and handling of operations.

- *Conscientiousness:* Preciseness and being organized is an important facet of a leader's character. This character gets factored during the later year when the leader is involved in the strategic and operational planning process. Start is made during the grooming days of the officer, being meticulous in approach does pay, as it imbibes the quality of being careful and concerned.
- *Extroversion:* Character of companionability is a perquisite in a leader, this helps in bondage and acceptability with the team. Socially confident leaders brings openness in the behaviour of the team, builds comradeship and team spirit. This character provides greater understanding among the group and the leader. *Best of human behaviour is when there is equal balance of extroversion and social acceptability, one who can maintain the required proportion will be a better manager and a leader* - team and leader equation becomes more tenable when both display equal openness. Being in contact with the men and understanding them, makes the leaders astute in optimal utilization of the human resources. Rightful employment of the team is possible only when the leader is aware of each member's operability and associated capabilities. *Potential of any person is not only suitability, but also identifying capability with the demand of assignment/ task and sustainability of performance* - this assessment of men under command is possible only when the leader has knowledge of the men and is socially adaptable with the team.
- *Audacity:* I consider this as a character, even though it is a part of personality of a leader. It comes from within and creates a separate identifiable personality. Being audacious is part of human nature and is situation dependent. This character encompasses combination of aptitude of resilience, boldness, courage and risk taking ability. Audacity in a personality is built and developed through repetitive exposure to challenges. In making of leaders, audacity is an integral part of training and grooming.

- *Creativity:* Every individual is creative by nature and this characteristic is the prime source which creates an identity of personality and is idiosyncratic by nature. During grooming of leaders, scope of enhancing this character assumes importance. Basic aim is to imbibe the qualities of ingenuity, innovativeness, resourcefulness, initiative and compatibility/adaptability with the group. Creativity attributes helps in developing the aforesaid soft skills in leaders. Creativity is to be considered as one of the important factor in independent decision making ability.
- *Exploratory Aptitude*: Human mind is always inquisitive, it wants to explore new avenues, experiment with ideas, try out ways and search for answers. Every human-being is an explorer. This character in human-being develops the aptitude of investigation, examination and probing. Leadership personality must have a good quotient of this character to carry the team through the tasks. It also helps in increasing the proficiency of the leader and forming the habit of going into details. This aptitude also makes a person alert and proportionately develops the capability to take calculated risk. Every leader must imbibe this character at the very first stage of command of a body of troops. Another important aspect of this character is that it makes the leader adventurous, bold and daring.
- *Originality:* Individuality and novelty are aspect of originality, which brings freshness to ideas, concepts, strategies and thought. Blind following without reasoning will never make a good leader; the team will always be hesitant in accepting such leader or trust his/her authority. Originality in approach and thought is a big motivational factor in accepting challenges. It would be apt to quote Liddell Hart from his book "Thoughts on War 1944" *"Originality is the most vital of all military virtues, as two thousand years of wars attest. In peace it is at a discount, for it causes the disturbance of comfortable ways without producing dividends, as in civil life. But in war originality*

bears a higher premium than it can ever do in a civil profession. For its application can overthrow a nation and change the course of history in the proverbial twinkling of an eye".

- *Responsibility:* This is one of the basic of leadership character; leaders are responsible for all their actions. It is on his/her displayed responsibility that the team generates their confidence on the leader, at no point of time he/she can pass the buck or the blame to anyone else. Just to highlight the importance of responsibility I would like to quote Field Marshal Montgomery, *"Regimental spirit and tradition can be a powerful factor in making for good morale, and must be constantly encouraged. But in the crisis of battle, a man will not derive encouragement from the glories of the past; he will seek aid from his leaders and comrades of the present. Most men do not fight well because their ancestors fought well at the battle of Minden two centuries ago, but because their particular platoon or unit have good leaders, is well disciplined, and have developed the feelings of comradeship and self-respect among all ranks and on all levels. It is not devotion to some ancient regimental story that steels men in the crisis; it is devotion to the comrades who are with them and the leaders who are in front of them. Therefore, it is essential that in our training we select men who possess within them the potentialities of leadership and, secondly, we develop those potentialities. This is best accomplished by giving the leaders responsibility. The mere fact of responsibility will increase the leaders' powers of decision and make him confident of his ability to handle any crisis".*

Self-Belief

In order to lead and take independent decision, leaders must have self-belief. This is a value which one must possess to influence and be accepted by the team as a leader. Factors which contribute to this value are confidence in self, professional competence, confidence in the team, faith of the superior and pragmatic perceiving of ground realities depending on the tasks or objectives. Self-belief is one of the factors which directly influence the aptitude of fortitude, resilience, vigour and determination in the leaders. Self-belief of the leaders creates roller coaster effect on the team, the consequential effects are:

- Self-belief sets momentum in addressing and accomplishment of task, it acts as booster for the team to achieve the set target. Self-belief is also factored by positive attitude, optimistic outlook and awareness of one's strength and weaknesses.
- Positivity of self-belief depends on the degree of confidence and determination. Positivity of self-belief creates an environment of vigour, positive vibes and is an effective motivational factor for the team.
- During the moulding/grooming stage, self-belief is developed by making an officer pass through tough schedule of training and physical hardening to improve the mental and physical robustness and psychological conditioning with the aim to bear prolonged stress and strain. Leader and team endurance compatibility must be ensured and achieved.
- Practice in participative leadership and indulgence in activities of the men under command brings bondage with the team and improves interpersonal relationship, this builds trust and faith and develops solidarity and/or *espirit-de-corps*.
- Enrichment/enlargement of professional competence gives boost to the self-belief. This builds the confidence of the team on the leader.
- What is important for a leader is to successfully synergies the team, task and objective, this is best achieved when the leader's self-belief is at the optimal point and the level of confidence is well established with the team and within each member of the team.

- Another aspect which is associated with self-belief is the level of maturity; this adds to its value and is a guard against over or under estimation/assessment.
- Over confidence in self-belief is detrimental and adversely affect the working relationship with men under command, this is especially so when the level of maturity is not commensurate with the task at hand.
- Capability of self and the team, being pragmatic and realistic in assessing the capability builds self-belief. This helps in decision making and planning.
- Self-belief creates vibrancy in character; it gives confidence to the leader to lead from the front and set personal example.

Dynamism

Dynamism in a leader not only gives identity and recognition, it generates vibrancy, enhances the personality and develops relationship with the team/group. The aspect of stability in leadership qualities are governed by the level of dynamism which one possesses, thus during the grooming it is emphasized that *"leader with vigour and enthusiasm must also be prudent"*. The factors which govern the dynamisms are psychological build up, degree of tolerance level, flexibility, sense of judgment, speed of response, commitment, honesty of purpose, passion and courage of conviction. Dynamism in itself will not have an effect if the leader is not able to link with the team or create an environment of commitment.

I am of the view that *"Potential of any person is not only suitability, but also possessing capability in respect to demand of the assignment/task and sustainability of the capability/performance during the course of the said assignment"*, therefore, the consistency factor of dynamism has to be maintained by the leader to influence the team and this is possible when the leader is dynamic in his outlook and approach. Catalyst leadership and drive are said to be the prime mover in dynamism, it decides the participation quotients of leader and the team. When passion gets generated within the dynamism of the officer and the team, then the spirit to achieve and succeed is said to be optimum.

Dynamic leaders must have and be groomed to posses the qualities which bring purpose in the functioning and towards achieving the desired target/objective. Dynamism in a leader is thus an important impetus which generates positive vibes in the team, some of the aspects which support dynamism are:

- Self-control when under stress and when facing odds/ reversals.
- Transparency and openness in dealings and detesting from ulterior motives - Gives confidence and builds faith and trust.
- Courage of conviction, being candid, prudent and having integrity of high order - Builds strong bondage between the leader and team.
- Morale fiber - Gives impetus to honesty of purpose.
- Looking beyond the immediate goal, catering for contingencies and visualizing the future course of action - Gives the direction and purpose to the team and builds confidence.
- Leading the team from the front and building the team spirit - Builds the self-belief and gives confidence to both the leader and the team.
- Believe in professionalism and the team capability - Builds working relation, commitment and team spirit.
- Attitude to sacrifice self interest and giving predominance first to the organizational interest - Makes the leader a better manager of human resources. Improves the trust and faith on the leader, interpersonal relationship and image of the leader.
- Empathy towards human concern and feelings - Builds compassion in approach.

- Competency level in par with the group/team and growth of professional knowledge - Qualifies a leader as judicious and astute.
- Responsibility and accountability - Increased dependency of the team on the leader.
- Passion in approach and commitments - Boosts the drive to succeed.
- Supportiveness - Builds the team proficiency and faith.
- Delegation and freedom of action – Builds an environment of equal participation within the team and sharing of responsibility.
- Set personal example - Makes the team to participate with commitment.

Moulding and grooming, therefore, is the first essential step towards making of a leader. The acceptance of the leader within the functional environment of an organization is not achieved until the organizational values and ethos are not comprehended and followed by the leader. In Armed Forces we call making leaders as grooming and in industry it is termed as orientation. However, there is a lot of difference between grooming and orientation? In my view, grooming deals with transformation and adjustment of a leader and is an art and orientation involves making the leader adjust with the environment and is considered as a practice.

In this chapter, I have tried to bring out the issues which young leaders in the organization must dwell upon. What is important in the initial stages is establishing the leader's identity with the working environment and creating a sense of belongingness towards the organization. For this, no training schedule or routine classes are required, this can be best managed through on job training and interactive workshops within the organization. But, whatever may be the technique, what is important is planning the induction of the leader.

The grooming is possible only when there is continuity and consistency. The organizations have to be more focused and try to hold on to the trained and experienced leaders as they are the one who develop the subordinates as leaders. Another aspect which is important at this stage is developing the spirit of affinity and sense of belonging. Following measures will help in developing the affinity of the leader with the organization and which I feel are important imperatives and must be considered:

- Confidence building by providing professional stability.
- Ensure continuity in the leadership development.
- Extending scope of the leadership practice to all levels and stages.
- Provide opportunity to improve professional competency.
- Increase scope of decentralization and freedom of action.

There is a requirement of having defined system in vogue to address the issue of grooming and training of leaders and it is the only way which can make better the "practice of leadership".

> *"The first act of leadership is coming to grips with yourself, who you are, where you are, and what is of value to you, and shaping yourself by acts of conscious will into what you want to become".*
>
> —Fenwick W. English

2 Leadership Approach

"The real test of leadership is not if your men will follow you in success, but if they will stick by you in defeat and in hardship".

—Field Marshal Slim

The topic of leadership have been covered in manuals, books, pamphlets and articles, it is a beaten topic having varied school of thoughts and recommended courses dealing with nature and approach to leadership. In this chapter, what I intend to cover is shaping of a leader, development of leadership qualities and leadership in face of odds or reversals or demanding situations, which are the actual testing grounds of the leaders and qualities which make men to follow. In one of the informal discussion with one of the Vice President HR in a corporate get-together, his comments on leadership I felt was rather matter-of-fact and candid, he said *"what we are taught in the management school, its applicability is round about 20 percent; rest is one's own ingenuity"*. In Armed Forces, leadership is an honour bestowed by appointment and considered as a duty and responsibility towards the men under command and the unit. Therefore, the emphasis is on values, ethos and the notion of service before self. The development of the leaders is a process which is a quotient of exposure - experience - growth

- combatant service, in other words, leadership development is not sacrosanct to any defined/set parameters but is dependent on the variable situations and exposure to command of troops. This has made me to always consider leadership a constituent of combination of style and outlook of approach towards the functional demands. Lots depend on the assessment of the ground realities as obtainable in the given situation, proficiencies to accomplish the task and the traits potential of leading the team.

Methods and techniques laid in manuals are only for reference. Leaders who know and understand the ground, the situation and have confidence on their men will evolve their own approach which might be different from the manuals but proves to be the most appropriate and effective in any given environment. The applicability of leadership traits and qualities will depends on the outlook, each individual will be having different attitude towards the approach and style with number of variables in existing personalities and characters. This is where the concept of adaptability to different style and approach of leadership technique comes into the forefront. Human or natural and acquired traits are dependent on physical, functional and organizational environmental factors, variables spectrum of human behaviour have a direct influence on the leadership techniques, therefore, all leaders cannot use the same formula. Due to this, in the present prevailing work environment both in Forces and Corporate sectors the 'Ideal leader' concept has been taken over by 'Good leader' concept.

The approach and style of leadership in Armed Forces have always been purpose based and factors which influence this type of leadership is the operational environment, team/group vis-à-vis leaders' dynamics, invariable factor of discipline and service before self. Moreover, the Armed Forces regulations and acts have the factor of 'obedience to order' as an integral part of soldiers' discipline, this makes the leadership more challenging as accountability of action is exclusively that of the leader as question of participation/non participation of the men does not arise. When it comes to decision making, irrespective of outcome the leader is solely responsible by appointment.

Leadership by appointment does not make leaders. It is when the person is put through realm of situations repeatedly that traits get developed. But in order to be accepted as a leader, officers have to exemplify each trait which is expected of a leader and acknowledged by the team or group. This becomes more predominant in constantly changing circumstances in a combat zone, where the leaders have to adapt to various changing roles. Thus leaders' adjustments to the changing environments, the changing group/team dynamics depending on the prevailing situations and the ultimate goal/interest therefore becomes demanding. The fixation to set pattern of traits/approach by a leaders in such an environment will be a non starter and detrimental.

Leadership is basically a sound balance of competence, self-belief and responsibility, credibility and commitment and trust and faith ratio. Therefore, at any point there cannot be two similar leaders with the same style and approach. Keyword of leadership thus is 'ingenuity' with 'originality'.

What really makes the men follow the leaders/manager? One can list all the traits, but what matters the most is the style/approach to leadership. Each of the traits is interrelated and coexisting within the preview of each other's definition in the style and approach. I am of the opinion that there are certain basic traits which are common to style and approach to leadership which are 'must have' and these are courage, conviction, communication skills, credibility and compassion; I call them 5 Charlie's. These basic traits develop other valuable traits and bring changes to the approach towards leadership.

The style of leadership is the most discussed and have number of interpretations and variants. I have never advocated adaption of a style as I felt that tendencies creep in, to duplicate someone else. What is more important than having a fixed style is the approach towards leadership. Approach gives the scope to adjust the leadership qualities in meeting the prevailing operational situation and have very positive impact during conduct of operations/command of troops. A leader has to have the vision and conviction to achieve, his approach and style must have power to inspire and provide impetus to the energy of the team/group to get things done.

The effective approach and the style is personality dependent and choice of the leader parse, certain approach and styles which have proved effective in varied operational situations are listed. These are my perceptions and I firmly believe that any leader cannot survive by adapting any one of the approach or style exclusively, there has to be variety and variations.

Styles of Leadership

There are no definite and fixed styles of leadership. When human behaviour itself is not constant and is influenced by the environmental factors, thus adapting to a style and maintaining the consistency of performance within the preview of the said style, it is not possible. In fact, leaders should know and understand the basic facets of all the styles and accordingly adapt depending on the environment and the situation. The styles which I found effective in the command of troops both in field/combat and non-combat environment I have enlisted five of them. These are my perception of basic style and their permutation combination can further create other styles:

• Leadership by Example

In my opinion, this is a style of leadership; just being in the front is not leading by example or leading from the front. The style demands dynamism and character, it involves :

- *Self*: "You should be able to do what you expect from others" this is what an officer must learn before he takes to leading the troops. Leading from the front or by example is one of the ethological requisite of an Armed Forces officer. Leading from the front or by example is easier said than done especially in a fluid and uncertain combat environment. Three primary requisites for the leader are self-belief, audacity and courage of conviction. These requisites requires four abilities they are ability to take risk, independent decision making, understanding of ground realities to carry out mid course corrections and ability to exploit the windows of opportunities. Officer must have will power and capacity to endure the associated stress factors of uncertainty, isolation and reversals. To be a leader firstly, the officer must get accepted as true leader by the troops and secondly, one has to lead and make men follow. Leading from the front/setting personal example has to be made a practice rather than a rule. One thing must be remembered that once you are in it you cannot back track or give up, whatever may be the outcome or at the cost of life, the leaders have to take the team through the mission. In leading from the front or by example the leader is accountable for all the decisions, actions and the results, it is not an one time effort but part of the ledger of his/her daily work. Another important aspect is the consistency in the performance level, till such time the degree of commitment with performance is not consistent then leading by example or leading from the front is difficult. The men are to follow the leader and to make do so the level of trust and faith has to be very high and this is possible only when the men have faith in the competency of their leader.

- *Levels:* The officers are expected to have the level of competence and professional knowledge minimum at par and ideally above the team. The acceptability of the leaders is an important factor and the support given by the team is based on the level of confidence and faith on the leader and it does matter in combat. In isolation it is not possible for any leader to lead from the front or set example. The basic facet is the team-leader quotient of commitment to task; this plays an important role in giving confidence to the leader to lead from the front. Participative leadership increases the level of commitment and brings it to the matching frequency as that of the team. Important aspect is the level of compatibility between the team and the leader, it is not just that the level of the leader has to be higher than the team as also that the team must match up to the leader's level of proficiency, morale, motivation and commitment. Thus it is the responsibility of the leader to bring the team up to his/her level to create matching compatibility. The level in the context of leading from the front or by example is also governed by passion and the will to achieve at both ends.

- *Team or Group*: The bonding of the leaders with the group is a very important factor in the practice of leading from the front and by example, it is related to the dynamics of the team/group's willingness to achieve, level of motivation of the leader and the group, cohesiveness of the group and viability limits of the leader and the team to reach the objective/target. Thus group/team and the leader have to be in synergy. *Interpersonal relationship of the leader is not only based on perception, traits, personality, and interaction, it is the personal involvement of the leader with the group/team.* The confidence so developed makes the leader to lead from the front. I have seen leaders faltering mid way due to fault lines in maintaining the momentum and fluctuating group dynamism in the face of reverses. Synchronizing with the group therefore has to be considered by the leader before setting out for an assigned task. *Every individual is an entity in itself, with varying personality spread over the spectrum of behaviour, capability and drive. Synchronizing these with that of target/goal and with the team is leadership. Leadership is thus involving each individual to the demand of the set target/goal.* If this is achievable than leader is successful in leading by example and the said example is followed by the group to reach the selected target/goal.

• Flamboyant Leadership

Grandiose in character, distinctively differentiates a leader from the group. This attribute is not very common, it is very few who can develop this attribute and in some it is a born quality. This attribute is a special quality and style specific. In a given and defined environment the attribute creates an entity to stand out in a group and be recognized as the leader. The demonstrative traits in this style have finesse and are temperamentally inclined. This style of leadership is not always situational dependent; it is demonstrative and 'way of life' by nature. The style creates an impression on a group and this makes the group responsive to the leader.

This style is action centered and where the leader is able to highlight his/her traits that make the group accomplish the given task. The disposition of the leader is such that it compels him/her to lead by performance and carry the team along. The style creates an aura which is one of the motivational factors for the team. Personality gets projected through compulsive attributes of the characteristics of this style and is situation specific and/or situation dependent. This type of leader believes in enforced personality and ostentation, it gives this type of leader a flamboyant attitude and makes him/her committed to leading by example. Personality of such leadership gets 'acceptability' biased on degree and frequency of success achieved and feelings generated to match the vitality of the group/team. In this style, the organizational interest is at the forefront. Possibility of dramatics in personality projection cannot be ruled out in totality and need to be guarded.

In combat environment this style of leadership especially in adverse situation gets personified by the projection of the character of the leader, charismatic personality make troops under command to give their best and taking risk to stride along with the leader. In order to keep the aura alive, such leaders put themselves in the forefront to prove and live up to the expectation created among men under command. Such leadership style has been very successful and history of warfare had seen many successful campaigns under such leaders.

This style personifies qualities of perseverance, consistency in projection of boldness, prudence in decision making and taking of calculated risk. Adaption of ingenuity and originality in approach in reaching the set goal of the assigned task is one of the very ingredients of this style, thus:

- Extraversion is a born characteristic of this style of leadership; such leaders are outgoing, energetic, posse's positive emotions, assertive, social and seek stimulation in the company of others. Statesmanship and verbosity are two of the characteristics which distinctively distinguish such leadership from other leadership styles.
- Task goal relationship is addressed by creating stimulations in the group, making them believe in genuineness of purpose. Creativity and professionalism in approach creates the desired inputs which responds to the incarceration of impression formed on the group by the leader's personality. The idea is to create an environment where the team or group swears by the leaders.

• Leadership by Empowerment

Leaders are made by appointment and selection, this type has a different and a separate style of leadership technique. Authority gives a stratum to leaders and he/she has organizational backing. This style have very distinctive characteristic as compared to other styles. The leaders in this case have to develop the requisite traits, personality and character through regularized training.

In this type of leadership the first step is to create acceptability equation with the team, the leaders have to establish their entity as part of the buildup to get accepted. Persona analyses and its compatibility with that of the environment and the team have to be carried out before trying to establish the bestowed authority. In the course of functioning, leaders have to weigh their trait compatibility with that of the team and adjust. Therefore, development of traits is very essential aspect of this style of leadership. Leaders have to be very cautious of their actions; authority gives the right to command but acceptability of the leaders cannot be enforced, this would require proving oneself in all spheres and keeping standards at par with the expectation of the men under command.

Leaders in this system are very calculative and watchful, maximum percentage of leaders falls in this category both in Armed Forces and the Corporate World. Two end of the spectrum in this type of leadership are positional utilization and positional influence. Positional utilization is using the appointment conferred to take out the maximum output from the team, who are under the obligation of obedience of order, the aspect of willing/unwillingness of acceptance is totally discounted. The other extreme of this is positional influence, where the leader even though being conferred with the authority uses leadership traits in influencing the team/group under command. The attitude of authoritativeness and leadership by persona gets applied in this style of leadership, the proportion of applicability is situation reliant and dependent on the power vested.

Leaders and team relation gets developed over a period of acquaintance and corresponding working equation. Leadership traits and personality projection in this style of leadership is dependent on the amount of interest the leaders takes on the team and interest of the team on the leader. There are traits, qualities, methods and techniques which a leader adapts to influence the team will depend on the leader and the projected personality. The leader is required to make his presence felt by being competent professionally at par or above the competence level of the men under command and application of human relation skills to lead the team. However what makes a difference in this style of leadership and degree of success is – the adaption of self with the environment, earlier the better.

Leadership by empowerment does create a quotient of comparisons between the leaders and members of the group. The question of comparison by members of the team with that of the leader in the initial days is a very common human behavior and it is due to this very reason the question of acceptability comes up. Thus leaders have to establish their entity in the team/group on the professional and managerial front, in Army it is often quoted, "to be a leader, you have to make people want to follow you, and nobody wants to follow someone who doesn't know what is to be done". The approach of the leader has to be pragmatic and in consonance with the competency level of the team/group, a very apt quote of Lieutenant General Arthur G. Trudeau US Army which gives out the basic, the will to command "Acquiring the art of leadership is simply a matter of mastering certain techniques, understanding men, and building up those sterling qualities that give effective full expression to your natural talents. The average man can be a good potential leader provided he is willing to work diligently at being one". Taking initiative, representing the group, involving the group in arriving to a decision, putting forward of plans with one's personal imprint, ingenuity, pragmatic resource assessment and ensuring achievability of the target or making it within reach of the team/group are some of the imperative's which provides the leaders a separate entity from the group. Earlier this is achieved; the better it will be for the leader by empowerment. An empowerment leader has to really prove, a very common phrase is most applicable here and I repeat "no man is a leader until his appointment is ratified in the minds and hearts of his men". The effectiveness of this leadership is dependent on the leader and time taken to get adapted into the system.

• Environmental Leadership

The environmental leaders are the one who nurtures team/group or organizational environment to influence the emotional and psychological perception of individuals in the team/group or the organization. An understanding and application of group psychology and dynamics is essential for this style to be effective. The leader uses organizational culture to inspire individuals and develops leaders in the team/group. An environmental leader cultivates a leadership enriched environment; it brings out the best from the environment and inspires the individuals individually in the group. It nurtures the organization's interest. Armed Forces are echeloned at vertical and horizontal functional levels, in order to influence the complete spectrum to accomplish task jointly such leadership have a vital role to play.

This type of leadership takes predominance when operating in decentralized organization and echeloned chain of command from sub unit to formation levels, as the leader has to nurture the participating leaders in chain of command within the various sub groups/units under their direct operational command. A military operation will have a multi faceted composition of units/formations, each having different dynamics of operability, plans will have various phases and each phase of actions will have defined involvement, multi strata of command structure will be prevalent at each phase and that too echeloned at various levels. Thus command during a military operation/action is actually simultaneous management of forces and decision making processes.

Environmental leadership concept have been in vogue and practiced in the Armed Forces since ages. Here the organization develops leadership abilities and categorically acknowledges the role of the team/group and the leader, it concentrates on growth and enhancement of the leader and the group. Directions and directives create an environment of sense of purpose, facilitating the leadership to build visions, organize the vision into a mission and decision making at each echelon of functioning. This type of leadership is most effective in decentralized command structure and where freedom of action exists. The leader facilitates operations by developing overall command at each level. The leadership is not about changing mindsets or ways of functioning, it is to cultivate an environment that brings out the best, inspires the team, create a working culture that motivates and install confidence of collective action. In the forefront are the organizational interest and the interest of command.

• Directive Style of Leadership

There is a misconception that directive style is - autocratic in nature - highly hierarchical - it lacks flexibility - high headedness is predominant - maximizing control - people have to be driven and supervised. The literary meaning of directive if taken, it is to command obedience or make people obey. One can call this type as instructional leadership style and it is given to be understood that leader in this style disseminates the worked out plans or the intentions by passing executive instructions or directions, the meaning of the word 'directive' then gets changed. This style of leadership is based on the concept of decentralization. When the ground variables are never constant, situational changes are frequent, opportunities are restrictive and limited, where the possibility of intimate control is not possible as the operational spectrum is wide spread, in such an environment the concept of directive style of command is effective. This style of leadership is governed by principle of intention and providing direction to intention, this has the maximum applicability in the assorted environmental field of large scale operations. The intentions or set objective as decided by the high command is the basic parameters on which each echelon of leaders works on. In Armed Forces it is addressed as 'Directive Style of Command'. Some of the important facets of this type of leadership are:

- *Decentralization of Control:* One of the important ingredients of Directive Style of Command is decentralization; the degree depends on the spread of the functional areas, multiple spectrums of operations, levels of subordinate command and their involvement, duration of operations and the ground situation as prevalent. Overall intention as given out by the high command will dictate the actual scope of decentralization. The most important value which one must possess as a leaders is 'trust, faith and confidence' in subordinates. This is essentially based on the concept of distributed leadership.
- *Delegation:* Delegation of task and responsibility is a function of authority; it is participative pursuit and profiling of responsibility at all the level of command. At no time leader is devoid of his/her accountability during the process of delegation. Buck will always stop at the leader. Delegation of task and the responsibility to functional level provides scope to initiative, ingenuity, interest and sense of accomplishment. In Armed Forces where the operational variables are not constant, area of operation is large, not possible to have intimate control on all the operating teams in the area of operation and degree of fluidity of operations is high, it becomes prudent to delegate task and responsibility to lower echelons of command to achieve the target and meet the intention.
- *Freedom of Action:* Delegation and freedom of action are complementary. Freedom of action gives room for maneuver to the subordinate to plan and conduct operations with passion, ingenuity and originality. Exploitation of opportunities, flexibility in approach and resolve to meet contingencies and reverses is better ensured by enhancing the scope of freedom of action at each level of functional command. Freedom of action facilitates

speed in execution, maintenance of momentum, initiative to exploit the windows of opportunities and level based decision making. But the most important factors which are required to ensure for apt applicability of freedom of action are prudency in decision making, application of common sense, having vision and perception of outcome of the vision – without which freedom of action is ineffectual.

- *Competency and Awareness:* The leaders in this style have to be aware of the environment, its peculiarities and the response levels. Leaders own working knowledge and competence level must be high in the areas where the directive style of command is to be applied. Capability of analyzing the requirements of the intention of the high command and conceptualizing of the directions based on the intentions is an important aspect of exercising this leadership style. Faith and trust are two important factors on which this style stands. Some of the issues which the leaders should incorporate in the environment are :
    - Internal supportive systems
    - Confidence in the system
    - Transparency
    - Recognition of efforts
    - Communication and feedback.

Rapid changes in technology, strategies and mission accomplishment techniques with overlapping of boundary of operations and paradox of uncertainty are factors which govern the leadership style. What is important is the confidence of the chain of command on the leader and faith and trust of the leader on the men under command. General John J. Pershing US Army aptly sums up *"To get the best out of your men, they must feel that you are their real leader and must know that they can depend upon you"*, the leader who believe in the directive style of command has to maintain the creditability consistently, it is only then that the command will have their trust and faith bestowed on to the leadership.

Leadership Approach

What is the qualification of good leaders? When this question is asked, there is no definite answer as perception of good leaders is full of ambiguity. But let me make an attempt, I feel that leadership is a combination of approach and style which one applies in meeting the demand of the selected task/objective. One must not confuse with trait and approach, the approach is the outlook and the temperament of the leader which he/she has developed during exposure to command. Effectiveness of the command and responsiveness of the team to the style and leadership qualities determines the approach. Approach is the art of addressing the management of the team and is totally a personal perception; it is factored through application of leadership techniques. I am highlighting various types of approaches which a leader can adapt depending on the situation:

- *Open Approach:* In this approach the leader creates an environment of ingenuousness. The basics of this approach are approachability and candid submission of views by both parties i.e. the leader and the team. The team looks upon the leaders to take views of the team before coming to the decisions. Team expects its self esteem to be respected and considers the leader as guardian of the team. In the open approach what the leader must look for is participation and commitment of the team. In such an environment, the leader must also be prepared to take disapprovals as well. Leader in this approach makes self approachable and takes the team in confidence. Mental mobility and flexibility are essential traits; this makes the leader accommodative and develops the power to convince with logical reasoning. Understanding of the team functional parameters, prevailing conditions and its effect on the team and the team psyche are mandatory. Moreover due to application of human factors in optimizing the output and maintaining the momentum under environment of changing human behaviour due to the demand of the task and persuasion by the leader is an important facet of command. In this approach, the leader with resilience, participative leadership and protectionist temperament will be open/ adjustable and adaptable. To gain confidence and to work within the functional parameters of the team such leader are open to discussion and welcomes ideas from the team. Such type of leadership approach is applicable when the situation is fluid, changes in orders are very frequent and the proportion of uncertainty is high as there are no fixed courses of action. This approach is suitable for open ended tasking, high risk missions and tasks requiring voluntary participation. Leader has to maintain the transparency and close loop interpersonal relationship in this approach. Decision taking rests on the leader and he must be accountable, passing the blame will be detrimental and break the cohesiveness.

- *Egalitarian Approach:* Involvement of team and optimal engagement of each team member keeping in consideration their expertise/specialization are basis of this concept. The leader has to be aware of team's work competency and have intimate knowledge of each team member and their proficiency levels. Participation of the team in the functional process is an important aspect of this approach. It is very similar to Open Approach but only difference is the involvement of the team in decision making. Leader makes each member of the team responsible in the task. Sense of equal responsibility brings fineness in activities and guarantee involvement. The democratic equation is very prominent; responsibility delegation is an important facet of this approach. To make the concept a success and result oriented, leader must back up the team, maintain the impetus, keep motivation going and must be ready to share the credit for success. One thing must be very clear leader cannot absolve himself of his responsibility, leader has to be a brave heart to bear the responsibility of failure, however in this concept recovery and corrective actions are very fast due to established relationship of the team with the leader. Blame game is a strict NO in this concept. This type of leadership approach is apt in group task based operations, specialized operations and task involving multiple options.

- *Acceleratory Approach:* It is an equation between the group and leader's enthusiasm. The drive, vigour, vitality, dynamism and determination are the basic ingredients of acceleration. Both leader and the team have to be at the same pedestal and intensity. To reach to a successful conclusion to a mission, the leader and team's contributory dynamism have to be at the same proportion, any large tilt in the scale will be retrogressive and counterproductive. In this approach, the leader must identify the positivity in each member of the team and match up to the combined dynamisms of the team. What is very important in this approach is to channelize the dynamism and give direction; control by the leader over the team has to be assertive. Willingness on the part of the leader to take on the challenge straight-on must be oozing through each action undertaken in accomplishment of the assigned task. This type of leadership approach is mostly applicable in highly intensive and high risk tasks environment where speed is an important element of success. Leadership by example also pays high dividends in this approach. Here the leader maintains the pressure to ensure there is no drop in acceleration, the most important factor is to sustain the momentum. Such leaders are always in a hurry to complete the task and lookout for the next impending tasks. Such an approach pays good dividends where time lines have to be achieved or task has to be accomplished on a fixed date line.
- *No Nonsense Approach:* Certain factors which are predominant in making the team responsive and one

among them is no nonsense approach. Leader is strict and follows the book. This approach requires proportionate level of pragmatism and transparency while fixing responsibility and accountability within the team. Other important facets in this approach are reasonability and sensibility; it is on these factors the leader has to base his decision and distribution of work. The reasonability of set standards and sensibility will depend on the demand of the task and level of competency of the team. Leader's presence on the work floor/ground is a must. The leader must ensure that the target set is within the reach of the team/group. The firmness and steadfastness of the leader has to be strong and he must not buckle under pressure. Transparency plays an important act of binding the leader and the team. In this approach, the important factors are discipline, following the orders and standard operating procedures (SOP) and clear cut instructions. The Leader has to ensure that at any cost there is no ambiguity in orders and plans. Strictness is an important component of this approach. The approach is more applicable to sensitive task which are SOP based and requires high quality of proficiency like fire fighting or bomb disposal or clearance of land mines.

- *Translucent Approach:* In this concept, the leadership demonstrates candidness, ingenuousness and honesty of purpose. The complete plans are thrown open giving out all the pros and cons. It prepares the team to take the challenge and makes itself responsible in achieving the set target. Human nature is such that when it knows what the outcomes are, it prepares itself and works out contingencies. Leadership using this tactics have to keep number of options ready in case any apprehensions cropping up among the team about the feasibility of the operations, alternatives thus are must and should be made available to keep the interest and participation level high. In this tactics, tasks which have multiple options are best suited and the team selects the target and sets the mission. The leader is the coordinator and director.

- *Urgency Approach:* Leadership in this approach creates an atmosphere of convincing urgency and influence the team temperament. The urgency in this regard has to be in organizational interest. What is important in this approach is establishing quotient of urgency and team efficiency. The leader has to create the sense of purpose in the urgency. The first sense of purpose is to meet certain fixed and planned target, the requirement of urgency must be visible and the team must willingly involve itself in supporting the leader to achieve the target. The second sense of purpose is that leadership maintains an environment of urgency by fixing the time; the leader has to decide the quantum of applied urgency at each stage of work and keep regulating. The leader has to guard against too much of urgency, as it can bounce back and lead to inefficiency syndrome within the team. Dynamism in leadership in this approach has to be consistence through the entire duration of the urgency.
- *Minimalistic Approach:* "Make plans simple in its content and for execution, so that a dud must also be able to place himself in the plan with least quantum of supervision, so that when the plan is faced with uncontrolled environment or when odds are against, it is able to effectively run through", my senior subaltern had said these words during a company exercise. A simple and clean plan which is understandable, easy to assimilate and without any ambiguity will bring efficiency in execution. It is the leader who should simplify the plan to suit the quotient of efficiency of the team. Tasking of each member of the team based on capability and aptitude, creating attitudinal coexistence based composite task force and select group tasking are some of the methods which makes complex plan into a simple plan. Here the leader is a regulator, he must be aware of all contingencies, alternatives and be in constant touch with the plans as the plan keeps unfolding.

One must also remember the idiom, "simple plans are not always that simple as one perceives", its execution is dependent on how much the leader is able to simplify the procedures and keep the quantum of output within the ambit of functional efficiency of the team. Simple demeanor of the leaders is another factor which makes things look simple and one gets associated with the simplicity of the leader, things start looking lot easier.

- *Inspirational Approach:* An inspiring leader must get intimately involved with the team psychometrics and aware of the points of initiator which energizes the team responses are two important considerations which are essential in this approach. What is important is synchronizing the team potential, level of motivation and momentum to be achieved through inspiration. Inspirations have to be planned keeping the team competency and level of proficiencies, same repetitive inspiration techniques will not have the same effect as was in the previous use. Working out techniques of inspiring, the leader has to have ingenuity and ability to cash on to the motivation created. Aspects which must be borne in mind are:
  - Level of involvement of the leader in accomplishment of the assigned task. Leading from the front and leadership by personal examples.
  - High competency and proficiency levels. Professionalism in approach is a good initiator of inspiration.
  - Meeting the expected standards of the team. Commitment of the leader must be visible.
  - Giving credit to the team, highlighting of the achievement/standards achieved and incentive to deserving. Ensuring total transparency is a must.
  - Discipline in the team and self discipline of the leader.
  - Ingenuity of the leader e.g. catchy maxim for a task does inspire, the maxim "Yeh Dil Mange More", really paid in Indo Pak conflict in Kargil Sector (J&K) 1999.

- *Optimist Approach:* It is the aura which a leader can generate of positivity and optimism; this creates an environment of commitment and responsiveness in the team. People follow those who persist with hope. Positive mind will always work a way out, 'Hoping for the best' is human nature and when this is systematized to a given coherent momentum, the passion gets infused. Sense and attitude of positivity is very important facet. A quote by Rick Warren, which I had jotted down from a quotation board which is very pertinent here "Leaders inspire, they maintain a hopeful attitude even in the face of reversals, men do not follow discouraged leaders and they follow those who persist with hope". Taking prudent risk is very much part of this approach, but gambling and experimenting with probability will be counterproductive. However, the leaders in this approach need to ensure:
    - Build a pace which is sustainable.
    - Maintain steady motivation levels.
    - Build the team.
    - Confidence and competency in the team.
    - Establish high, attainable, clearly comprehensible standards.
    - Have confidence in subordinates.
    - Encourage and reward prudent risk taking.
- *Protectionist Approach:* Parent child equation between the leader and team is one of the factors which positively contribute in enhancing productivity. Protectionist approach creates an environment of assurance in the working relationship. Here the leader gives full support in terms of involvement, professional guidance, confidence building, meeting requirements and projections, follow-ups, shouldering responsibility and motivation. In this approach, the team is leader dependent, 'under my wings' outcome is predominant in this approach. Higher the credibility of the leader, higher will be the dependency.

'Looking over the shoulder and under the wings' syndromes setting in within the team is a big drawback of this approach.

- *Persuasive Approach:* In this approach the leader uses the persuasive skills to get work done. The basics for this approach is to make the intention very clear, follow this with clear orders and briefing and lastly give freedom of action and liberty to ensure execution. Monitoring and feedback are two important facets of this approach. In other words the influence of the leader has to be always present. Faith of the leader on the team and that of the team on the leader has to be high. Leading from the front is an important element of this approach; its relevance is more pronounced in this approach as it gives creditability to the leader. Understanding of nuance of the task, realization of ground realities, close working relationship, professionalism and competency and proactive attitude gives authenticity to persuasiveness. Those leaders who follow this approach must learn the art of how to make people dream and aspire.

Prerequisite of a Leader

There are certain cardinal prerequisites which a leader must possess; these are different from traits and approach. These prerequisites give distinctiveness and creditability to leadership. In order to maintain such distinctiveness and to be effective, leaders must have:

- Vision and ability to translate it into reality.
- Ability to take independent decision.
- Power to convince and clarity of thoughts.
- Passion to achieve and instinct to survive.
- Accountability for actions and decisions.
- Habit to follow up, monitor and take feedback.
- Self-belief and confidence.

- Courage to live up to ones convictions.
- Be catalyst of professionalism and development of the team.
- Compassion and concern.

There are some leadership comportment's and habits which do pay dividend during command of the team and build trust and faith on the leader. The leaders must imbibe these habits which give credibility to their competency and ways, they are mundane yet very important:

- Remain cool and calm, do not be in a hurry and wait for the storm to pass over. Readjust and regain to get along.
- Develop 'It will look better tomorrow' attitude this gives confidence and hope.
- Get angry and lose your head when warranted, then get over it. Do not keep it to your heart.
- Always show 'Yes I can do it' attitude. Volunteer to take on challenging task.
- Go into details, never be in doubt, if required check and recheck again.
- Avoid having ego of your position. Mix up and participate.
- When you choose or given the best, stick to it and manage. Do not ask for a change.
- Do not let anything stand in the way of a right decision.
- Never allow anyone to take your decision.
- Recommend rightfully and only deserving.
- Be demanding when it comes to meeting the deadlines.
- Don't take counsel of your fears or naysayers.
- Always stand by the side of your team especially in reversals/failure.
- Carry your team.

Leadership is very much an individual projection of personality in leading a team/group, no two leaders are same and neither a clone can be created. Individual human behaviour has direct influence in the style, approach, quality of leadership and degree of effectiveness to control and to lead the assigned team. Leader must have a single aim that is to get the leadership ratified by the men under command and the organization, it is only then that leader is said to be effective. The organizational ethos and values also have a role to play, regimentation of the leader and the team which is an important facet of interpersonal relation is very much governed by the established ethos, values and traditions. Leadership in a regimented environment of Forces as compared to the Corporate Sector is somewhat different, so are the challenges. What I have tried, is to high light leadership issues in this chapter which had paid well when it came to leading troop into the battle. Field Marshall Sir William Slim had described the leadership in a very explicit and lucid manner, I quote *"It is that intangible force which will move a whole group of men to give their last ounce to achieve something without counting the cost to themselves, that makes them feel they are part of something greater than themselves".*

Tips to Effective Leadership

Here I would be quoting the great military leaders and scholars' to bring out the essential of leadership. These quotations are very intimate observations on leadership by some of these great military commanders of their time. As a conclusion to this chapter I am jotting some of the very pertinent ones which I have always believed makes the leaders and leadership qualities worth emulating:

> *"Our job is to develop bold audacious leaders, competent enough to know the difference between risk and gamble, and willing to take risk to get inside the decision cycle of the enemy in order to wrest the initiative from him. We must develop commanders who trust their subordinates, who delegate responsibility and authority to them, and who encourage them to exercise initiative within the framework of their intent".*
>
> —Gerald T. Bartlett, Lieutenant General, USA.

"There are no desperate situations, there are only desperate people."

—Heinz Guderian.

"The commander must go up to see for himself, reports received second hand rarely give the information he needs for his decision"

– Field Marshal Rommel.

"If you think you can and you are right. Just be passionate about it. And if you lack passion develop it because success never comes till you are passionate about it"

—Carl Von C Clausewitz.

"We represent the example to the world of what values really mean. We are value based organisation and we need to recognise that. All of us in leadership position must be able to exemplify values. Talk is not enough; you must be able to back up your words with deeds"

—General Dennis J Reimer US Army.

"Preparation for war is an expensive, burdensome business. Yet there is one important part of it that cost little, study"

—Napoleon.

"Do not repeat the tactics that have gained you one victory, but let your methods be regulated by the infinite variety of circumstances"

—Sun Tzu.

"It may be of interest to future generals to realize that one makes plans to fit the circumstances, and does not try to create circumstances to fit the plans"

—General George S Patton.

"To get the best out of your men, they must feel that you are their real leader and must know that they can depend upon you."

—General of the Armies John J. Pershing.

"I do not fear an army of lions, if they are led by a lamb. I do fear an army of sheep, if they are led by a lion."

—Alexander the Great.

"Discipline can only be obtained when all the officers are imbued with the sense of their lawful obligation to their men and to their country that they cannot tolerate negligence. Officers who fail to correct errors or to praise excellence are valueless in peace and dangerous misfits in war."

—Gen. George S. Patton, Jr.

"Acquiring the art of leadership is simply a matter of mastering certain techniques, understanding men, and building up those sterling qualities that give effective full expression to your natural talents. The average man can be a good potential leader provided he is willing to work diligently at being one."

Lieutenant General Arthur G. Trudeau.

"Last, but by no means least, courage of one's convictions, the courage to see things through. The world is in a constant conspiracy against the brave. It's the age-old struggle- the roar of the crowd on one side and the voice of your conscience on the other."

—Douglas MacArthur

"What are the attributes of leadership? The first, the primary, indeed the cardinal attribute of leadership is professional knowledge and professional competence. Now you will agree with me that you cannot be born with professional knowledge and professional competence even if you are a child of Prime Minister, or the son of an industrialist, or the progeny of a Field Marshal. Professional knowledge and professional competence have to be acquired by hard work and by constant study. In this fast-moving technologically developing world, you can never acquire sufficient professional knowledge."

—Field Marshal SHFJ Manekshaw, MC.

"A true king has the confidence to stand alone, the courage to make tough decisions, and the compassion to listen to the needs of others. He does not set out to be a king, but becomes one by the equality of his actions and the integrity of his intent".

—Chanakaya

"Personal leadership exists only as the officers demonstrate it by superior courage, wider knowledge, quicker initiative, and a greater readiness to accept responsibility than those they lead."

–Field Marshal Sir William Slim

"Practice what you sermonise, action speaks louder than words."

—Heinz Guderian.

The tips are very many, what I have listed above are the one which in my perception makes a place for the leader and gives him recognition. What matters in leadership is that it should leave a mark on the men under command and they must swear by their leaders.

At the end of this chapter, I would like to discuss certain negative traits in a leader, during my stint with the Indian Corporate Sector, I was involved in the appraisal/promotion discussions and observing the HR recruitment process, I found that these said negative traits are considered as very undesirable, no one takes a call for these negative traits. Certain fixed mindset exists among the management; more stress is on the literary connotation and dictionary meanings. The aspect of positivity or the limit of the applicability of positivity is not taken into consideration. However, on the other hand these leadership traits in a combat environment does at times gives huge positive dividends, what matters is the circumstances and effect of the trait to deal with the circumstances. I am trying to compare some of these negative traits which in corporate is strict NO and how did I find these suitable when its application had positive outcome in many combat encounters:

Arrogance: in a leader is associated with the character of haughtiness, snobbishness, egoist, overconfidence and smugness. These in the scales of Officers Like Qualities (OLQ) is considered as negative and kept at bottom of the personality spectrum. However, when there is indecisiveness prevailing in the environment and changes in the courses of action are too frequent or uncontrollable due to the changing dynamics of the state of affairs on the ground, certain arrogance on the part of the leader is helpful in striding over the problem, it makes the team to stick together and get the task accomplished. It is the matter of prestige and the self esteem which makes the leader arrogant at that point of time. There are numerous examples in combat from capturing an interfering bunker from unassailable direction to rescuing a hostage from militants alive when hopes were remote. Arrogance gives a direction, an alternative and stubbornness in approach of getting the task accomplished, but too much of arrogance and frequent use can at times be detrimental or negative. Very close to arrogance is *Stubbornness:* it is the rigidity which is considered as negative. I have always felt that flexibility must have some element of rigidity inbuilt, it is only then the leader is able to astutely incorporate flexibility in his decision and implementation of the plans. Having a mixed quotient of this trait with other traits gives the leader sense of boldness and makes him audacious. Extremity of this trait is very negative and I have seen missions failing and units taking heavy casualties of own troops. Another trait which has closeness to the other two is *Obstinacy;* this trait has negativity of unreasonableness, pigheadedness and inflexibility. Whereas on the other hand the personality with this trait is determined, tenacious and is persistent, the positivity of this trait are important facet of leadership quality.

Skepticism and *Suspicion* are two aspects which are very negative in their interpretation. *Skepticism* negativity is pessimism, mistrust, doubtfulness and uncertainty, no recruiting officer will ever endorse a candidate with this trait, and certain amount of skepticism makes a leader thorough, careful and carryout introspection of plans before giving the orders for implementation. The iota of pessimism in the leader does helps in building/catering for contingencies or taking preventive measures. Similarly *Suspiciousness* is considered as negative attribute but in an investigative nature of job of police or detective this attribute is an important facet of the personality. The leader also must possess the investigative quality and element of suspicion helps in investigative approach in fact finding tasks or getting into the root of the problem.

Tempestuous person has the negative qualities of being violent, hysterical, uncontrollable, emotional and confused, whereas the positive side is being passionate and enthusiastic. The positivity of tempestuousness is very much part of the expected character of a progressive and leading by example leader. *Aggression* on the other hand is associated with violent behaviour, anger, hostility and antagonism. Any officer not having aggression is considered as docile officer, in order to be authoritative, to take bold actions and accept risk the leader must have aggressiveness in his personality. A meek leader will never fit well in a highly motivated and performing team. That killer instinct which is expected in an officer will be lacking, if aggression is lacking.

Rebelliousness and *Restlessness* are two very negative traits and I also vouch that these traits are unacceptable. But courage of conviction comes only when there is element of *Rebelliousness* in the leader, more over having all 'yes sir' leaders is also not advisable. The courage to say 'no' or disagree with the seniors does require a speck of rebelliousness in a leader. On the other hand if leader is not *Restless* he/she will not be able to meet the deadlines and give push to the team. What I had experienced is that restlessness at times had accomplished a task well before the stipulated time thus changing the dynamics of the combat situation and giving advantage to the main operational plan.

Therefore my advice to the recruitment fraternity is that do not out rightly reject a person who are having some iota of negative traits. Basically all human-beings have negative traits most of it gets dormant when the scales of positive traits are higher. In actuality what matters is a successful leader who can achieve. Recruiters those who can understand this and positivity of so called negative traits, there will not be a hindrance in rightful selection.

What I have discussed in this chapter are my views, thoughts and observations of human behaviours as seen in practice of leadership in the Indian Forces. Approach to leadership is very personal matter and it depends on the basic perception i.e. leadership is nothing but taking charge of the men, materials and situations in order to meet the mission requirements, no two leader will ever be the same and neither one can imitate the other. Actually if you see the leader is all alone and everyone is looking at him/her, this makes the leadership position very tentative, thus leader has to keep validating the approach, attitude and the responsiveness of the team to approach so as to establish the credibility or develop pragmatic outlook and temperament towards leadership traits which will provide definite results.

In this chapter I have quoted number of military leaders, I for one had always been very impressed by military quotes and taken these as reckoners during my command. These quotes in most of the occasion are remarks based on observations which had the backing of experience and in depth study of human behaviours in combat.

"Leadership is seeing the possibilities in a situation while others are seeing the limitation."

—John. C. Maxwell

3 Decision Making

"In any moment of decision, the best thing you can do is the right thing, the next best thing is the wrong thing, and the worst thing you can do is nothing"

—Franklin D. Roosevelt, President, USA

Decision making is a mental process; it is governed by internal and external environments within the organization, state of mental strength, quotients of perceptions, variables of controlled and uncontrolled situations, leadership outlook and temperamental state of the decision maker and the personal attitude of the leader. In today's environment decision making is an applied procedure based on matrix, models and formula. The reliability on human angle and instinct has been minimized with development of decision making tools. In fact, models and procedure are not as successful and what really matters is the human element behind the decision which creates the impact. The human part of application of logic and reasoning will always remain predominant in the decision making in spite of dependency on the decision making tools.

In Armed Forces the decision making is process based, however the human element is more dominant as no fixed module/matrix or procedure is practicable due to the very nature of operations which are varied in their content. The controlled variables and dynamics like in industry etc are nonexistent. Military Decision Making Process has heavy dependency on the human elements and in combat the famous OODA (Observe, Orient, Decide, and Act) loop is an adopted procedure. This procedure is well covered in various military manuals. In combat another factor is the speed in decision making, especially when situational imperatives are constantly changing. Decision making here is in race with the adversary's relevance of actions/reaction.

In spite of models, formulas and procedure we err in decision making, it is the human factor which matters both in the Corporate and Armed Forces. The human elements of tentativeness, hesitancy, lack of self confidence, cautiousness in implementation, indecisiveness, doubts in the mind and zero error expectancy/play safe attitude are some of the factors which influence the decision making. Similarly in the world outside uniform various models and scientific methods are incorporated in decision making, here time is not at premium and decisions are deliberate, then also there are lots of apprehensions which arise due to the human elements. Ultimately it is the human factors which have direct bearing on the leadership qualities and the decision taking ability. What matters is the 'human angle in taking right decision'. Decision making is a human response to meet the process of accomplishment of set goal. Leadership decision is to be undertaken in various circumstances and scenarios, some of the important ones are:

- Matters of routine requirements.
- Disruption or threat to the decided course of action.
- On emergence of a window of opportunity in course of a running plan.
- To facilitate acceleration in a process of operation.
- Compelled change of courses of action,
- Implementation and/or planning new strategy.
- Modification of established strategy.
- Meet situational challenges and changes to a plan.

- Meeting the deadlines.
- Change in variables in the factors considered in the plan.
- Retrospection of the ongoing operations, the set target and accomplishment of the objective.
- Reaction to a feedback/follow up.

Whatever the model, matrix, template are applied in decision making and facilitators used, yet the decision is based on human instincts, intuition, perception and temperament. Approach to decision making by the leadership is one of the important factor which is very individualistic in nature and personality based. In this chapter, I am not discussing the methods or models used for arriving at a decision in Armed Forces or the corporate world. Based on my observations of leaders at various strata, I am making an attempt to bring out what all human elements which influences the decision making processes and aptitudes to take right decision.

Decision Making and Leadership

In decision making the basic factor the 'Human' have two basic elements, temperaments and outlook. Success lies in purposeful application of the perceived outlook of the leaders to achieve the desired objective and secondly on how the temperamental variables are regulated and synergized with the process application of logic, reasoning and the situation prevailing at the time of decision taking. The attitudinal elements of outlook and temperament in the leaders thus have direct influence in decision making processes.

Outlook of a leader is based on the factors of attitude, personal values and ethics and individual perception. The other significant facets which influence the outlook are self-belief, level of professional competency, relationship quotient in the prevalent functional environment and quality of the personality of the leader. Decision making is in consonance with the proportionate relevance of the factors of outlook.

Temperament on the other hand is the mental state of the leaders while making a decision, while outlook may be constant on the other hand temperament by nature is not constant.

Decision it may be routine, tactical or functional, strategic or futuristic, in response to opportunity or demand of situation will get influenced by outlook and temperament of the leader. Therefore, decision based on outlook and temperament can be apt or inappropriate, bold or timid, prudent or rash and this will be dependent on proportion of degree and intensity of the factors governing the outlook and the temperament.

I am of the view that the decision makers are of three types, *first*, who is definite and confident, *second*, who is tentative but is optimistic and third who have fear of failure. The types are categorized based on human facet of behaviour and are governed by the outlook and temperament. In Armed Forces there is no scope to try the decision on a pilot project or have a sample application or the decision making is not an open ended process or having no restriction on time. On the other hand, what is important is 'right decision at the right time'. Plans may be war gamed or brain stormed to get options, in actuality when the time comes to taking decision, it the one who is faced with the problem and is confronting actual ground realities in a given situation has to take the final call. The communication, practicality, knowledge, competence, participation, courage of conviction, risk taking and accountability/responsibility are mandatory variable factors for arriving to a decision and these create an environment of viability. The accreditation of decision is dependent on the type of the decision maker. The aspects of type of outlook and temperament and their combinations which have bearing on military decision making process are:

- *Approach and Positivity:* The leader's outlook to approach towards the decision and the temperament of positive attitude, here the decision making is directly proportionate to the degree of positivity applied. The outlook must have the attribute of logic, purpose, practicality, spontaneity, concern of outcome and interest of the organization. Decision temperament of positivity comprises the will to succeed, persuasiveness, perfection, transparency and catering for contingency. The aspects of intuition and probability have very limited scope in such type of decision making. In combat situations the decision depends on rightful appreciation of challenges of changing situations and battlefield volatility, thus approach is practicality and candidness of application is based on the leader's temperament of positivity. Approach to be positive will need having a clear defined vision and focus so that it can match the temperament of positivity. However, what makes difference in decision making and success are – positive intentions in approach and temperament of positive bent of mind.

- *Rationality and Practicality:* In case of outlook being rational towards decision making, then practicability of application of the decision is mandatory factor which the leaders have to ensure to derive maximum output from the team/group. Prudence and common sense combination does bring out workable decision. Maintaining the balance between the rationality and practicality by the leader increases the viability of the making apt decision. Outlook of the leaders towards rationality is affirmative then decision making gambit must have judiciousness, shrewdness and reasonability. Whereas on the temperament side, practicality, sensibility and levelheadedness predominantly must be logically related to the outlook of rationality of the leader. The level of maturity of the leader is an important factor in this process.
- *Responsiveness and Speed:* Decision making process must be deliberate but time is an important factor for decision to be made effective. Time of response and speed/spontaneity are two factors, too long or too short of either or both - leads to inconsistency and indecisiveness in decision making. It is

important that response must correlate with temperament of spontaneity and definiteness of approach towards decision making and speed in taking a decision. Tendencies which retard the process of decision making are pendency and indecisiveness, higher the positivity in temperament in terms of response and promptness and speed in action less will be the said tendencies. In combat situation, the factor of speed in decision making is an important facet as the ground situation keeps changing and the OODA loop need to be faster than the enemy commander's intention and decision making. Opportunism is a related facet of responsiveness and speed; leaders have to factor it in their decision and plan to deal with contingencies. Keeping flexibility in the approach to decision and catering for changing ground situation needs prudency in the outlook and temperament of adaptability in the leader to make the responsiveness and speed coexistent in the plans especially when the time is a factor.

- *Standard and Consistency:* Leaders in the process of decision making need to have an outlook towards making a set expected standard of decisions, this can be achieved when there is consistency in all the decision taken by the leader. In this facet of human behaviour both the outlook towards achieving a standard in decision making and the temperament of consistency in the decisions, brings in the value of perfection in decision making. Temperament of fickle mindedness and erratic behavioural pattern will be detrimental. To establish a standard the consistency is a must, the troops under command develops faith in decision making capability of the leader when both are optimal.
- *Prudence and Passion:* When outlook of the leaders is prudent and practical, this must be complimented with temperament of passion. One has to be very passionate of his decision it is only then success will be ensured. The facet of prudency in the outlook of the leader lends to

practicality, sensibility, farsightedness and common sense in decision making whereas passion as temperament is proportionately related to the value given by the leader in his/her involvement, accountability, responsibility, integrity and honesty.

- *Credibility and Creativity:* Credibility and creativeness are essential imperative to decision making, outlook towards credibility and temperament of creativity makes the leader visionary and imaginative. In this a leader creates/maps a decision first before arriving to making the final call. Person having creative bent of mind will weigh all options, visualize the sequence of events unfolding and the effect of the decision, carryout suitability analysis and visualize the ultimate outcome. Giving credibility to decision depends on the value the leader gives towards sincerity of approach, trustworthiness of the group towards the leader, integrity of the leader, reliability factor and standing of the leader in decision making. Creditability therefore is outlook dependent. When it is a known fact that decision have factor of risk associated as in combat decision making, the facet of creativity and credibility are proportionately equal in value.
- *Insightfulness and Meticulousness:* When the outlook is of insightfulness and temperament is of meticulousness, the decision will be pragmatic. Insightful leader's posses' sharpness, ability to discern rightfully the requirement of the task and the related outcome and apply the acumen of the experience gained in the decision making. When the leader applies these in decision making, the degree of precision and accuracy in decision are proportionate. The higher the degree more right and deliberate will be the decision. Deliberation in character is predominant when insight and meticulousness are equally applied. In combat maximum dependency is on 'right decision at the right time' and in doing so leaders have to apply these two facets in right proportion along with spontaneity and speed.

- *Decisiveness and Answerability:* The outlook of leaders being decisiveness, this should be based on his/her conviction that the decision is right and workable. When the decisions have been taken and directions given the leader is answerable for the entire outcome flowing out of the decision. The leaders cannot and should not play the blame game, the confidence of the men under command degenerates and the level of faith and trust on the leadership deteriorates. Mistakes are always acceptable to the higher command when the leader is accountable to his/her decision. Important issue is to maintain the confidence/faith of the men and this is best done by learning from such mistakes and to do this the leader has to demonstrate resilience in approach. If the outlook is definitive to the spirit of decisiveness, the temperament to accepting responsibility and answerability towards the outcome must coexist in the personality of the leader; this makes the leader more acceptable to the team.

"He who has relied least on fortune is established as the strongest", leaders during taking decision must ensure this. Always relying on luck will never pay, as the law of probability on right decision is not based on fortune but on the ability of the leader. Higher probability of right decision will be when the factors of outlook and temperament are at right and equal proportion. Negativity is the only component that will make the leader indecisive. Decision makers in Armed Forces are appointment and rank based thus officer is duty bound to take decision and it is part of the command responsibility.

Decision Making is an Art

Frankly speaking decision is made and taken by every living creature in this world; even a chameleon when given an option of multiple targets of insects, selects and decides which one to strike. In day to day life every human-being takes routine, impromptu and deliberate decision. With all the models made available and scientific formulas worked out to facilitate the leaders in the process of decision making; one element 'the human mind' has always been a factor which restricted the scope of all such models and formulas. Certain aspect of decision making may be based on standard operating procedures, time tested traditions, ethos, routine and drills. It is ultimately the human state of mind which compels a person in taking the final call. Every military leader is trained in decision making process and to take decision is a bounded moral duty. With all the available aids, models, tools and templates in place then also everyone is not comfortable in making or taking decision. I have seen leaders in various situations some have knack of taking a decision, others learn through repeated mistakes, few play with alternatives and depend on fortune and there are some who do not take decision but wait for things to happen on its own. Decision making is an art, human character is never same and each individual will have their own ways of taking decision.

Art of decision making basically involves use of leadership attributes as facilitator and ability to implement the decision. Making the implementers comprehend the decision and understand the standpoint is also necessary and is part of the decision making process. To make the decision viable what really matters is the personal outlook and the associated temperament in the process of decision making as discussed above. The stages of decision making are basically three, before, during and after (follow-up). Each stage must be handled in their respective relative importance:

- *Before Decision Making*: The leaders in this stage have to prepare for the process. Foremost important is to have a right frame of mind, clear understanding of the directives in respect of accomplishing the assigned task and the terms of references which have direct bearing on the assigned task to arrive at decision. Next in the process which is essential is clear understanding of the situation on ground, factors which are effecting the operations and controlled/uncontrolled variables which are going to affect the decision making and are related to the assigned task. Finally, the factors on which will depend the implementation of the decision, understanding of the executing forces and its dynamics , resources being made available and the demands of the plan. Proficiency of the leaders and his ability in comprehending these factors has bearing on the decision making. The leader must consider:

- How much time is available to spend on this decision?
- Time factors for making the decision and its consequences?
- Opportunities missed if there is delay in decision?
- Is there any scope of changing/modifying the decision?
- Time for deliberations at arriving to a decision?
- What will be the outcome of the wrong decision?
- Tasking and responsibility?
- Resource position and availability?

- *During Decision Making*: This is the stage where the acumen of the leaders comes to the fore. Method of decision making adopted depends on the level of confidence and the quotient of answerability vis-à-vis responsibility. Decision is either independent or dependent based on individual professional proficiency and the level of self confidence or consultative or collective. Whatever be the approach for decision, the leader is responsible for the decision. Personalities of the leader have definite impact in decision making, basic factor in any sphere of decision making is the 'individuality' and this is personality dependent. During decision making what matters is how are the actions regulated and synergized to facilitate the decisiveness factor in decision making. This to a large extent is dependent on level of self-confidence of the leader, faith and trust of the team on the leader and credibility of the competency and professionalism of the leader. The aspect of organizational interest also needs to be factored by the leader. Certain essentials which require consideration during the decision making are:

- o Clarity of the objective and vision
- o Visualizations of sequence of implementation
- o Understanding of environmental dynamics
- o Lucid sense of purpose
- o Maximization of resource utilization
- o Timelines
- o Fixing of responsibility/accountability
- o Practicality of application
- o Faith in self and men under command

'Art' is understanding the genuineness of the need to take decision, generating alternatives, carrying out the prognosis of alternatives, choosing the best course where ratio of logic is maximum, obtaining pragmatic feedback and 'yes sir' people to be discounted in this process.

- *During Follow–Up:* Leaders must cultivate knack of ensuring that decision taken is followed and genuine feedback is obtained. This facilitates in mid course correction if any and apply contingencies to correct mistakes. As human factor is predominant at this stage of implementation, the art of knowing your men and having their faith in your leadership are important factors. Another important aspect is the acceptability of the decision, the leaders here have to impose their personality, ability to understand and control group dynamics which will influence the implementation of the decision. Personal involvement in nurturing one's own decision is a key factor which makes the decision fructify. The 'Art' is to progress the decision to successful conclusion. The leaders must always keep in mind that it is he/she who is responsible for the decision, to quote Field Marshal Montgomery *"Decision making is an art; however, it must be supported by valuation, logic, analysis and hypothesis which require scientific bend of mind. The Human Elements of prediction, probability, fortune, risk and predicament do have its influence in decision making. Ultimately what matters is not the approach adopted by decision maker but the responsibility of the decision irrespective of the outcome".* Mistakes will happen in the decision making instead of getting angry and loosing the cool, the leader must take a step back and ask answers to the questions of what is the root cause and what have I learned from the mistakes, what was the problem and how to prevent it the next time. When the leader retrospect's the mistake it prevents future mistakes, but also keeps the leader motivated to take on further tasks.

Techniques of Decision Making

Decision making is a technique; every person has his/her own ways of dealing with the decision making. Certain techniques used by the leaders in various situations and battle conditions in arriving at decision, I found these to be one of the effective way of coming to the right decision. Techniques are the ways evolved to come to a conclusive decision. In the book of management very many of them have been given and which are said to be the tools of decision making, the techniques which I am going to discuss are unique ones as these are very effective under combat environment and which I had observed being successfully used by the leadership in Armed Forces.

There are two type of decision makers, one who identifies self with the responsibilities - works for the institution - is source of strength of the men under command - have belief in the system - not self-centered/self-promoter and on the other hand the very opposite those who are careerist - own interest is predominant - lack compassion and empathy. Both have different attributes and ways to come to a decision. However, both types of leaders before evolving their ways of taking the decision have to ensure that the decisions are operable.

The functional and operational ground factors under which the implementation of the decision is to take place must be considered keeping the dynamic of the operating environment and the equation of resource optimization. I am highlighting some of the techniques other than OODA (Observe, Orient, Decide, Act), which I found rather unique but effective. I am sure same can be made applicable in the world outside the uniform.

- *Predictability Techniques:* The leaders here predicts two extremes of the outcome of the same problem, he appreciates the situations which have relevance to the decision making. In the process of interposing the polarized predictability within the frame work of the terms of references of the directives received, the leader compares these based on situation visualization or likely fallouts. In doing so the leader systematically builds up his/her own matrix of advantages and disadvantages or the pro and cons. Simultaneous addressing both the extremes of the predictability, the leader analyses and works out alternatives and contingencies neutralizing the negative extreme of both the ends. The decisions arrived in this tactics is a balanced one and are more practical and pragmatic as each angle of the spectrum of predictability is addressed and the odds/probability gets eliminated in the process. The method is "what can be the best possible or what can be the worst possible" comparative analysis, where the criticality of the operations is weighed in relation to the judgment of the prevailing situation on the ground.
- *Optimizations Techniques:* Dynamics which have influence in the decision making are the directives, given out terms of references, data base, resources both operational and manpower, ground/work platforms, prevailing environment and the target to be achieved. These dynamics when optimized to the requirement of the problems, provides clear options to work on the decision.

Important aspect is clear understanding of the dynamics and giving comparative values to each aspect of identified dynamics. Options have to be worked out giving degree of importance to each of the identified dynamics in the sequence of planning, to arrive at the selected course of action. Each dynamic will provide certain deductions based on the envisaged task/objectives, these have to be collated to arrive at a conclusive decision.

- *Target Response Technique:* The leader first decides on what he/she wants i.e. the aim and what is to be achieved at the target end or the targets expected response. The leader thereafter works backwards covering each aspect of the process and evaluation of application of decision. The hiccups are addressed and solutions worked out to tackle each of them. Doing so the feasibility of application of the decision becomes evident and the leaders arrive at the option of correctness of the decision. In case there are certain breaks and blockages in the chain, alternatives are worked out to tackle the same or methods work out to circumvent the break/blockages. The process is similar to reverse engineering technique. In this technique the leader has compared different solutions and options by considering the possible advantages and disadvantages of each. Such type of decision making is more applicable where the variables are constant and operational fluidity is limited, it is only then the target response can be logically appreciated.
- *Consultative Techniques:* When the decision involves inclusion of complete spectrum having the main and ancillary linkages in the conduct of operation. Decision making process in such a scenario is dependent on the consultative technique. The process includes *Domain Specialist Previews, War Gaming, Brain Storming and Discussions.* The complete strategy is dependent on the reviews of varied perception, judgments and convictions.

The said facilitators provides the inputs which are required for decision making, however the final call is that of the leader. The decision and accountability is that of the decision maker. This technique is possible when time is not at premium and scope of deliberations exists. The process is time consuming but the satisfaction of 'being party to the decision' syndrome of the participating groups makes the operability of the decision easier.

- *Building Block Technique:* The decision is divided into stages and each stage into parts, each stage and parts are tackled individually to come to an affirmative conclusion. This way the complete spectrum is addressed by the decision maker. At the end all the sum total are added to come to core decision. Aspect which must be ensured is the compatibility of each slab/stage with the related or connected slab/stage, it is only then the flow of the decision will be smooth. The slab which is not connecting will have to be modified/alternated to fit into the decision. This can be termed as 'building block' method.
- *Blend Technique:* Blending of number of options and contingencies/alternatives in the desired proportion to arrive at solutions is another way of coming to a decision. Use of combination of options gives number of alternatives having the same culminating end result based on which the decision maker can decide/take a call. As compared to sequential addressing of the problem to come to a decision, in this technique aspect of experimentation is predominant. The factor of risk is also predominantly high as combination of options is made with high dependency on probability. Decision maker has to plan for alternatives and mid course corrections to keep the blend intact. This technique depends on accuracy of validation of the options, applicability of the options, intimate follow up and monitoring. Leaders here must have adequate experience and must possess the ability of appreciating and studying the ground situation.

- *Appreciation Technique:* In this form all issues leading in sequence of importance to the core issue of the decision is addressed. This is called in the Armed Forces as 'Appreciation' of the decision. Each factor in the sequence which has direct bearing to the core point is analyzed in detail to arrive at deductions, based on the arrived deductions courses of actions are worked out. In the said process assumptions, constraints, resources, risk assessment, time factors and pertinent value of each factor are addressed. Suitability of the courses of action to the core issue is then analyzed giving out the advantages and disadvantages. Where the quotient of advantages is on the higher side in comparison to the disadvantages, the said course of action is deemed as appropriate.

Cardinals of Decision Making

There are certain cardinals of decision making which is expected from the commanders in the Armed Forces. I am highlighting some of them which I feel are essentials and enhance the confidence level of men under command on their officers:

- *Taking Decision is a Duty and a Responsibility of the Leader:* This is the basic mandatory requirement of decision making. Duty and responsibility are bestowed by the organization. This aspect can never be delegated to someone else. With duty is attached the loyalty and integrity. General George S Patton perceived *"Be willing to make decisions. That's the most important quality in a good leader"*, good leaders are identified with their ability to make right decisions.
- *Deliberation:* Decision must be deliberated; it must be supported by valuation, logic, analysis and hypothesis which require scientific approach. The Human Element of forecast, probability, chance, risk and dilemma do have its influence in the deliberations during decision making.

Deliberations are complete when the factor of reasoning has been catered.

- *Decisions not to be Kept Pending:* Pending of decision puts a questions mark on the capability and reliability of the decision maker. Delayed decision is still better but pending decision is committing suicide. It puts a doubt at your creditability!
- *Delays Increase Indecisiveness:* More the delay more will be the confusion. "Delay is a tactics and at times is good for reaching to a positive end result, but too much of it will bring slackness and indecisiveness" this is what I had been saying to my battalion commanders. Timely decisions are instinctive and instinctive decisions are mostly logical for it takes advantage of the opportunities provided by the ground situation. However, one must reason the decision and make use of the common sense.
- *Cater for Contingency:* No decision can be hundred percent accurate, factor of human element/influence brings certain amount of unpredictability and mindsets. When the flow of application is restricted due to certain unplanned variables which crop up in mid course, to make decision survive alternatives have to be worked out to tackle such interruptions. In a fluid situation, the best plans at times when tested can fail; it is prudent for a leader to have adaptable alternatives/contingency plans with same decision objectives to further the operations.
- *Audacity:* No decision is without certain amount of risk involved. In the environment of changing variables, risk is a universal factor. Decision maker must fathom the risk involved in the deliberations. Depending on the degree of risk both inherent and calculated, the decision makers have to make the final decision. Bold, audacious, prudent, and timid decisions are based on what is the decision maker's capability of taking risk and ability to put up with the associated stress factors. No risk and play safe in decision

making can be retrogressive when it comes to meeting/ achieving the desired objective.

- *Progressive and Introspective:* The decision must flow smooth during the process of implementation, it must reinforce the confidence of the decision maker. The effect of decision must flow into the process of implementation and results must be visible, it is only then that credibility of the decision maker gets established. Progressiveness of the decision depends on ratio of interruptions and corrective measures activated, lesser it is better is the decision. When impact and result of the decision taken is not visible to the environment it directly effects on the level of confidence of the group on the decision makers capability. In case of decision going wrong the leader must carry out self introspection to prevent mistakes and accepting the responsibility of a wrong decision, this is readily acceptable to the command if the leader learns from the mistakes committed, the faith and trust remains intact.
- *Comprehensible and Simple in Context:* The decision when communicated to the group must have clarity, should be concise, lucid and comprehensible by every member of the group which is to implement the decision. Ambiguity in decision will create indecisiveness in the implementation process and there will be many fault lines cropping up. Fault lines in the implementation create vacuums which the decision maker have to fill by altering the base decision or carry out too many mid course corrections, thereby the very entity of the decision gets changed.
- *Momentum:* Decision made should have the same momentum from the start to the end in the process of application. Decision should be alive and kicking, at no point of application there should arise an occasion to resuscitate and revive the decision. When the decision maker is not confident there will be gaps and this will lead to knee jerk actions at all levels, in such a situation

the need of resuscitation arises. When a decision over the decision passed have to be resorted to or review of decision have to be taken, this breaks the momentum of the process of application. Resuscitation of decision is always accompanied by the danger of the base decision getting changed. The difference of changing a decision, review of decision and use of alternatives to tied over a contingency encountered during the application of decision, need to be very clearly understood by the decision maker. When a decision dies its own death mid way, resuscitating such decision is waste of effort and time, it is better to review the decision or take a fresh decision.

- *Trust and Resoluteness:* Decision based on a structured analysis and made to follow a logical adopted course is said to be a measured decision. When this decision is backed by reliability, prudent planning and responsibility, the decision is universally accepted as apt and followed without hesitations. Decision maker must not buckle under any type of pressure, when the leader is confident of the decision and is resolute in his approach, it will make the decision pragmatic and viable in application. Momentary hesitation on the part of decision maker at any point will directly affect the confidence in application.
- *Objectivity and Transparency:* Benchmark of a decision maker is an important aspect in human resource management; this is shaped by perception of the group about the decision maker and degree of trust. Decision making and its subsequent fallouts directly effects the perception equation as prevalent in the environment, thus objectivity and transparency should be visible in the decision and its application. When objectivity and transparency is evident in the complete process, the perception of the group will be on the positive plinth and degree of acceptability will be correspondingly higher. Personal prejudice must never reflect in decision.

Guidelines are facilitators in decision making to decide on the right decision, one aspect must be very clear, each decision has individualistic character and no two decisions can be the same in all aspects as no two decision takers are same. Decision making will always remain individualistic in context and content due to the human behaviours, therefore the applicability of cardinals will vary in degree of applicability in each situation separately. In corporate functionaries what I have observed is that attitude of passing the buck and looking over the shoulders is a prevalent practice, lot of time is wasted in getting to perfect decision instead of right decision amounting to last minute fire fighting to achieve the set target. Perfect decision may have some gaps as the decision maker does not want any gaps whatsoever and it takes time to fill up the gaps. But right decision is sensible and intuitive backed by contingencies to cater for the gaps, here the leader is pragmatic and confident, therefore is judicious in his approach.

Never regret a decision which have gone wrong, take responsibility and learn from it. Good decision comes from experience and experience comes from mistakes committed. One must not fear taking a decision; it is a moral duty of the leaders to take decision. In conclusion to this chapter I would like to quote Field Marshal Sam Manekshaw one of the few Indian Generals who has been candid about his opinion, *"It is the ability to make up your mind to make a decision and accept full responsibility for that decision. Have you ever wondered why people do not make a decision? The answer is quite simple. It is because they lack professional competence, or they are worried that their decision may be wrong and they will have to carry the can. According to the law of averages, if you take ten decisions, five ought to be right. If you have professional knowledge and professional competence, nine will be right, and the one that might not be correct will probably be put right by a subordinate officer or a colleague. But if you do not take a decision, you are doing something wrong. An act of omission is much worse than an act of commission. An act of commission can be put right. An act of omission cannot."*

Decision making will always remain a controversial subject and there will be many critics to a decision, it is the human tendency to be critical of others view point. My advice to all decision makers, once you have ventured into a decision just go through with it and remember General Patton's phrase *"A good solution applied with vigour now is better than a perfect solution applied ten minutes later."* Opportunities cannot be sacrificed for want of decision.

> *"Great leadership does not mean running away from reality. Sometimes the hard truths might just demoralize the company, but at other times sharing difficulties can inspire people to take action that will make the situation better".*
>
> —John Kotter

4 Planning Strategy

"All men can see these tactics whereby I conquer, but what none can see is the strategy out of which victory is evolved."

—Sun Tzu

Before I deliberate on strategy, first the difference between strategy and tactics need to be understood. Strategy is setting the target and tactics is ways to achieve the set target, in other words, it is why! and what! Method to implement the strategy is the tactics. Tactics achieve goals and Strategy is all about setting the right goals. The terms tactic and strategy are often confused: tactics are the actual means used to gain an objective, while strategy is the overall plan, which may involve complex operational patterns, activity, and decision-making that lead to tactical execution. Quoting two quotes which differentiate between strategy and tactics *"Great leaders have a long-term vision of the future, and they avoid getting bogged down in the here and now. While they can be tactical when necessary, they maintain the strategic outlook necessary to guide their businesses to the best future possible"* and *"Tactics are the what. Strategy is the why. Tactics are the actions. Strategy is the planning. Tactics may achieve goals. Strategy is all about setting the right goals."*

The present day need for making strategy to an large extent been relegated to use of models and tools, the art of applying oneself in evolving and conceptualizing strategy have given way to the concept of favoured job addressing, departmentalized tasking or multiple tasking and planning, prioritizing and domain specialist concept. Whatever be the tools without evolving strategy the tactical application is not possible, computers can formulate plans but the primary requisites of strategy is the human element of visualization and thinking. The value and importance of strategy need to be understood by the leadership, it is the first logical step of starting the process of formulation of any plan or activity. Strategy is well defined by this quote of B.H. Liddell Hart, *"Strategy is a way of visualisation and thinking, a conscious and deliberate process, an exhaustive management and implementation arrangements and the skill of insuring prospective success."*

Strategy is conceptualized at the highest planning level and gets applied down the chain. Having vision is an important facet of leadership responsibility and it is this facet which decides the aim, scope and terms of references for the directives of the strategy. Based on organizational directives, strategies are conceptualized at each level of command/ function and the scope is decided, to apply the strategy to a phase or the entire operation or the duration of the activity in organizational interest. Strategy encompasses all the associated activities or the function in the area of operation which must include both the areas of interest and areas to be influenced. To make the strategy successful the chains of command at various levels have to be equally involved and ensure implementation through sound tactical plans.

Planning of Strategy

Strategy is logical appreciation of the process in relation to the visualised vision and the objective of the vision that is to be achieved; influence of human elements in the strategy making process will always subsist. Formulating strategy for an operation is a pathway and this paves the way for making plan, directives and instructions to run an operation. The planning of strategy is a technique which is dependent on logical reasoning and certain basics imperatives which must be considered by the leadership are:

- *Vision:* The strategist must have vision, visualisation of the ultimate objective to be accomplished need to be framed and the field over which the strategy is to be applied need to be defined. Vision encompasses giving of the meaning, identification of the target objective, integration of efforts and appropriateness of relative ground situations in relation to the desired objective. The prospects of the idea of the vision and its adequacy, relative importance of the fields on which the vision have to rely upon and synthesis of the environment which is directly related to the vision are some of the issues which warrant consideration. Aspect of the spread of the vision and the duration of applicability need to be established, accordingly the vision may have short term/long term prospective or combination of both. To make the vision a reality the strategy should have total objectivity-Vision precedes strategy and strategy is the roadmap to the vision. Vision must be understood by everyone in the environment and easily comprehended. The vision must first identify where you are now, follow it with what is the future and the road map to the planned objective. Once this is considered and clearly defined, the next step is obtaining the answer to what is to be achieved and where all the vision is to be applied and lastly who all will be involved. Here I want to put a word of caution, there should not be any confusion with the term vision and visionary, the visionary may or may not be realistic, it is imaginary perception whereas vision is always realistic and is an idea, imaginary or utopian approach to vision will never get perceived in the right perspective of strategic thinking.

- *Identification of Aim and Scope:* As a starter, the leader has to first decide on the aim of the strategy which he/she is planning and ensure it is in consonance and within the vision ambit. Aim has to be definitive in nature. The scope of the strategy giving out the scales, restrictions and limits has to be worked out in relation to the selected aim. Terms of references and directives as given by the top controlling authorities/management have to be catered while deciding the aim and scope. These are the very foundation of planning any strategy. There are certain issues which must be borne in mind while deciding the aim and the scope:
    - Practicality
    - Achievability
    - Sustainability
    - Scope confines and/or terms of references
    - Simplicity
    - Clarity
- *Considerations:* Before arriving at the strategy, the considerations on which the plan is to be based must be identified. Consideration addresses the question of 'what all and when'? The scope and terms of references facilitates in deciding the considerations. Considerations must answer the questions - *what do you want to do - how you want to reach to the point where you want to go - what do you have and what do you need - when and at what time - what are the strength and what are the weakness - what is in favour and what is not - what can stall the plans - how to respond to such situation and contingencies - what timelines should you plan and how to be applied* and lastly *what thereafter.* The factors and issues of each consideration which are essential for making strategy must be highlighted and listed out by the planner. Considerations that have been obtained then must be connoted in order of importance. The considerations give completeness to the process of preparation of planning of

strategy. Following must be considered to work out the framework of the plan to apply the strategy:

- o Situation as prevailing on ground
- o Information/data base availability
- o Resources required in application of strategy
- o Environmental imperatives, intelligence inputs with regard to preparation and application of strategy
- o SWOT (strength, weakness, opportunities and threat) both internal and external
- o Visualised contingencies
- o Supports from internal and external resources
- o Coordination and liaisons
- o Key Success Areas/Key Result Areas
- o Harmonization of the field of applications
- o Modification, reappraisal and evaluations of systems
- o Responsibilities and accountability
- o Communication and follow-ups
- o Process and/or phases of application

- *Potential Analysis:* The consideration will facilitate in making a framework of the strategy. The aspect which must follow is to carry out an appraisal of the potential and capability of various resources which are to be applied in the strategy. Here pragmatism is of importance. Over and under evaluating of the potentials of all the players in the strategy should be avoided, this creates ambiguity in the mind of the strategic planner. Right assessment of potentials gives the planner the confidence in taking right decision and calculated risks. The potential analysis facilitates:
  - o Synergy of effort and agencies
  - o Appropriateness of application
  - o Integration of resources
  - o Sense of purpose in plans and event control
  - o Resilience in employment of resources
  - o Support requisition
  - o Corrections and modifications of plans when warranted

- *The Plan:* The final plan is derived out of the tentative frame work, as at this stage all the inputs are available with the planner. The plan will get formulated by proper application of logic and within the purview of the aim, scope and the objective. The aspects which require attention at this stage is the human element of the plan and which will always remain individualistic in character. For strategy to be effective and successful issues which must be incorporated in the plan are:
  - First thing which must be very well understood that it is "man behind the machine" i.e. human resources who are going to make the strategy work, therefore the plan must be easily understandable, assimilated, taken on board and absorbed.
  - The sustainability of the strategy depends, on the willing response the plan can generate. Therefore, the plan must be transparent, having a purpose and certainty. Plan must not be paradoxical in nature, ambiguity will break momentums.
  - The plan must have in built scope for freedom of action at tactical and execution level.
  - The organisational values and ethos play an important role in imbibing the spirit of belonging and pride. The strategy during the planning stage should imbibe these values and ethos.
  - The plan must cater for human concern and growth. This will sustain the momentum and facilitate task enlargement in the application of the strategy.
- *Deployment of Resources:* Based on the aim, scope and the objective the resources allocation is planned, deployment of resources in right quantum and at right time is an important facet of strategy. There are three type of leadership, when handling resources, *first*, who believes in equal and balanced distribution of resources and caters for reserve, *second*, who believes in putting maximum mass at the point of decision and *third*, type who is cautious in employment and believes

in drip-let/installment employment technique, and with progress of the application of strategy keeps reviewing the employment of resources. All three have their pros and cons. The equation of employment of resources is based on three factors - task, situation and time, based on these factors the quantum gets decided. The application of the resources depends on its importance, potential, capacity and relevance in the strategy. The deployment of resources thus will be governed by:

- o Relative importance of sequence and priorities of the strategy
- o Decision points which have relevance in sustaining the strategy
- o Timeframe and timelines of the strategy
- o Decided acceleration and speed
- o Frequencies of anticipated contingencies and contingency plans
- o Economy
- o Reserves for anticipated opportunities and modification of plans

- *Development of People Plan:* It is the human resource integration, which forms the basic parameter of making strategy successful. It is men who are the ultimate decider of the outcome of any plan, for strategy alone cannot achieve the objective. It is important that unique value based relationships are developed between men and the planner. This is possible when men understands the strategy, values its purpose and accepts responsibilities thereof. It is then the set outcome of objective/target becomes achievable. When planning, human resource must be considered as one of the core issue on which the strategy is dependent, important human aspects on which the planner must focus are selection, value of commitment and participation, familiarization with the environment, preparation to undertake the strategy and stimulation of responses. Having right man at right place will sustain the strategy. Human resource being versatile variable will require intimate handling and periodic reviews. What is important is creating mental setup and stimulus towards strategy; this can be best achieved by integrating the people and the plan. Understanding of the men who are to apply the strategy and strategic employment of resources is equally important as much as considerations, understanding the fundamentals and working out the concepts for the strategy.

- *Integration and Synergy:* Once the above factors have been worked out, in order of sequence first integration followed by synergy of the resources need to be applied. The compatibility factor in this regard must be kept in mind, mismatch will create problem in implementation processes. The ambit of integration will be from inception to completion of the objective of the strategy. Factors which should be considered in integration are – justification, shifts, classification, adeptness, adaptability and compatibility. Integrating any resources and/or agency facilitates in identifying the point of integration, suitability and processes of incorporation. Synergy means more than coordination, it is art of synchronization to obtain unison and harmony of the process implementation, and synergy is a force that creates an environment of spirit of achievability, responsibility and unity of purpose. Synergy is tenable till its spirit is kept alive and is nurtured. Factors which impact synergy is justification of mechanism, relationship with process mechanism, inter and intra association within the process, component's value contribution and objective vis-à-vis component's relationship. Maximum optimization of resources is depended on integration and synergy.
- *SWOT Analysis:* Strategy cannot be complete without catering for contingency planning and backup plans. Strength, Weakness, Opportunity and Threat (SWOT) analysis is a mode which enables in working out the

contingency plans and evaluates the requirement of reserves to meet the contingencies arising in the strategy. To sustain the strategy, contingency planning must be prudent and resilient. Perception of SWOT have to be rational and relevant, over cautiousness and lack of pragmatism will be misleading as it can result in over/under assessment, this will directly impact the contingency plans.

- *Force Multipliers:* Strategist while planning strategy must consider using force multipliers which helps to invigorate, energise and provide impetus. Force multipliers are those components which have inherent capability to accelerate the process of implementation and provide advantage over the existing resources. The force multiplier can be new technology or specially trained work force or components which have additional/enhanced capability and potential which provides position of strength or advantage. A simple thing like introduction of a new weapon system to tilt the balance with the adversary, the said weapon system is considered as a force multiplier. The plan must include force multiplier either from the start or can be added during the course of the operation. Strategy planner must always be in search of such force multipliers, need to carry out reviews to identify them and incorporate them at appropriate time.
- *Tactics:* The tactics is planned and applied at the execution level; the strategist involvement in this field is restricted. There are two schools of thoughts :
  - Some strategic planners are of the view that the core issue tactics must be planned by them, this brings in consistency in implementation, as the core issues are directly associated with the key issues of the tactical plans. The aim and scope are inter related with each other, thus it would be prudent to plan the strategy and tactics simultaneously. Such addressing is basically to avoid variation at conceptual level of both

strategic and the tactical plans of the strategy. Here the planner is involved at both strategic and tactical level. Communication with the subordinate command is direct and intimate. As the planner is intimately involved, the planner is able to review the progress and adopt corrections on ground.

- The second school of thought believes that strategist must follow the directive style of command, where the directives are issued by the strategic planner and execution of the strategy is delegated to subordinate command those who are responsible for planning the tactics in implementation of the strategy. The accountability factor and responsibilities shift to the subordinate command with the latitude of freedom of action, this develops the scope in terms of initiative and independent decision making at functional level. In this style of control the strategic planner have to adopt a system of follow up communication and monitoring. In this option the planner has a constant overall holistic view of the progress and thus is in a position to carry out constant review, modification or mid course corrections.

Therefore, the strategy planning is a deliberate process and sequential application of factors/considerations as discussed above. The process can be summarised under the following steps:

- Obtaining information data base
- Identification of issues to be addressed
- Assessments of ground of operation and ground realities
- Environmental scanning
- Potential/capability utilization plan
- Risk assessment
- Process implementation plan
- Issue of directives
- Review process

- Readiness/preparation
- Control/monitoring

Putting into Operation the Strategy

The next important aspect is putting into action the planned strategy; this is the sole responsibility of the planner of the strategy. This is the stage where the planner has to apply, plan the process application and streamline the control and review system. Very many plans stay on the drawing board for want of apt application and process control. It is not the plan but putting the plan into action which matters the most, this is a responsibility from which the leaders cannot be absolved irrespective of the level. The combat considerations which are important facets of putting the strategy into operation are:

- *Terms of reference*: The components who would be responsible to execute the strategy must know the terms of reference, the terms of reference must bring out:
  - What is available and what can be allotted?
  - What additional can be made available and in what time frame?
  - When to start and when to complete?
  - What are the time lines?
  - What all support will be given?
  - Who all will be supporting the operation and till what time?
- *Directives*: Once clear terms of references have been defined, this must be followed by the directives on the conduct of the strategy. This must not be confused with the terms of reference which is the given parameters on which the plans are to be based, where as the directives give out the methods and modus of operation or tasking for operations. The ubiquity of directives will be dependent on the degree of freedom of action given at the executior level. Directives have to be highly structured and cover the

conceptual application of the plan; it should give directions of actions to make the application of strategy purposeful and focused. The directives must not include tactics of applying the strategy; this should be best left to the executives of the strategy as they have intimate awareness of the situation and ground realities. The directives are basically functional parameters which are given out as a guideline on which the plans at tactical level of execution of strategic plan are planned. Here there should not be any ambiguity, uncertainty and vagueness; this will create confusion down the line. "*Clean and clear directives and correct and accurate distribution of means is the great art of deployment of effort, add to these 'the right' generalship the plans thereafter will flow on its own*" was Napoleon's observations on strategy of battle.

- *Responsibility and Accountability*: Selection of core group for implementation of strategy is an important factor, single handed operational handling by the strategic planner is not possible. Depending on the spread of the spectrum of the strategy, the scope of the core group has to be decided. The core group selection will be based on the fields of the components that are going to participate, domain specialisation, experience, and the command and control structure. Timelines and criticality state of the operations are two aspects which must be monitored continuously at all the fronts of the strategy to maintain the momentum and continuity; therefore decentralisation of responsibility becomes a necessity. Decentralization of responsibility is a function of authority and if the field of the strategy covers a large canvas it would be prudent to delegate authority and responsibility to the created command and control structure. It is participative quest in decision making which makes the executors of the strategy more responsible, this also makes the leader accountable to the task entrusted. This process depends on the magnitude of the strategy, bigger the magnitude larger will be the decentralisation and delegation.

- *Orientation and Preparation*: Once the terms of reference have been made explicit, directives spelt out, command and control structure worked out; responsibilities delegated the process of planning at execution level sets in. Strategist must orientate the core group with the plan and carry out deliberations on the conduct, issue guidelines, fix functional parameters in reference to vision and to put into action the conduct of the strategic plans. The core group will thereafter proceed to prepare the participants for the task and/or set the vision vis-à-vis objective stipulations of the strategy. This should be followed by familiarisation (reconnaissance) of the respective functional/operational areas by the participating component heads and the participating units.
- *Control and Monitoring*: The person who is planning the strategy need to work out the command, control and monitoring structure to implement the plan. Over and above the central and functional structure of command and control, the planner need to monitor the implementation and progress of the plan, this is necessary to carry out review, evaluation and midcourse corrections.
- *Feedback, Reviews and Evaluations:* Mechanisms of feedback have to be instituted so that the progress can be evaluated and review of application of resources can be carried out. Feedback must be taken from functional and the command levels. Command and control reporting chain, operative level assessments and individual feedback methods must be adopted to get the true picture. Multiple feedback channels provide confirmation, authenticity and truthful check back. The strategy planner must keep evaluating the progress based on timelines and objectives to be achieved, constant evaluation will help in reviews and corrections were warranted. Ideal course for the planner

will be to ensure that plan flows without interruptions and corrections, however with the fluidity in the operations and constantly changing variables the strategist have to resort to reviews and application of contingencies. To keep the plan on track and ensure successful conclusion of the strategy frequent reviews and reappraisals are mandatory.

Military History through the ages has seen great battle strategies, there are certain identifiable leadership qualities which such strategist demonstrated:

- Vision and foresight, clear understanding of objectives to be achieved.
- Astute planning and eye for details. Unambiguous judgement of the situation, retrospective analysis of failures and consequences and bottle necks/holdups.
- Clarity of thoughts and observations, bold decision taking and audacious approach.
- Temperament for creative ideas and ingenuity in application. Individualistic and original concept in planning.
- Passion in planning and execution of the strategy. Strive for excellence in conduct.
- Confidence in one's own decision making and conduct.
- Preparing and confidence building of participating forces.

The strategy planning can never be delegated to the subordinate command. The organisational interest is supreme in the planning process; the values and ethos also have a big role to play in giving direction to the strategy. The strategy cannot be compared with the process definition and management, it is largely concept based on which the functions and process get governed. Every leader must have the knack of making strategic plans or plan out strategy. Strategy is both the art and science, it involves setting of objective/goals, determining actions to achieve the said objective/goals, and mobilizing resources to execute the actions. Carl von Clausewitz defined military strategy as *"the employment of battles to gain the end of war"* and B. H. Liddell Hart's definition of strategy is *"the art of distributing and applying military means to fulfill the ends of policy"*. Thus ultimate question which the strategist must answer is how wherewithal be optimally used to achieve the ultimate visualized goals/objectives.

> *"You have to be fast on your feet and adaptive or else a strategy is useless*
>
> —Charles de Gaulle, French General and Statesman

5 Setting Up Tactics

"Strategy without tactics is the slowest route to victory. Tactics without strategy is the noise before defeat".

—Sun Tzu

Tactics is the applications of ways, methods and means in support of the strategy and facilitates meeting the overall strategic objective. *"Tactics are the what. Strategy is the why. Tactics are the actions. Strategy is the planning. Tactics is the path to achieve the strategic goals. Strategy is all about setting the right goals,"* a very apt quote by Lynn Parker which differentiate tactics and the strategy. In tactics the operations are tackled at execution level and are more specific, intimate and very personal. Leader's personality has a big role to play; the veracity of the tactics depends on skill, attitude, perception, outlook, approach, motivation and commitment towards the organization. Negativity in any one of the aforesaid characters creates inconsistencies and gaps which impinge on the quality of planning and execution of tactics.

There is a distinctive difference in application of tactics and standing orders/standard operating procedures (SOP); I have seen many people who are confused on this aspect, as they infer that "it is the successfully applied tactics which becomes a standard operating procedure or the standing orders". In my opinion *firstly,* no two tactics is the same, *secondly,* repeated tactics may not always be successful as the situations and variables of the said situations may have changed and lastly tactics is not a routine activity. Tactics is never dependent on matrixes or set procedures, each individual's perception and the approach to the objective/goal is different therefore, there will be number of tactics to address one single task. Tactics is an application of a plan at execution level and is leader dependent. On the other hand, the standing operative procedures are guidelines or instructions which are commonly applicable for bringing uniformity during conduct of a routine or everyday activity. Like a beat patrol doing patrolling as per SOP but when the said patrol is attacked by miscreants, the actions which follows is the tactical handling of the situation.

It is at the tactical level were the strategy is executed and leadership plays an important role here. Strategy may be planned at the highest or conceptual level but at each stratum of application of the strategy, tactics plays an important role. Therefore, at each level below the strategic level and between the work floors, the leadership at each stratum has to evolve tactical plans to implement the strategy successfully. The individual perception of the applied tactical plan has to be in consonance with the strategic thinking. The tactics which had been used in one particular strategy cannot be replicated or repeated in the new strategy, for each new set of strategy even if the scope being similar new set of tactics have to be evolved depending on the changes of factors, variables and the timelines. Each new attempt will be providing avenue of application of new tactics, to quote Sun Tzu, *"Do not repeat the tactics which have gained you one victory, but let your methods be regulated by the infinite variety of circumstances"*, tactics is situation and occurrence dependent and will keep varying with each application, it is leaders' very own way of handling the task.

Planning Tactics

Planning of tactics is similar to strategy but the difference is in the level of planning, tactics is more focused and down to earth in relation to the ground situation. Tactics at lateral and vertical spectrum of execution, combine to make a strategy work. Strategy is broad based but tactics is precise. Planning and executing tactics is an art, however it must be supported by knowledge, logic, ingenuity and passion. I find that now-a-days the functional level planning of tactics has been relegated to fixed matrix tactics as there is lack of personal involvement and ingenuity. Cautiousness and cut-copy-paste syndrome have cropped up, over supervision and no risk syndrome is the second factor which curbs the initiative of the junior leaders and lastly looking over the shoulder for help have become a common phenomenon as freedom of action are restricted by the seniors who believe in incident free career graph. Tactics is a casualty in such an environment.

Working out combat tactics is the command responsibility of the military leaders at all levels of command, there are certain basic qualities which the leaders must have or develop to do justice to tactical planning and application:

- *Competency and knowledge:* These are the foremost important qualification. Leaders must be having detailed knowledge of the task and the task requisites/considerations. Leader's proficiency and competency level must be high, for the men under command he/she is the ultimate. The analysis of the data input, understanding of the ground, the logical consideration of task requirements, optimization of utilization of the allotted resources, appropriate tasking of men and material and command and control of the team are important functional factors. Knowledge, therefore, is an essential requisite and the experience/ acumen of the leader are the added linked factors which have direct bearing/influence on planning of the tactics.

The tactics evolved by the leader and the quality of tactics is proportionate to the level of competency. Professional shrewdness is an important facet of a good tactician and this is possible when knowledge is appropriate. In tactics following questions have to be answered which are knowledge based:

- o Why and what is the purpose? How is it going to meet the overall strategy? What will be my role?
- o What are the technical and practical aspects? How will these be applied and what all have to be considered for application?
- o What are the tactical implications and how are these going to affect the plan?
- o What will I require or have to bid to make the plan working?
- o Who all will be participating in the plan?
- o What is to be monitored and what will be the control mechanism?

- *Appreciation of the factors:* The acumen of the leaders in accurately appreciating the factors and the operational environment is important to apply the plan. Appreciation of the environment and area of operation (which can be geographical limits, technical ground of operation, work floor, etc.) are important factors which facilitate in planning of the tactics. Acumen of the leader depends in judging the operability of the stipulated plan or the factors within which the tactics is to be applied and this will depend largely on the situation on ground, assessment of each of the inferred factors, peculiarities of factors vis-à-vis its relation to task and the imperatives of the planned operation to meet the assigned target. If these are rightly appreciated the tactics will flow with the plan. The contingencies and courses of action to negotiate the tactics are determined through the said process. The technical and tactical visualization of likely fallouts and actions to meet the said contingencies thus are part of leader's appreciation. In a fluid environment the process of appreciation is continuous. In fixed and invariable environment appreciation applied will vary with change of application of operative procedure or any changes in the course of the task within the preview of the operative tactical plan. Prudent leaders must develop this art, as this will give impetus to innovative ideas in planning and executing the tactics.

- *Attitude:* The degree of positivity in attitude during tactical planning and on ground application is one of the factors which the leader has to reckon with. The degree of commitment and involvement determine the degree of positivity of approach, no two leaders can be alike when it comes to attitude. Another aspect which determines the attitude is the outlook of the leader, the way of thinking creates different pressure point during application of tactics. Survival instinct of the leader and faith on the team competency are two important aspects of attitude which gives impetus to commitment and involvement. Leader's attitude to achieve, boldness in approach, resourcefulness to resolve problems, courage of conviction and support to the team makes the application of tactics astute. The right and positive attitude establishes the leaders within the team, determines the intensity of participation and working out of the right tactics within the capability. In the words of Chanakya, *"The tactics which does not have the leader with right approach, it will not succeed"*. Thus right appreciation or giving value to the tasks, supporting elements, men, material and communication is important facet of approach to any tactics.
- *Optimism:* Optimistic leaders are good tactician. Optimism is directly related to sanguinity and confidence in approach of the leader. The degree of optimism determines the leader's aptitude towards decision making, risk taking ability and ability to sustain the operations.

Most of us confuse optimism to be associated to providence, dependency on probability of success and the hope of succeeding. In actuality it is positivity of thought and outlook in a leader which determines the approach to be adopted in application of tactics and the achievement of the desired result from the said tactics, optimism gives positive flip to the leader's outlook and approach.

- *Trust:* Trust is two sides of the same coin; on one side, it is the trust in subordinates, in men under command or in the team and on the other side, is the trust of subordinate, men and the team on the leader. Trust is dependent on credibility, reliability, conviction and commitment. When levels of both sides of the coin are balanced, trust is more dominant. *"Trust is like a good cheque which never bounces but one who issues it must maintain a good balance in his account always and every time"* this was what my platoon commander used to say, trust is to be neutered and sustained. It is the equilibrium of proportion of trust which matters, when the trust is maximum on both sides the tactics is the gainer. Trust determines the level of decentralization and delegation of responsibilities by the leader. If the level of trust is high the tactics will have a smooth run, there will be passion, aggressiveness and determination to achieve the target by both the parties. Degree of combined willpower and determination to persevere in face of odds is trust dependent, higher the trust greater will be the resolve and purpose. Trust provides the scope of taking calculated risk by the leaders in tactical application of the plans.
- *Passion:* Vibrancy of the leader is reflected through passion for involvement, excellence and faultless execution. Passion for involvement by both the leader and the team creates an environment of commitment, will to achieve and unison. In tactics passion is in relation to execution and excellence. The passion for excellence generates innovativeness, ideas, ingenuity in approach and resourcefulness, the buoyancy

of tactics comes out of the passion for excellence. Passion in execution of tactics brings momentum, speed and energy. Cohesion of the team is better achieved when passion of execution exists at the leader and the team end respectively. In tactics where the complete sequences of actions are more related to the actual situation on ground, passion plays an important role in meeting the challenges in right way keeping the sensitivity of the desired objective/goal into consideration.

Planning of tactics is the art and skill of employing available means to accomplish an end. Tactics is doing what you can with what you have, it is planned at functional level and the spread covers both lateral and vertical levels of the job platforms. Strategies have number of tactical operations at lateral and vertical execution level, combination of series of tactical operations makes the strategy meet its objective or the vision. The process of planning tactics involves:

- *Study and Reasoning:* Detailed study of the area of operation followed by logical deductions derived from the factors identified which have direct influence in tactical application of men and material in the said area of operation is the perquisite of tactical planning. Deductions streamline the process of application of the plan, men, material and contingencies while executing the envisaged plan. Deduction should bring out the :
    - o Timelines
    - o Possible combinations of options of courses derived from the ground and the functional environments
    - o Peculiarity of area of operation and its support to meet the objective
    - o Inherent natural qualities which will support the task
    - o Identification of bottlenecks/blocks and how to overcome the same
    - o How are the resources to be employed to advantage in reference to the area of operation and the task?

- o How to exploit the concerned factors which has direct bearing in the process to one's own advantage.

Assessment of the ground/functional environment on which the tactics is to be applied must be known in detail, ground in actuality includes the complete spectrum of the areas of operations. For a military commander, the ground will be the terrain, whereas for a consumer goods manufacturer it will be the market and the production lines. Till such time the leader himself carries out the assessment and arrive at the logical deductions, feasibility of applying the same in the real time and in own terms will put tactics in a weaker position. Deductions help in working out the various options and courses of actions. The applicability of the tactics in various scenarios of application in relation to target/objective get streamlined through this process

- *Resource Requirement:* Optimum utilization of the resources is in relation to the task and the demand of the ground/ work platform. The issues which have direct influence in deciding the relative importance of the resource and its application is the task, terms of reference of usage and rightful employability based on optimizing the resource capability. 'Right resource at the right place' is the desired objective, here very many leaders gets it wrong and indulge in trying out or experimenting with resources. Another tendency which usually crops up is 'what I have is not sufficient or it is not good enough', without rightfully exploiting the optimum capability and coming to conclusive decision, these tendencies must be avoided. A good tactician is the one who uses his ingenuity to make use of what is available. "Correct and accurate distribution of means is the great art of utilization of effort, add to these 'the right' management and leadership acumen, this gives completeness to the plan", there is no end to cribs when it comes to availability of resources and the results not being up to the mark, thus resource engagement is an important element of successful tactics.

- *Options:* The ground and resources open up options available for application of tactics. Each course has to be evaluated in the backdrop of the task and comparative advantages/disadvantages. While working the options, points which require consideration are the suitability, sustainability and vulnerability of task and the tactics being employed in handling the said tactical task. Options worked out must be comprehensible and modus of application of options of courses of action must clearly come out to meet the stipulations of the ground situation, resources, time and the target requirement. While taking decision on the option to be selected, the leaders have to apply logic, contextualize it to the situation as obtainable on ground and ensure that there are no hindrances in execution. The skill lies on how to make the right selection of the option.
- *Timelines:* After the options have been worked out, each of the options time management have to be calculated. It would be prudent that timelines are worked out in both forward and backward calculation. While determining the timelines all possible interruptions must be incorporated in the calculations. Leaders have to take decision on :
    - o What should be the duration?
    - o What are the process/activity involved, should the process be in phases or continuous application and what must be the timings?
    - o How long the applied tactical plan to be sustained to derive the target or create impact?
    - o Timings of resource availability, sequence of application and time frame of the plan?
    - o What will be consequence if timelines are not met? What cushion timings to be catered in the plans? Time for contingencies?

- *Selection of Course of Action:* It is at this stage that final decision is taken in selecting a course of action. The inputs at this stage is adequately available to make a final decision, two unequivocal aspects which need to be ensured *firstly,* decision is of the leader and *secondly,* leader is responsible for the outcome of the decision. The option selected must be within the purview of achievability, capability and quantum of resources made available. Play safe or no risk syndromes are detrimental as such an attitude brings in too much of cautiousness without taking an attempt or the plunge, this adversely effects the actions to optimize the tactical plan to its planned conclusion. In selecting the right options the issue of exploiting the windows of opportunities or taking prudent risk to carry out mid course corrections or decision to apply planned contingencies to break the logjams will depend on the approach and competency of the leader. While selecting the option one has to guard against going in for an over ambitious option as this may lead to the tendency of experimentation; compulsive taking of chance and dependency on outside intervention, these create breaks in the flow of the application of the tactical plan. A prudent leader will go in for balanced options which supports the confidence/trust of the team, optimization of the resource output, which is within the capabilities of the team, which can sustain the momentum of progress and meet the time lines. At times, combination of options to decide on a course of action pays good dividends in terms of maximization of utilization of resources and exploiting the advantages of all the options, one has to be careful as combinations may create frictions and this does break the focus, one is reminded of the idiom "too many cooks spoil the broth". This phase is the final stage of decision making on which the desired result is dependent however, the responsibility totally lies on the leader.

- *Risk Assessments and Contingency Plans:* All plans must have backups, scope for recovery, reserve and cater for contingencies. Once a course of action has been decided risk assessment and actions to handle the risk need to be planned, this would be the first step. The second step would be to keep a reserve option always open in case the assessed risk changes the scenario or windows of opportunity coming in the way due to the said risk can be exploited/adequately handled. The third step would be to work out various contingencies to deal with unplanned issues or the uncontrolled variables cropping up due to the risk contemplated to be undertaken. The selected option/plan are complete when the aspects of unforeseen occurrences have been catered and actions have been identified to address these occurrences.

Tactics are the specific actions or sequences of actions to make the operational plan functional. If one have more than one strategy then different tactical plans for each strategy will be required. The tactics is the art and science of management, direction, control and manoeuvre of forces that have been made available to achieve a task/target. The planning sequences have been discussed above, there are certain characteristics which a leader must possess which makes the tactical plan and tactics employed work, I am highlighting few of the crucial one's:

- *Briefing and Instructions:* This is one of the most important aspects of application of tactical plans; the leaders must carry out detailed briefing and pass instructions to the command in a very exhaustive manner so that there is no ambiguity and the plan is rightly comprehended. This involves tasking of each individual, resource allocation, support, schedule of each task and procedure of feedback. Communications procedures have to be clearly spelt out during the briefing to ensure speed in passing of orders/ instructions, maintaining the contact, obtaining feedback, follow-up of execution and monitoring the progress of the plan. The frequencies of briefing have to be decided by the leader this is to ensure that there are no gaps; it will also depend on *firstly*, the number of phases in the plans, secondly incorporation/discontinuity of resources, thirdly, occurrence of change or compulsion of taking recourse and lastly the level and/or degree of confidentiality. *"Simpler the plan better is the control"*, one detailed briefing is the best way to ensure continuity of momentum set in force at the launch of the plan. Too many briefings create confusions and display the uncertainty in the leaders. Detailed and comprehensible briefing makes the plan look simple.

- *Review and Evaluation:* The tactician must review the progress of the plan from time to time, this should be done basically to demonstrate the involvement of the leader and give confidence to the teams. Review should not be with the aim to change especially when the set course is meeting the objective. Frequent changes are not advisable, as with any major change a new plan automatically gets evolved and the original plan gets relegated, moreover if this is so then the selected course of action in itself is faulty. Midcourse correction is part of evaluation, and evaluation is the process of assessing the progress of the plan. This gives the leader scope of putting impetus in the plan and timely resuscitation to maintain the momentum of the plan to final conclusion. Taking feedback from the environment at regular interval is must to keep the hand on the pulse to gauge the progress and attainment of the result.
- *Influencing the Team/Group:* What is important for a leader in tactics is how to influence the team. There are number of methods available to the leader to apply , here I would like to give out certain effective tactics in leading the team, all of them or most of them are practiced and part of character of a military leader:

- *Demanding Attitude:* In this tactics, the leader has full control and authority to employ the tactical plan, the leader in a way dictates the terms. This tactics is more applicable where there is little time or urgency is of importance or deadline cannot be compromised or the task is less desirable by the troops. This method is productive only when the leader is able to create the challenge and make use of the trust of the team to meet the urgency of the task. Personality of the leader here is very important. Certain negatives which one must guard - it must not be overused, no one likes 'barking' of orders or mistakes made by the leader covered under the guise of authority 'I do what I want, no one can question'- these are detrimental to the confidence and trust/faith of the team on the leader.
- *Involvement:* If the leader can get others involved in the process and is committed, the team will adopt the leader's goal as theirs and become committed to its attainment. Involvement is a very powerful influencing tactic as each member of the team is made to feel the onus of the plan and responsibility towards the perceived onus, 'we work and fight very strongly for things that are our own and when we are answerable'. Involving people succeeds when the credit of achievements is attributable to all participating member of the team and this depends on the faith and the creditability of the leader.
- *Encouragement:* With the encouragement, the leader motivates and gives impetus to the confidence of the team. Leader here is a mentor and makes an endeavour to exploit the potential of each member of the team through encouragement. In this tactics, the freedom of action is given ample opportunity. Motivation and encouragement of one confident and proficient member can be used in getting others to take the challenge

individually or collective by the team/group. Leader has to keep in mind that persons can commit mistakes and opportunity must be given to improve/correct, this attitude sustains the encouragement.

- *Masking*: The leader uses indirect tactics, team is made to perform task similar to the actual task with similar degree of intensity and leader does not reveal the real task. The actual intent is to camouflage the tasks which are very critical and secrecy is to be maintained or purely in the interest of any specialized operations having high risk which can make the team tentative. The leader in this case creates a parallel objective which has close association with the actual and indirectly facilitates in accomplishment of the intended task thereby building the confidence level and generate passion. In combat such high risk tasks are very many. I have witnessed many such tasks and observed that once the parallel task is achieved the men when given the choice of the actual intended task have volunteered making use of the confidence of success achieved, thrust and intensity of efforts.
- *Credit:* This is a perfect initiator of motivation and morale. The leader here shares the credit and shows that people involved in the task are all equally important. The leader while giving credit must ensure that genuine men are not sidelined and the men whose contribution are not there get highlighted by purpose or default. Leader must bear in mind that individual unsuitable for one job may do a better job at a different time or at a different place or in a different task, thus do not discount any one in your team. Give opportunities equally to all men under command to prove.
- *Guidance:* In using the guidance tactic, the leader gets the men to involve directly. The commitment gets an impetus; the leader in such a scenario is catalyst and

guide. A good leader in the run to make the men accomplish the task must be candid and disclaims own ability and in doing so encourage men who are competent to do the job. Honesty makes men regard their leader with respect and willingly take on the responsibility. Leader in this tactics exploits the competency and proficiency of the team and acts as the facilitator.

- *Persuasion:* Another important influencing tactic is persuasion. In persuasion the leader influences by conferring with team to arrive at a settlement which both the leader and the team find acceptable. This is not very relevant in the Armed Forces however in corporate sector persuasion is required in certain circumstances especially when there is conflict of opinion in the perceived method of execution and the target set by the leader. This type of situation arises when leader and the team are equally competent or when the leader and team have same level of proficiency or when both parties' interests are at stake. Persuasion with appropriate reasoning and logic used by the leader is an important facet of this tactics. The team takes persuasion when they have the confidence on the credibility of the leader.
- The leader's selection of a particular tactic to influence the team/group in any given situation will thus depend on the under mentioned components:
    - The leader's competency and the team's proficiency
    - The outlook of the leader and the team members towards the task.
    - The leader's and team's temperament
    - The leader's intent, goals and objectives and team's perception of the same
    - The position of the leader and authority vis-à-vis team's acceptability of the leader.
    - The importance of timelines and completion of the task within the schedule

- The type of commitment required to complete the desired task
- Rules, policy and terms of references as applicable to a given situation/tasks
- Righteousness of the intent and honesty of the purpose in respect of the intended/assigned task.

Putting into Action the 'Tactics'

The most important part which the leader plays is 'putting into action' the planned tactics; this is an art of leadership. Very many of us may be of the opinion that a well planned tactics itself will roll into action and will reach desired conclusion. This is possible when all variables are constant throughout the process of application. On ground, the things are different, number of forces play active role in the application processes, there are balances and counter balances at all levels of application. Application of tactics demand certain leadership qualities on which the very concept of implementation of plans are dependent. In combat there are certain leadership qualities which directly influence the application of tactics and provide source of inspiration to the team:

- *Responsibility of the Leaders:* The leader is responsible and accountable of the decision. Blame game will break the cohesion of the team. Leader must have courage of conviction and courage to stand by the team at all times. Leaders must have courage to accept the failure. The creditability of the leader depends on this factor.
- *Clarity of Objectives:* The objective/goals should be explicit and clear, at no point of time there should be imagination or delusion in the plans. Delegation and freedom of action is best when the objective/goal is clear and no ambiguity exits. Exploitation of opportunity is optimized when the process of application is clear and there is no vagueness in

the orders/instructions. When clarity of objective is there the factor of reach vis-à-vis ability gets better addressed.

- *Righteousness of the Leaders:* Degree of transparency of the leaders is one of the factors which proportionately increase the level of confidence in application. Leaders' approach towards handling of each segment of the plan has to be without any prejudice or favour, a fixed mindset will create blurredness and perceivable biases, and therefore openness in leader is desirable. Leaders have to be righteous in their approach so that the tactics and its application do not get dominated with personal biases. The team commitment is an important facet and tactical execution is dependent on this facet, righteousness gives impetus to the team's commitment.
- *Focus:* Sustaining of focus is a very critical part of leadership approach in handling of the application of tactics. Any diversion in focus will directly affect the outcome of the tactics. In order to guard against this tendency, the leaders have to firstly identify the key focus areas, secondly carry out relativity analysis of each of the focus areas and lastly localize the focus areas based on the tasking and grouping. Wavering of focus level will proportionately affect the correctness of procedures, evaluation of progress and the end result of the tactics.
- *Practical Approach:* Leadership must be aware and adapt to the realities of the ground situation, tendencies of the human factors affecting the tactical plans and uncontrolled variables specific to the task must be accounted for and the leader must be aware of its effect on the plan. The practical approach depends on the apt use of common sense. Pragmatism in approach need to be maintained throughout the application of tactics. Two more crucial facets which are must in tactics are anticipation and foresight; this gives sound backing to pragmatism. Practical approach keeps the momentum going and increases the scope of ingenuity in application of tactics. Quote by General George S Patton

gives lucid view on practicality in adaption of tactics *"It may be of interest to future generals to realize that one makes plans to fit the circumstances, and does not try to create circumstances to fit the plans."*

- *Temperament:* Leaders temperament have direct bearing on the application of tactics, disposition displayed are the indicator of the motive and degree of involvement. The proportion of positivity in temperament will determine the level of motivation of the participants in the application of tactics. Propensity of application depends on the degree of sustainability of the temperament of the leader. Ability to execute is the key to successes and this is dependent on the temperament and outlook of the leader.
- *Proactive Engagement:* Leaders have to be proactive during the engagement of the tactics. The aspects on which the spirit of proactive engagement is reliant are innovativeness in approach, resourcefulness, leading from the front and being the role model, urge to survive and resilience instinct. Proactive approach of the leaders provides impetus to commitment and increases the instinct to anticipate. Reactive approach slows down the pace and level of audacity.

The originality, ingenuity and innovativeness are basic ingredients when putting a planned tactics into operations, the leaders self-belief, survival instinct and competency have a major role to play. Tactics involves common sense which the leaders must be having; many a times tactics fail miserably as the leaders had not applied their mind and common sense and was solely dependent on adaption of tested techniques and/ or was hesitant in taking any calculated risk. Conditions which make the tactics a failure and which the leaders must guard against are:

- Repetition of the tactics
- Shallow reconnaissance/surveys
- Shortcuts

- In hurry to achieve the target
- Overconfidence
- Taking things for granted
- Too much interference and changes
- Implausibility in the scope of the tactics
- Involving of non players
- Rumours, guard against it for 'someone can be waiting to out-manoeuvre your tactics'

At the functional level a good tactician must have certain characters which make the applied tactic sustain during the process of implementation; these are survival instinct of the leader and it must include creativity, originality, flexibility, persistence and cunningness. The leaders familiar with ground can only make tactical plans as they have intimate knowledge of the ground and are aware of the imperatives and its associated level, dynamics. In my opinion a strategist can make a grand strategy but when it comes to making functional level tactical plan, it must be left to the leaders at ground operation levels.

"There is no "approved" solution to any tactical situation."

—General George S Patton

6 Motivation

"The real test of leadership is not if your men will follow you in success, but if they will stick by you in defeat and in hardship".
—Field Marshal Slim

Motivation in Armed Forces is an issue which the corporate sector is always inquisitive about; questions asked are *"what make a soldier put service before self?"* and some are very blunt they are curious as to *"why soldiers readily put their life at stake?"* Here I would like to quote from an article by Lt General PG Kamath, Indian Army *"Why does a soldier gives his life for a cause? What makes him charge through a fusillade of bullets and splinter against sure death and injury overcoming the instinct of self-preservation? Why is he prepared to make his ultimate sacrifice and bid goodbye to the world? Why does he not think of his loving wife, his innocent children, his aged parents and the living world of mirth and bliss, knowing he has not even spent a quarter of his life? Why all his near and dear ones pale in to insignificance and he sees only his mission like Arjuna only seeing the eye of the bird? All this questions can be answered in two words, his pride. It is his professional pride."* Motivation is fulfilling this pride.

There is no denying of the fact that all the theories of motivation are equally applicable in the Armed Forces. The recognition, advancement, growth and desires, etc are factors which are equally applicable in the Armed Forces motivation concept and are similar in context with that of the corporate motivation concept. In leadership what matters is how to motivate. It is said that motivation involves both heart and mind. Being a state of human psychology, the degree of applicability of the motivation theories and identifiable factors/considerations will never be same for all, as each individual perception, frame of mind and view-point will always be different. Motivation will always remain intangible and elusive by nature; it is the human character of satisfaction which is never constant or consistent. Frequent changes in human behaviour are dependent on the working environment and the emotional quotient in any given situation.

"Motivation is the starter of morale; morale is the generator of motivation." Both are state of human psyche, the question now is – what is the difference between motivation and morale? Motivation is creating enthusiasm of doing something whereas morale is degree of confidence felt at a given point of time; both are situation based and are state of mind. Motivation is said to be successful when an individual's emotional needs are channelized to create sense of self-esteem and pride in the professional and social front. The balancing factor of motivation and morale is the demand of the job. It must be made very clear to the leadership that these human facets are controllable and vary in degree depending on constituted environment, personal outlook and the mind set. "Pride and self-esteem" is the fuel of motivation, the state of these two aspect is dependent on equation of the quality of leadership, leader's mental makeup, outlook, psychological acuity and relationship quotient of the leader with the members of the team.

Leadership is solely responsible to motivate the command. The leaders directly influence the level of motivation and are responsible in generating motivational practices. In applied motivation which is part of the institution/organizational human resource initiatives are not being included in this chapter, the leadership has no or very restricted role to play as applied motivation is governed by policy matters, however such applied motivation policies does provide scope in developing leader's personal motivation initiatives. Leaders by their ingenuity and innovativeness have to create their own initiatives to generate motivation and at the same time sustaining the existing level of motivation based on the demand of the task or the objective. Alongside this is the aspiration of each individual which requires separate addressing. I am of the opinion that motivation cannot be momentary and single purpose oriented in nature, what matters is the sustainability of level of motivation and this is a challenge to leadership.

Leadership Basics of Motivating Men

Motivation is intangible and unpredictable in nature. It is dependent on the mental state, attitude and outlook. The equation of motivation thus encompasses perception of the individual and the group, reasoning and level of understanding, degree of sensitivity towards the situation/ground realities, judgment of the attitudes, expectations, degree of involvement of the leader and the group, human and organizational values and finally the objective or the goal to be achieved. Motivation is said to be successful only when momentum gained is maintained as well as remains constant firstly throughout the period of the job/functional tenure and secondly task specific involving the complete cycle from origin to completion of the said task/objective. 'What motivates' men/employees, these have been well covered in theories and books, my stress is on how leadership can give shape to motivation. There are two basic fundamentals which the leadership has to ensure firstly to carry the team/group and secondly make motivation responsive in terms of output. In spite of differences in each individual's perception level with regard to the degree of motivation and its level of attainment, the basic fundamentals do create an impact on motivation and factors governing it:

- *Involvement:* The process of motivation needs involvement of the leaders, each individual member of the team and the team/group as an entity. The interests shown by each of the participant have direct bearing on the motivational factors. Sense of involvement have to be developed and reinforced by the leaders, this correspondingly affects the spirit of participation. Involvement of the leaders has to be participative by nature and the leader's presence in activity cycle must be visible. Another aspect of involvement is how each of the parties identifies themselves with the organization; the degree of closeness and spirit of association with the organization plays an important role in motivation, this has to be cultivated at team and individual level. A leader connecting with the organization and the men under command is an important aspect of command responsibility and one has to work for it. Involvement must not be confused with regimentation; regimentation is the process of adapting whereas involvement is connecting with the team/group.
- *Purpose:* Any cause/task or objective must have purpose, this must be clear to each participating member of the team. Purpose is directly and proportionately related to involvement and commitment, better is the understanding and assimilation of the purpose higher will be the degree of involvement and commitment. There should not be any ambiguity in the purpose, as selection of courses of actions, rationality of the task and clarity in orders are dependent on this aspect; this in turn creates better understanding among the members of the team and apt role analysis of each of the participating individual. Motivation and purpose are correlated, purpose gives impetus to motivation and motivation on the other hand gives meaning to purpose. The purpose must answer the following questions of an individual, if the answers are positive then purpose will motivate:

- o Why I am being asked to do this?
- o Why only me?
- o How does this affect me?
- o What do I achieve, is it worth the effort?
- o What will be the value of my contribution?
- o Will my contribution help the purpose?

The purpose gives the impetus to motivation, it should be well defined to assist in building self-confidence and enhance self-belief. The leader, therefore, must be clear of the purpose and build up the attitude of positivity towards the purpose in each individual of the team. There are two types of purpose, selflessness of purpose and purpose with motive. Selflessness of purpose is said to be in the organizational interest, confines to the values and principles of righteousness and having no hidden agenda. Purpose with motives on other hand is aligned to conflict and friction, self is predominant and has a hidden agenda, and this creates the 'in doubt' syndrome in the individual and the group which adversely affects the faith and trust equation. The leader must make it apparent and evident to men under command the genuineness and truthfulness in the purpose, it is then that motivation will have a positive impact on the psyche of the team.

- *Challenge:* Whatever may be the task, leaders must build perception of challenge. The task in which challenge is inherent, then leaders must use the challenge as the spring board to create self-belief, confidence and perseverance in each participating individuals. It is not possible for each participating individual to be motivated; it also does not mean that all those who are not motivated are not capable; therefore the leaders have to adopt ingenuity in their approach to create an environment of accepting the challenges within the group. Challenges have contagious impact and are initiator of motivation. The challenge is there in all tasks, most of the time this is either not visible or are considered as mundane, the art lies in making the challenge testing to meet the quotient of the self esteem and the pride.

- *Camaraderie:* Cohesion, unity, interpersonal contact, participative leadership and organizational ethos are important facets which have direct bearing in creating an environment of comradeship. Establishing an association with the unit/organization is the step towards developing the sense of belonging and trust, the concept of creating a sense of 'Regimentation' and imbibing the spirit of being a part of the organization are the basic imperatives of motivation. In return of the commitment men expect support and assurance from the leader/organization, this helps in building the confidence level. When belongingness and camaraderie are established at the functional levels within the organization, the team is said to be motivated. Man is said to be motivated when he is assured of the mental and physical wellbeing by the organization, the leader and the team. A very crucial aspect in developing the spirit of comradeship is making an individual know that his being part of the team/organization is truly acknowledged and valued. Trust among each participating members will depend on the degree of comradeship, whereas comradeship is correspondingly related to the level of cohesion existing in the team, which in turn is directly related to the level of trust and faith among each member of the team. Thus camaraderie achieved and the sensitivity of comradeship among the team members depends to a very large extent on the leader's attitude and his/her approach.
- *Openings*: The leaders must endeavour to provide equal opportunity to all the participants. Opportunity must be within the scope of the aim/purpose, to meet the target, to take on the challenges, induce commitment and provide prospects to prove 'one's worth'. The opportunity can be individualistic or for the group/team. Opportunity must be equally distributed in the complete spectrum of the

assigned task, here transparency is of utmost importance and nepotism must be avoided. When openings exists it motivates, each group member feels that he/she is part of the task and their contribution is valued. The scope of opportunities and openings which is generated in the process of task accomplishment will help the leader to assess the job enlargement or the job enrichment of his/her team for future endeavours. "*Human behaviour is diverse; getting a team to same plinth of motivation is a difficult proposition. The best motivator is the job itself, pride in the job, value of contribution, meeting the challenges, exploiting the opportunities which lie in the course of the task and accomplishment of the goal*", opportunity thus opens an avenue towards achievement and in the process makes task accomplishment a definite possibility. Factors in which involvement of the leader is hundred percent and those which meets the demand of the professional pride of each member of the team, will motivate.

- *Passion:* Passion with earnestness at each level gives impetus to motivation. Building up of passion among the participants depends on the type of work environment, prevalent situation on ground, transparency in the overall system and equal opportunity of effective participation. Passion generation process in the Forces involves:
    - *Firstly,* enlargement of self-confidence by giving impetus to the level of job satisfaction, the value of each individuals contribution and the pride in the profession. Leader has to recognize each of the participating individual's capability and proficiency
    - *Secondly,* the understanding of the significance of the ultimate goal and corresponding importance of involvement of each participant
    - *Thirdly,* recognition of the effort

The above are important elements and force multipliers of the passion generator. Passion is volatile and have tendency to swing between low and high scale, therefore sustaining the passion at a constant level is a big challenge to the leader. Passion is contagious, it spreads among the participating team and in turn motivates. But the foremost requirement is that the leader must be passionate about the mission/task, towards leading the team from the front and have an attitude to achieve.

- *Transparency:* This is one of the vital basics. Where there is lack of transparency, none of the aforesaid basics are viable, lack of it in turn create frictions and fault lines in the functional environment and has negative impact towards motivation. The leaders during planning of the assigned task and handling of the team during the execution of the task have to maintain a high standard of transparency. Leader has to make all efforts to keep the team in picture of the motives, purpose and the intent; this brings confidence in the team. To make the transparency authentic the leader has to display genuineness of application of the plans giving equal attention to each participating member of the team, carry the team along and have courage of conviction to stand with the team. Selflessness of the leader here is a great motivator.

Motivation Builders

The issues of career progression, promotions, pay and allowances and incentive are factors of motivation, these are equally applicable universally. In the Armed Forces motivation has an additional facet that is keeping the spirit of 'service before self ' alive, thus it is more confined to the purview of duty and operational responsibilities. In corporate, motivation is more of a facilitator in improving the functional efficiency, here the issue of organizational values, service before self and pledge to serve the nation are not applicable, to a large extent motivation is related to productivity and outputs/profits.

Motivation builders are the dynamics which must be present at all the functional levels and be part of leadership considerations. Motivation builders are based on organizational ethos, beliefs and values. To optimize the level of motivation these builders have to be developed to a desired level in relation to the organizational requirements. The leadership plays an important role in development of the motivation builders; it is the leaders who create the atmosphere for the motivation builders. The motivation builders are:

- *Entity and Acknowledgment:* Foremost important aspect in motivation builder is to establish the entity of the individual in the organization so as to create a sense of belongingness and pride. This must be followed by acknowledging the individual's entity in the group/organization. Till such time the acceptability and accommodative factors between the individual and the group is not optimized, motivation is a non starter. Motivation is achievable when the equation of value given to the entity and acknowledgment of the individual by the group/team is well established and the individual feels the pride of being one of the participating members of the group/team. The degree of sense of belonging is dependent on this equation, higher the degree better will be the scope of motivation.
- *Self Actualizations:* The leadership needs to create an environmental climate where realisation of one's talents and potentialities are established. Self-actualization is a process when a person desires to use the individualistic abilities, competence and the reach to achieve the maximum. Such climate within a group creates an impetus for motivation. When an individual gives the best and strives beyond the self-actualization limits, the motivation is at its optimum. Leaders must value the self-actualization of an individual. Self-esteem and pride of the individual is proportionately linked to degree of recognition/value

to self-actualization and corresponding confidence levels established between the individual and the group.

- *Relationship Equation:* The interpersonal relationship plays a vital role. This brings in the sense of comradeship and the cohesion which is essential for motivation. Till such time an individual is not able to create space within the ambit of functional relationship, he/she will not be able to give the best. Moreover absorption in the system will depend on the individual's initiative to get adjusted, therefore faster the individual is able to establish the adjustment equation in the team, better will be the scope of acceptance and absorption. Potential analysis and suitability assessment by the leader plays an important part here in optimizing the deployment of the individual and helps in development of relationship equation. In combat the team dynamics plays an important part in outcome of result as every component has to take part in its designated role for the achievement of the overall aim. If the relationship equation is good the environment is conducive to motivation. Creating such an environment is leadership responsibility. Potential of an individual and deployment must be in accordance to the team dynamics and correspond to the team competency levels, misfits must be avoided as it breaks the team cohesiveness which in turn reduces the motivation level. Lot depends on the attitude, approach and outlook of the leader, initiating relationship initiators within the team is leadership responsibility, if this is befitting then the motivation is said to be sustainable.
- *Perception Building:* Sensitivity, awareness, understanding and opinion play an important role to form the perception. When an individual has clear perception of the organizational values and ethos, understands the importance and significance of the task and requirement of value addition in form of personal commitment to the overall aim/objective, then the performance and

involvement will be proportionate to the opinion formed by the members of the team. It is command responsibility of the leader to get the perception of the individuals, unit or team to a single bandwidth level so as to have same frequency of willing participation. The basic aim of perception is to make the participant make belief in self and the organization. The climate thus created is the motivation builder.

- *Values and Commitment Equation:* Every organization has its values which are built over the years; these values give an image to the organization. Values get derived from the organizational culture, ideology, ethics and ethos. Climate of motivation is optimum when commitment is corresponding with the values and the values are recognized by the individuals. Values give impetus to commitment and when the equation is at same plinth, the motivation will be optimum. Approach to commitment has to be positive – willing - responsible by each member of the team; leadership here is expected to play the role model.
- *Recognition and Ethics:* Recognition of accomplishment is one of the important elements of motivation. Every individual desires to be recognized for the work. Some of the organizations set standards for achievements and plan out corresponding recognition in terms of incentives. Even though this practice facilitates motivation but is very restrictive by its very nature i.e. benchmark of selection, thus the question of levels of competency vis-à-vis the standards set vis-à-vis the selection process will always persist, subjectivity cannot be stopped from creeping in to the assessments. The second alternative is that field is made open and ample scope of betterment provided so that achievement can be preferred not only within the ambit of duty but beyond it, however this will create an environment of unhealthy competition. Thus fixation

of recognition and free for all notion, both can be degenerator of motivation and have negative impact, if best and deserving are not recognized. Other aspect which is equally important is the ethics of transparency, openness and rightful judgment in giving recognition; these must be visible to all the participants. Favourtism and parochialism must be avoided. Motivation is high if the recognition is ethical and leader is the one who must be in the habit of ensuring this. Recognition should be based on 'the best and deserving' and fair, this must be supported by ethical approach and encouragements from the leader.

- *Involvement and Reach Equation*: On the degree of capability / proficiency and the extent of reach, the involvement and performance of the individual and the team is dependent. Motivation gets a boost when the input of involvement is maximized in relation to the reach which must be within the capability or the level of proficiency. It is on the leadership to take the call on optimizing the capability and define the reach, the involvement will then commensurate with the reach and capability. Here I want to quote two Army phrases *"You have to risk going far to discover just how far you can really go"*, the reach and capability will get decided when the leader and the team operates to the maximum possible achievable limits. Endeavour to know the limits will determine the actual reach which must commensurate with the capability. The second one is *"A pessimist sees the difficulty in every opportunity; an optimist sees the opportunity in every difficulty"*, therefore, the exploitation of opportunity and degree of difficulty will provide the test of reach and capability. Motivation thus will be the challenge, optimism and positivity in the approach to achieve. The equation here will be correspondingly proportionate between achievement and the combination factors of reach, capability and commitment.

What I feel the leader must keep in mind while creating the motivation builders are the working environment, intensity of engagements, pressure and related reactions, stress of such engagements and mental frame of the members of the team. The motivation builder's applicability will depend on the leadership environment and the attitude of the leader, some of the builders can be juxtaposed with the situational requirement, personality of the leader and the team dynamics. Leader's ingenuity and innovativeness does matter, a word of caution the leader must not play with the sentiments of the team/the members of the team. Hanging of carrots is not the end all of motivation, what matters is leader's association with the team and its sentiments and in the process help them to aspire and recognize their worth.

Component of Motivation

Motivation is not singularly dependent on the leadership but also the components of environment, which constitutes to create climate for motivation. What matters is how the leadership exploits the climate generated to boost the motivation. The conduciveness of motivation is dependent on basically three facets, the organization ethos and values, both individual and group/team's perception to motivation and the motivational scopes at work. The motivation of Armed Forces and that of the corporate are similar i.e. to obtain the optimum output at the point of effectiveness. The only difference is the degree of selflessness, in Armed Forces selflessness is predominant as compared to the corporate. Following components of motivation as practiced in Armed Forces which are unique and make for selflessness in commitment are:

- *Organization:* The foremost is the organizational ethos, tradition and values. The basic character building of an individual is based on these factors; it is when an individual starts identifying himself/herself with the organization, individual self-esteem, pride and sense of honour are shaped. The second important aspect is the organizational concern for the individual; when the individuals are confident that their interest will be looked after by the organization, the degree of selflessness will be higher and selflessness in turn will give impetus to fortitude, courage, resilience and determination. The third important aspect is functioning philosophy of the organization; this encompasses the work culture, interpersonal relationship values, communication accessibility, openness and recognition of achievement. Lastly the human resource initiatives of the organization keeping the ambit of the work environment and expectation of the participating work force. These gives impetus to degree of involvement and commitment. The organization in actual terms provides the platform for motivation and the expectations are dependent not only on the environment created but assured affectivity of the initiatives. Seriousness of interest in implementation and sustaining the climate of the genuineness of human resources initiatives by the organization has corresponding effect on the degree of motivation.

- *Leaders:* Firstly, leaders themselves should be motivated, it is only then they can motivate the men under command. Secondly leaders have to be visible to the command; this is best achieved by participative command, involvement and attachment with the team. Thirdly leaders have to make the men under command confident of their leadership traits, develop trust, faith and be fair in all dealings this is best achieved when the leader is professionally competent, upright and selfless. *"When odds are against, uncertainty is prevalent, dangers lurking and probability of failure is high and morale is vulnerable to collapse, here the leader who gives the hopes and is in the forefront of happenings will be most successful in reviving the spirits and motivate"* quoted by Sun Tzu, Chinese military philosopher, the importance of the leader having self-belief and being the role model at the time of crisis cannot be denied, motivation and morale is sustainable against the odds when the leader has the spirit to survive, courage to face the odds, withstand the pains, does not lose the confidence in the men, able to keep the command united and have perseverance to bounce back - this is what matters actually. Lastly the leader who leads from the front, sets personal example and has courage of conviction will always be appreciated by the men and the said faith will create the climate for motivation. These four basic characters of the leaders are a must to motivate the men and the group. Another aspect which the leaders must keep in mind is the relationship equation with the men, it must be closest with no fault lines, this has a big say in motivation.

- *Team*: The team dynamics have a role to play. The team's composition, composite behaviour, competency, degree of perseverance, interpersonal affiliations, involvement and commitment to the tasks, mutual and inter-personnel support, spirit of continued existence as a 'force to reckon with' are the motivation initiators. The confidence for achievement and altruism is based on the team dynamics. In the face of the odds it is the team/group which gets the best out of each member. Team's fighting spirit, cohesion, willpower, determination, killer instinct and perseverance directly influence the individual personality of its members and this in turn gives impetus to motivation. It is important for leadership to have an intimate knowledge of the team and understand its dynamics. Higher is the functional and inter-personnel relationship equation greater will be the scope of motivation, and the comrade-buddy support factor in a team are essential initiators of motivation. The team contribution in building individual member's professional competency, preparing the mental makeup to meet challenges, mutual supportiveness and building cohesion level provides momentum to motivation.

- *Regimentation (Affiliation):* Making an individual part of group is 'Regimentation' in Armed Forces; this is not same as establishing association there is difference which must be understood. Regimentation is creating an affiliation and bonding to make an individual identify with the group/organization and in the process make to imbibe the values and ethos. The pride and honour of being part of the outfit creates selflessness towards the duty and the responsibility bestowed. The degree of regimentation and affiliation will determine the level of motivation. The respect of the organizational values and self-esteem (Izzat aur Imman) get imbibed once the affiliation/regimentation gets matured and developed during the process of career in the organization, these are the two most prominent factors of motivation.
- *Culture*: The organizational culture is one of the factors which make an individual feel comfortable with the work/functional and social-inter personnel environment. Interest, involvement and morale are dependent on this factor. Tradition, ethnicity, organizational philosophy and customs are important facets of creating a culture. The way of life in the functional environment is based on the culture enunciated by the organization. When the vibes generated are positive the culture is said to be definitive, this motivates the individual to give in their best. The aspect of welfare, career, recognition, standards and ergonomics depends on the organizational culture, thus motivation to a large extent depends on the support of the organization.
- *Training:* When an individual is well trained and is aware of the expected job/trade content of the profession, he/she is confident and this confidence lends to motivation. A well trained man is better prepared and is not hesitant, to quote Sun Tzu "If men are unaccustomed to rigorous drilling, they will be hesitant in battle". Training not

only brings confidence but also increases awareness, brings compatibility within the team, appropriateness in employment and job satisfaction, this directly influences the inclination to perform and achieve. Training is a good motivator as it provides the opportunity to job enrichment and job enlargement; these two elements result in making an individual responsible and responsive, when this equation is at the positive spectrum the subject is considered as motivated. A word of caution, it is only purposeful training which motivates.

Leadership and Motivation

Leadership is the main player in motivation; leaders are in constant contact with the men under command and it is they who keep their men motivated/stimulates motivation. The question is of leader - team equation, when this equation is strong and lends to meaningful relationship, the motivation level of the group will be higher. The attributes which a leader must possess to motivate their men are:

- Higher level of competency, this must be higher than the competency of the group/team. A professionally competent leader is a respected leader and followed.
- Must have clear vision and well defined goals. Confused leader cannot motivate. Nobody wants to follow a leader who does not have the sense of direction?
- Ability to craft intellectual stimulation and generate passion
- Self-confidence, courage and conviction in leader creates positive aura. Men don't follow discouraged leaders; they follow a leader who persists with hope and stands with the team.
- Maintain neutrality and transparency in human resource handling and in personal conduct. Personal reputation of leader generates motivation vibes.

- Keeping the interest of the team and the organization above one's own is one of the most important elements of motivation.
- Develop confidence of the group. Optimizing potentials, giving opportunities and providing experience develops confidence. Continued endeavour to enhance the proficiencies make the team/group successful.
- Realistic in approach and persistence-resoluteness in execution
- Establish credibility by leading from the front and personal example.
- Be focused, have a sense of purpose and a clear understanding of the mission/task
- Encourage meaningful communication with/within the team.
- Promptness in acknowledgment of achievement and giving credit.
- Empathy and compassion towards men under command.

Leaders are key motivation drivers, they have to plan effective motivational strategy based on intimate knowledge of their men and the group dynamics of the team. Other important facets are maintaining and sustaining the motivation throughout the command of the team, the level and degree of motivation must remain constant but fluctuations will be there as situation and personality dependent factors will be changing. What do we expect from the leader to make motivation viable are high energy levels, initiative, passion in command, responsibility for the decisions taken, enthusiastic approach and resoluteness in execution, these in real terms motivates the men under command. To quote General George S Patton US Army *"Inspiration does not come via coded message, but by visible personality"*, leaders should be seen by the command, it is only then they follow. The question is what qualities in a leader which motives the men to do extraordinary, I am highlighting certain factors which give impetus to motivation to perform beyond the call of duty:

- *Trust:* The leader must have faith and trust of the team and the team on the other hand must have trust and faith on the leader. This is a two way process and mutually responsive. The proportion of trust and faith is more dependent on the leader, the quantum will depend on how much he/she can generate and the dependency level maintained between self and the team. Obedience, initiative, selflessness and courage are trust dependent. Trust and faith is also dependent on the professional competency level of the leader and the team, professional leaders and competent team will trust each other , when levels of trust of both are balanced it is considered as most dominant factor of motivation. Trust is a great motivator; it boosts the self-esteem of the individual and relates to the extent of confidence bestowed.
- *Credibility:* The credibility of the leaders is a very important factor in motivation; credibility is dependent on the proportionate levels of integrity, sincerity, honesty and uprightness of the leaders. When these factors are on higher side the credibility is on the higher plinth. The level of confidence of the group/team on the leaders is based on the credibility factor; motivation in turn is dependent on the creditability factor of the leader. Credible leaders are capable of raising the motivation level in the team by action, personal example and being in the forefront. An important aspect for credibility which must be borne in mind is the belief developed by the team on the leader and men must swear by their leader.
- *Personal Courage:* Courage, it not only encompasses the audacity to face the odds it also contains the combination of physical and morale courage. To quote Sir Winston Churchill "courage is rightly esteemed the first of human qualities." Leader is expected to have courage of conviction,

courage to take initiative, courage to take calculated risk, courage to have total transparency, moral courage to point out , courage to stand and support the team for a just or ethical cause and courage to lead from the front. When the team is guaranteed courage, boldness and high order of moral fiber from their leaders, the motivation is high and individuals/team willingly commits themselves to higher performance levels even beyond the call of duty

- *Intend:* Leaders having understanding of the future and can define the goal appropriately to give a definite direction to their visualization/aim is said to be pragmatic. Command expects leaders to have a sense of direction and aptly convert the aim into achievable mission. Team/group is motivated when the directions are well defined, every member's perception of the purpose is same and mission is unambiguous. Larger the gap in perceiving the importance of aim, higher will be the scope of condemnation in the ranks. The viability and acceptability of vision depends on the steadfastness in relationship of leader and the team, if this is maintained both will be mutually sustaining the vision and be committed to the fulfillment of the said vision. The intend therefore is not a single entity, it is conceptualized by the leaders but important aspect is the team/group identifying itself with the intend, which in itself is very much mandatory. This correlation when is at its optimum level then motivation is said to be responding to the leader's vision. Most of the people are of the opinion that vision is applicable to senior management/authorities and not very much applicable to junior leaders for whom intend only matters, I am of the opinion that, when vision is considered as foresight of the courses to meet the selected or desired objectives then it is applicable to all the levels of leadership. Vision includes aim, intend, purpose, hope, achievement and results thus it is applicable to all the levels of leadership, the only difference is the level at which the vision is planned.

- *Resolve:* Resoluteness, determination and steadfastness are the important elements of resolve. When the positivity of these factors is on higher spectrum of the character of the leader, the team/group is proportionately influenced. In Armed Forces this is called the 'GO' and it is this 'GO' in the leaders which motivates the team/group. Will to give 'a fight at all cost' in a leader and the survival instincts are great motivator.
- *Affinity:* Association with team/group is essential; this develops affinity, compassion and concern in the leaders. When the leader identifies self with the team or the group and same is reciprocated, the functional relationship turns into a parent child relationship. The lesser the gap in relationship more will be the productivity of the leader and the team/group. The environment thus created should be such that the team/group swears by their leaders. In this case the level of motivation will be high. The leaders have to be fair, respect the human sentiments, contribute to cohesiveness of the group and sustain the affinity in order to be effective.
- *Outlook:* Positivity in a leader's outlook makes him/her enthusiastic in pursuit of the aim, takes initiative to accomplish the mission and make prudent decisions. When the outlook is positive, the vibes created are positive among the team members. Positivity in outlook gives impetus in building motivation. Another aspect which is an important imperative of positive outlook is leadership taking responsibilities of decision and actions; this makes the team commit itself to the leader and the mission.
- *Discipline:* If the leader and the team are disciplined, the outfit is considered as motivated. Discipline make the leader and the team take the right path, follow rules, respect the law and value the ethos and principles of the organization. It brings cohesiveness and provides direction to accomplishment of the aim or the mission. Discipline in

the leader brings systematization in approach and pursuit, deliberations in decision making, responsiveness to directives and orders and effective application. The leaders have to enforce discipline in right prospective to make the team respond to the orders, quote of General Patton sums up the importance of leadership and discipline,"*If you can't get them to salute when they should salute and wear the gear you tell them to wear, how are you going to get them to die for their country?*" Discipline boosts motivation and this in turn creates sense of commitment in the team.

- *Openness:* The leaders must be approachable and reachable, this makes the men have faith and trust in the leader. The aspect of openness is leader's truthfulness and forthrightness; the team must be kept well informed of the all aspects of the task, their safety and security, likely fallouts and contingencies. A well informed worker is better motivated and develops confidence on the leader. The level of transparency must be high as this would answer most of the questions which might be lingering in the mind of the individual and the team. Most of the time the leaders falters by distancing themselves from the team, the position ego adds to the gap and selfishness is predominant. The commitment is proportionate to the scale of openness, and both gives impetus to motivation.
- *Judgment:* Rightful and correct judgment by a leader is another factor which is considered as great motivator. Common sense and righteousness are two important components of judgment; their application brings prudency in the process of judgment. This builds confidence of the team on the leader.

Motivation is not only a state of mind of an individual alone, it is a commitment to self and desire to fulfill the said commitment for obtaining maximum satisfaction. Therefore, motivation must be nurtured and upheld, must not be allowed to remain momentary. Leadership has an important role to play in maintaining the momentum of the motivation. There is a saying in Armed Forces *"He who is motivated can only motivate others"* and this is aptly applicable to a leader. Motivation is most discussed issue, so many opinions and writes ups, number of formulas and matrixes are in vogue but what matters is how you generate it when the basic variable of human behaviour cannot be fathomed and is never constant. This is where the leadership qualities comes into the fore, the issues which I have enumerated is from observation of varied leadership techniques used in motivating the troops in combat.

Certain quotations from my collection which I feel appropriately sums up 'motivation':

"Motivation is the art of getting people to do what you want them to do because they want to do it."

—Dwight D Eisenhower

"The secret of discipline is motivation. When a man is sufficiently motivated, discipline will take care of itself."

—Sir Alexander Paterson

"Be an example to your men, in your duty and in private life. Never spare yourself, and let the troops see that you don't in your endurance of fatigue and privation. Always be tactful and well-mannered and teach your subordinates to do the same. Avoid excessive sharpness or harshness of voice, which usually indicates the man who have shortcomings of his own to hide."

—Field Marshall Erwin Rommel

"Regard your soldiers as your children, and they will follow you into the deepest valleys. Look on them as your own beloved sons, and they will stand by you even unto death!"

—Sun Tzu

"The characteristic which higher command always looks for in any officer is honesty. Honesty in thought, words, and deed. Second to honesty and courage of purpose, I would place an unselfish attitude as the greatest attribute of a leader. Place

the care and protection of the men first; share their hardships without complaint and when the real test comes you will find that they possess a genuine respect and admiration for you. "To do otherwise means failure at the crucial moment when the support of your men is essential to the success of the battle".

—General Alexander M. Patch, US Army

"If you are going through hell, keep going"

—Winston Churchill

7 Morale

"Morale is a state of mind. It is that intangible force which will move a whole group of men to give their last ounce to achieve something, without counting the cost to themselves."

—Field Marshal Sir William J Slim

Morale is *"the level of individual's psychological well-being"*, it can also be said to be the *"mental and emotional condition of an individual or group"*. Morale is a state of mental well-being as perceived by an individual. There is a thin line between morale and motivation; some are of the view that they are two sides of same coin. However, I feel that morale and motivation is two different facet of human behaviour but they are correlated and mutually dependent. It is when mental well-being is good the state of mind is good, thus when morale is high the motivation is correspondingly higher. The confusion between morale and motivation will keep cropping up time and again in the minds of leadership but one thing will always be constant that is, the end product in both cases are the same, both are 'human energizers'. A man with high morale is motivated and motivated man has high morale. However, some may argue that it is not necessary always that person with high morale is motivated and one who is motivated will always have high morale. Morale is mental well-being whereas motivation is the state of mind; here the common factor is the mind. Contended man will have a high morale and degree of contentment factors in motivation.

"The foundations of morale are, I think, first, spiritual, then mental, and lastly material. I put them in that order because that, I believe, is the order of their importance." This quote of Field Marshal Sir William Slim gives out the basic constituents of morale and defines the purview of mental well-being. The morale therefore is dependent on the belief, emotional state and rational physical desires. When these are fulfilled the contentment is achieved and which in turn moderates the state of morale. Leadership has an important role to play in facilitating the degree of contentment to an optimum level and sustaining the achieved state of morale.

In corporate environment morale is linked to job satisfaction and productivity and in Armed Forces morale is linked with the level of involvement and commitment of the combatant with the organization. It is not necessary that high morale is equated with success but in defeat also high morale counts, similarly it is not necessary that satisfied man who's all demands are met will always posses high morale, on the other hand man who is deprived and made to face hardship can be having higher morale. John J. McCloy, Assistant Secretary of War USA, opined on the state of morale when soldiers are in face with challenges or facing reversals *"May I say a few words about 'morale.' A good soldier's morale is something like a lady's virtue-you don't talk about it; but there have been so much said about it recently that I want to add my bit. Above all we must rid ourselves of the notion that morale is achieved by giving somebody something. Real morale is more readily achieved by depriving soldiers of something rather than giving them something. Hostesses, movies, soda fountains and what have you, have their place, but endurance of hardship, sacrifice, competition, ability to outdo another unit, the feeling of inner strength- in short, the knowledge that he is tough, hard-bitten, and able to take and inflict stiff blows, gives the soldier morale, and the more he has to put up with things and overcome obstacles, the more it develops."* Therefore morale is something more than job satisfaction, productivity, contentment and well-being. The instinct to survive and spirit of resilience to face up to any challenges, makes an individual contended with the efforts which in turn gives sense of satisfaction, this gives boost to morale.

Morale is willing commitment of self in the overall interest of the organization and the pride in doing so. The working and the organizational environments thus have to be equally responsive and supportive in keeping the level of the morale sustainable or give boost to it.

Constituents of Morale

I had always taken morale on the value of expression of General Slim and during my command of troops followed it as code of command. If one looks into General Slims order of priority first spiritual, then mental and lastly material, the first two priorities are psychological and the third is physiological which is also dependent on the mental state? In the sum total morale is the mental state of well-being as well as spirit to face up to challenges in course of the job performance. As the human behaviours stands, the priorities can always be interchangeable depending on the individual's perception of well-being and contentment. Constituents I am discussing are based on the priorities given out by General Slim on foundations of morale and are very relevant in the present environment in Forces.

- *Spiritual:* This is a very large canvas as it covers the inner self of the individual and personal beliefs. These are very close to the person and individuals are very sensitive about it. In the functional environment the aspect of spiritually linked morale factors which directly influence the commitment and productivity are:
  - *Beliefs:* In this category religious, social and personal beliefs fall. It is the respect which is given by the

organization to the individual's beliefs. In the organizations with diversity in caste, religion and personal beliefs, each individual case cannot be addressed in isolation and handled separately; the concept of unity in diversity thus is more applicable in such organization. A group spiritual factor which meets the individual spiritual needs is more applicable in such a setup. The question of individual sensitivity still has to be addressed. Measures which boost the individual belief factor and morale are:

- Individual needs and beliefs must be respected
- Time to be spared and granted to the individuals to practice their beliefs
- Opportunity to attend social, religious and spiritual functions must be provided
- Respect of religious sentiments
- Participation and support from the group during specific needs
- Feeling of 'part of the family' approach to be reinforced
- Group spiritual affiliation to support the individual belief
- Organized group participations to accommodate the individual spiritual need
- Freedom to practice spiritual events within the purview of the organizational requirements
- Foster the cohesion within the group to handle the individual spiritual needs
- Fostering 'unity in diversity' to meet the groups spiritual need and supporting individual feelings/ sentiments

o *Values:* Values are developed based on the upbringing and the environment in the family, society and the work platform. These social factors create an individualistic state of mind. Values in course of life become the spiritual beliefs. Honesty, integrity, loyalty and truthfulness are the by-products of values and which are also spiritually dependent. When the values of the organization match with the individual values, the morale is said to be high. Transparency, positive and constructive work philosophy, respect and recognition to the individual's values are some of the important components which have positive impact on spiritual aspirations and beliefs. Level of morale fibers created due to values imbibed in an individual is proportional to the resultant spiritual belief and faith. The value as practiced by an individual and organizational ethos plays an important part in generating morale.

- *Mental:* The state of mental frame of mind which is both psychological and physiological reliant, directly influence the state of morale. The mental state encompasses a very large spectrum and is unpredictable in nature. The level of maturity, logical sense in perception modulation, degree of sensitivity to the spiritual beliefs and temperament of tolerance are based on individual's mental state influence and these in turn influences the state of morale.

  Aspects which have direct influence on morale are:

  - *Sense of Security:* The sense of security is an important facet in morale. Personal, family, social and lastly environmental securities are vital imperatives of morale. When these are addressed by the organization in the right perspective it develops a sense of confidence in the men and that of the team on the organization. Sense of security is dependent on the degree of sensitivity of being secured. It is a human psychology of feeling 'secured' not only about personal self but also of the near and dear ones which is important. Promotion, career progression, pay and allowances, family care, education of children, medical, insurance and leave are the aspects which enhance the security prospects. When the said aspects are provided to an individual at the organizational level or through his own efforts aided by the organization or at his own initiative with the support of the organization, the morale will be moderate to high depending on the satisfaction derived. Leadership has an important part to play as it is a vital link and executor between the individual and the organization on issues related to sense of security.

- *Safety:* Psychological factor of environment of safety is an aspect which influences the state of mind. Safe work environment increases involvement, participation and commitment towards the task. Safety of life and limbs is an important factor which gives impetus to morale. Safety encompasses the quality and standard of equipment, floor and tools, protective gears, work procedures, well sensitized co-workers, training and observant supervisors who have concern for their men and assurance of family safety. Safety is leadership dependent; safety is part of planning, decision taking and execution of the job. The confidence of safety which the men under command have on the leader is a real morale booster; it is at this point a soldier takes risks and attempts difficult tasks for the leader and the organization knowing that he is in safe hands. Higher the factor of safety the state of mind is more stable and thus morale is considered as high.
- *Unit:* The team/unit/organization are important platforms of morale. The ethos and associated values, achievements, reputation and honour, sense of pride, alliance and bonding of being a part of an elite unit/organization boosts the morale. Such units have certain standards and expectation from the employees, which an individual takes it as a challenge/privilege; this determines the degree of commitment and involvement in meeting the said standards and expectations. Morale is said to be proportionately dependent on the value given to individual's self-esteem and sense of pride of being associated to the said team or the organization.

These have an immense impact on morale especially when individual is made an important member of the team and in turn considers self as privileged; the team is equally responsible to give credence to the individuals self-esteem and pride so generated by joining the said team. A proficient and efficient team will always have high morale. The other important aspect is how does a unit accepts an individual in its fold and bring him/her to the desired standards. When an individual finds that team has given him/her the place, groomed, trained and supported the career progression, this increases the level of commitment in an individual to live up to the team's standards. Contributing to the team's achievement heightens the morale. In both the situations, the leadership has a big role to play in making an individual a part of the unit or the team.

- *Equipment:* Mental state is also dependent on the state of equipment, its technology, effectiveness and efficiency. The confidence of workers is proportionate to the standards of equipments in the work floors or the work stations. Equipment and technology is correlated to the degree of efficiency and output and vice-versa, worker's morale therefore is proportionate to the degree of efficiency achieved in handling the equipment and/or 'know' of the technology. Common saying in Forces "An army with better weapon systems have ascendency over the adversary having less better weapons" and "It is a man behind a weapon who is the ultimate decider of the outcome of war, it is important that a relationship is developed between man and the weapon, this is possible when man associates with the weapon and have trust and faith, it is then that both are said to be companion", the importance of the equipment and morale relationship is an age old issue, a better equipped person is always confident.

- *Training:* A well trained man will have high morale. Training is linked to confidence, self-belief, efficiency and productivity. Training provides the platform for development and the related issues are levels of confidence, increment in acumen, reduction in the competency gaps and increased employment opportunity. The ability of withstanding the job demand, facing up to the competition and enhancement of qualifications makes a person contended, this has positive bearing on the state of mind and sense of well-being. Other important aspect about training is that it reduces the skill gap among team or the group members and gives an impetus to morale through equal participation. Meeting the commitment standards of the team and living up to the expectations boosts the morale, training has a big say in building bondage and cohesion in the team. The troops who fight the best, do so, not because of their nationality or clan, but because at that point of time they are better trained, having better morale and ably led in the battle field, in Armed Forces training have always been considered as a tool which boosts morale. Another quote which had really impressed me and highlighted the importance of training and morale is that of Mark Twain - *"There is nothing training cannot do. Nothing is above its reach. It can turn bad morale to good; it can destroy bad principles and recreate good ones; it can lift men to angel-ship"*. Good training does bring enrichment in competency standards and level of proficiencies thus making a person more confident and having a changed outlook.
- *Support:* Biggest factor in mental satisfaction is support; it may be support from people back at home, organization, team or the group and the leadership. When the support is positive, the morale will be high. An individual feels secured when he receives support from peers, colleagues and the leader in the work place. The

mental stability, feeling of selflessness and dedication is generated depending on the type of support given. More than materialistic support the assurance of morale and psychosomatic support during the performance of job which is more important. Question is what does support encompass – basically it must encompass the professional development, personal well-being and psychosomatic support in calamitous situations. The leaders and the team have a big say in this. Morale will be dependent on the credence of assurance of support and the perceived expectation of support by the individual. Leaders have to ensure that support must not be mixed up with obligation this would be counterproductive.

- *Recognition:* The requisites of recognition include giving credentials to individual's place in the team as part of the organization, credit and credence to performance and acknowledgment of the achievements. Recognition of an individual in the team, the credence to the team and the individual on performance and recognition of the contribution towards the team achievements are the boosters of self-belief and confidence of both the individual and the team, when these are proportionate to the perceived expectation of both, then individual is said to be mentally contented and morale is said to be high in the team and that of the individual member of the said team. Recognition must never be used for pampering or doing favour, for it would offset and have negative impact on morale of the individual's and the team. Rightful recognition of performance and achievements creates sense of attainment of success, enhances the self-belief and develops reverence for the values of the organization and the leader. This factor has total psychological impact on an individual, the team and the leadership. Recognition is apt when the leader values and respects the participation and contribution of each member without any prejudice and give equal opportunity and space to perform before deciding the most deserving for awards or incentives. It is only then that recognition is said to be righteous, in that case men have faith in the leader and it does keep the morale high.

- *Motivation:* This has always been linked with morale; both are complementary to each other. Motivation gives impetus to morale, whatever be the source of motivation when it sets in, it automatically generates morale or when morale is high person is said to be motivated. In Armed Forces both must coexistent to achieve success. In corporate I have observed that a person with high morale need not be highly motivated, morale is high because the person is contented whereas performance and productivity quotient in relation to HR initiatives makes some of the persons get into 'my limits' syndrome then the motivation gets restricted. Whereas a highly motivated person in corporate is looking forward and wants to achieve the maximum till such time the scope exists, he/she is motivated till that extent or limit, stagnation is not acceptable thus before the limit the individual does job hoping, however morale in such case will be moderate. The sense of duty; culture of comradeship, espirit-de-corps or solidarity , cohesion , affiliation and bonding to the unit/team and service before self (selflessness) make motivation - morale complementary to each other in Forces. Motivation cannot be linked with stick and carrot policy, it cannot always be materialistically related, motivation's relation with selflessness vis-à-vis personal gains needs to be weighed in the right perspective to make it sustainable. When motivation is sustainable the morale will correspondingly be high. Placing innately passionate and motivated individuals around the organization helps in keeping the other employees' morale high.

- *Responsibility:* When an individual understands his/her position and responsibility associated with it, he/she is said to be motivated. There are two important facets of responsibility, *firstly,* responsibility brings reasonableness in attitude, prudency in approach and develops passion to achieve and the *second,* aspect is accountability of the responsibility. The faith and trust of the men under command is dependent on these two facets, leader who is responsible, accountable of his/her decisions and takes the blame of failure and gives credit of success to the men will be a morale boosting leader. Responsibilities makes the leader to lead by example and enlarges the courage of conviction, this develops the faith and trust of the men on the leadership and keeps the morale high of the team. Associated with this is the responsibility of the team, when each individual of the team is a willing worker and understand their responsibility and are active contributor to fulfill the team responsibilities the morale will be on a higher plinth as individual feels proud of being part of the responsibility.
- *Contact: "Contact unwinds mental knots",* an apt and frequently used phrase. All problems are resolvable when contact with the men is there and through value based communication, these two are great equalizers, when nothing works it is contact which opens avenues and breaks deadlocks, whereas communication cements gaps and relations tend to become accommodative. The approachability becomes easier and frequent, which in turn makes communication effective. When there is match of frequency due to contact and communication, it provides impetus to mutual understanding and frankness in approach. The impacts of contact and communication have direct bearing on the mental and psychological frame of mind. When the contact is open the morale will be high. Leadership's best

tool for keeping the morale of the command high is to effectively establish a relationship contact. However, all human-beings are not the same, each have different ways to perceive things thus leaders have to take care for the sentiments when establishing contact and communication. Leaders must learn to understand each man individually, bridge the relationship and communication gaps and cement the relation; this will depend on how well the matching frequency is established. Lesser the gap better will be the communication and high will be the morale.

- *Material:* Materialistic desire is one of the factors which meets the wants of the individual and gives certain degree of satisfaction both physical and mental and thus morale is dependent on meeting materialistic needs. There are certain basic needs which influence the state of mind and perception of well being, when made available at an acceptable quantum these fulfill the demand of wants and initiate a sense of approval towards the organization. Even though such basic material needs seems to be very mundane in terms of its existence in life of an individual, but are of value in making of morale, these are:
  - *Facilities:* The basic work environment, proper work place ergonomics, transportation, logistical support and provisioning, safety, medical and living accommodations and family welfare measures encompasses facilities and when provided gives boost to morale. Comfort from guaranteed availability of facilities at work place keeps the morale high. Facilitating in adjustment and settling down in the organization is another important facet of boosting the morale, when an individual is assured of support in terms of facilities to make the stay and settling down comfortable, this creates bondage. When assurance of support is prevalent, morale will be high.

- *Entertainment:* Any activity which breaks monotony of work is entertainment; it can be games and sports, cultural activities, outings, team/group competitions, work place meets and get-togethers of both men and their families, etc. Space for entertainment must be catered in the schedules and need to be planned, the frequency have to be calculated keeping the pressure of work, saturation levels of the team and individuals and reclamation time to energize. Entertainment has to be constructive and devised with logic to meet the organizational vision, work ergonomics and human stress relaxations.
- *Leisure:* Every individual needs a break. This can be in terms of leave for social obligations, organized vacation, rest to recoup, free time to spend with the family or on self, celebrations and festivity, planned trips professional or otherwise, holidays and organized events. These have direct impact on morale, the mental well-being of an individual depends on how much time he/she is granted to unwind self, regulate the level of stress and relaxation from work/environmental anxiety.
- *Leave:* There are certain obligations towards the family, social engagements, supporting family trade, settlements, acquisition of property or constructions, untoward incidents and medical treatments. Such leave do not fall in the category of leisure but are essential part of life. When an individual is guaranteed leave of absence to meet his/her requirement which he/she considers being important and a necessity, the morale will be high. Uncertainty creates anxiety which adversely affect the productivity. Here the morale is in relation to level and degree of anxiety which in turn is dependent on guarantee of leave. Leave is to be used as revitaliser and energizer, there are number of ways

to plan leave what is important is that it must cater for choice and unplanned request. Planning of leave serves the interest for both the unit/organization and the individual, as commitments to work remains energized and after leave rejuvenation of spirits increases the productivity levels. The concept of encashment of leave has materialistic connotation but judicious spread over the service must be considered, as no leave does put pressure on the worker who is without any break and brings down efficiency levels. Morale is sustainable by the leadership if leave is considered as essential human rejuvenator.

- *Incentive:* For morale, sense of satisfaction and realization of well-being are by themselves the primary facets of incentives. Even though incentive is more closely related to motivation but incentive in terms of benefits obtainable for well-being is associated with morale. Small community incentives like tea party for accomplishment have positive impact on morale. Community incentives with no distinction, universal applicability and equally beneficial to all are more effective in boosting morale. Incentives for morale and motivation, therefore have to be planned separately. Materialistic incentive does indirectly create avenues to influence the morale, what is important to keep note of is that materialistic incentives must be job related, applicable at the work floor and should facilitate accomplishment of the task by the team. Productivity related community incentives, may be in term of bonus or rewards for team proficiency will have a positive impact on the morale.

Leadership and Morale

Leadership is the most pertinent morale generator; it plays a predominant part in the state of morale and sustaining it.

Leadership and morale are inseparable and will continue to be so, it is the leader who is the initiator and generator of morale and the quality of state of morale is based on the quality of the leadership. Basic factor in any sphere of operations is the 'Human', thus the leader's balanced application of 'heart and mind' in handling of the troops, in planning operations factoring of conditions that govern the morale and building of the human momentum for the operations are basic imperatives of management of morale in Armed Forces. In this context I would like to quote Field Marshal Slim *"When odds are against, uncertainty is prevalent, dangers lurking and probability of failure is high and the morale is vulnerable to collapse, spirit is said to be high when in spite of reverses hope to succeed is always there"*, it is the leader who bestows the confidence and hope, thus morale of the men is directly related to the morale of the leader. Certain identifiable fields which link leadership with morale and applicable to both the leader and the men are:

- *Trust:* One of the very important factors in relationship and morale. The mutual trust between the leader and the men is the bondage. First and foremost is that when the leader identifies self with the team in every possible way and team recognizes the leader, then the commitment and involvement of both the parties is equally responsive in terms of identical level of morale. And when the team has a high level of cohesion, the trust is said to be high. When the spectrum of trust is on the higher side the morale of both the leader and the men is high. To get the best out of the men, the faith, trust and dependency on the leader is must. The feeling of confidence comes when trust mutually exists. The morale in this case is commensurate to the trust bestowed by the leader. Trust is a morale multiplier and need to be appreciated by the leadership. Building of trust will depend on latitude of dependency, recognising the value of commitment, the level of competency of both the leader and the team, credibility of the leader and assured support from the leader. When the leader thinks that he is part of the team and there is no distinction between the leader and the team when it comes to accomplishing the mission then the level of trust increases. Building trust is a leadership responsibility and living up to the trust bestowed must be the leader's duty.

- *Respect:* Outlook towards respect directly influences the morale. Every individual must be treated as a value entity that is an integral part of the team and the leader has to give credence to the self-respect of each man under command irrespective of profession/trade or level of proficiency attained or the outlook or personal opinions or the personal sentiments. When the leaders respects the feelings of each individual of their team, it develops binding of inter-personal relationship and mutual trust. The morale is proportionate to the level of respect which the leader confers on the men under command.
- *Rapport:* Morale is also dependent on the degree of rapport between the men and the leader. When this gap is less the morale is said to be high and when the gap is large the men distant themselves from the leader and this adversely affects the morale. Leaders have to create a relationship, have a bonding and know their men. Leaders have to ensure compassion, projecting and giving due recognition to their men and encourage oneness to develop a positive and responsive relationship. Relationship have two aspects human and professional, one without the other makes relationship incomplete. Rapport is based on the degree of inclination in the type of relationship being maintained by the leader, when human relationship is profound the leader is said to be sensitive, whereas when the professional relationship is profound the leader is

said to be insensitive and when both are balanced the leader is said to be having cordial rapport with the men under command. Professional leader must establish professional rapport, thus both human and professional relationship must be balanced, it is only then the leader is considered as 'meaning business'. Men like optimum combination, too much of sensitivity amounts to pampering and too much insensitivity creates clash of interest and disassociation.

- *Ethics:* The values and principles of the leaders have an influence on the morale of the men. These values and principles are the ethics which are applicable both in the work environment and the relationship; these have to be constant and uniformly applied, any fluctuations in this regard will question the credibility of the leader. Ethics in the character of the leader which have direct influence on the morale are attitude, conduct, decisions, approach, commitment, association and dealings. The leaders have to be transparent and noticeable while practicing the values and principles. Unbiased and candid ethical approach is good for morale of the team and the men, and leaders have to ensure that all their practices are consistent in all spheres of dealings with their men and within the team. Maintaining the standard of ethics by the leader is a vital qualification.
- *Fortitude:* Leader's courage (both moral and physical), resilience, perseverance, determination and ability to take on stress are some of the dynamics which construct a positive outlook of the leader and the morale of the men to a very large degree is reliant on this aspect. Initiative, enthusiasm and self-confidence are mandatory ads-on of the said dynamics which makes the fortitude positive in a leader. These give the leader a standing and recognition. A leader must demonstrate the vibrant aptitude in handling/dealing with situations and courage of conviction when it

comes to taking stand. There is a phrase in Army *"Those who command themselves, command others"* the dynamics of fortitude should be first developed within the leader and it is then the leader can expect the same from the men. When the men see the positivity in the fortitude then their trust and morale gets an impetus and a positive flip.

- *Creativity:* A creative leader must possess ingenuity, adaptability, risk taking ability, tenacity and should be a catalyst. Creativity inculcates the spirit of participation, involvement, productivity and originality. When the men find their leaders being creative, the morale is correspondingly on the higher range. Along with creativity is the responsibility, it is then that men will support their leaders and willingly commit to the task at hand. To quote Dwight D. Eisenhower, *"Leadership consists of nothing but taking responsibility for everything that goes wrong and giving your subordinates credit for everything that goes well"*. On the other hand when the creativity is supported and encouraged by the leader, positivity in the performance of the men is predominant and morale gets a good boost. With creativity comes initiative and it is initiative which supports creativity. A creative leader will encourage the command also to be creative; this is best achieved when the command is made to take initiative. The team/group in the process of taking initiative and trying to make their contribution novel are going to make certain mistakes or might err which the leader must accept. Leaders must be able to underwrite the honest mistakes of their subordinates if they wish to develop their initiative and make them creative, this is very much an important necessity to support creativity among the men. The leaders must inspire the team by demonstrating enthusiasm for creativity. The morale will be high where such an environment exists and more so when the leader supports this by setting personal examples.

- *Training:* Up gradation of proficiency and keeping the work force up to date with the latest are two important facet of keeping the morale high. Training has an important role to play in making morale high. A well trained worker has recognition and responsibility; this gives a boost to morale of the individual. Leadership has to focus on training activities of their team and must aim to have uniformity in its application, this makes the team complete in proficiency and also brings a balance within the team. Aim of the training is to gear up the team to an expected standard to meet the demands of the job; this is a great morale booster as it enhances confidence and increases the scope of employability. Leadership have a important and constructive role to play in proper selection, giving equal opportunity of training to their men, build up expertise levels and ensure suitability of deployment of their men based on proficiency achieved. This process must be transparent and honest, it is only then right person will be doing the right training and rightfully employed. Training adds value to an individual's personality and this gives boost to morale.
- *Communication:* Is a two way process, it cements the gap, builds the level of understanding and trust. Here I want to quote General Slim describing relevance of communication and relationship equation between officers and men *"If you want to talk to men, it doesn't matter whether they are private soldiers or staff officers, if you want to talk to them as a soldier, and not as a politician, there are only two things necessary. The first is to have something to say that is worth saying, to know what you want to say: and the second, and terribly important thing, is to believe in yourself. Don't go and tell men something*

you don't believe yourself, because they'll spot it and if they don't spot it at the time, they'll find out. Then you're finished". Communication cannot be restricted nor have a closed loop, it has to have a purpose and meaning. Must not be associated with gossip or chatting or oration. It involves establishing contact, speaking out your thoughts, sharing views and listening to others view points and ideas. Good communication starts with establishing link, followed by disseminations, ensuring assimilation and ends with feedback or assessment of the reaction. Effective communication therefore is giving convincing credibility to the need to communicate, assimilation of the content, influencing the commitment and persuasiveness to achieve the perceived goal. When communication is free flowing, meaningful and action/result oriented then it has positive impact on the morale.

- *Participation:* Leaders' participation not only in the functional/operational field but in social, community and shared activities is an essential part of command. Participation increases the acceptability of the leaders within the command. To get the best out of the men, they must feel that the leader is with them and must know that they can depend upon him/her; this can happen only when the leader is with the troops. The morale of men is dependent on the degree of participations of the leader; more intense is the leader's participations higher will be the morale.
- *Discipline:* Discipline is a mandatory requisite to good morale; disciplined outfits will always posses high morale. Leaders have to instill discipline among their teams, it is only then that negligence, errors, accidents and loss of life and limb is controlled. *"Discipline can only be obtained when all the officers (leaders) are imbued with the sense of their lawful obligation to their men and to*

their country that they cannot tolerate negligence. Officers who fail to correct errors or to praise excellence are valueless in peace and dangerous misfits in war" - General George S. Patton, discipline is an obligation and when it is enforced in its right prospective, it will be taken in the right spirit by the men, it is only then the effect will be positive on the morale. Uniform applicability of discipline is a must and need to be ensured by the leaders, any deviations or bias will be detrimental to morale. Good discipline will evolve when the leader is self-disciplined and is true in adherence.

- *Passion:* Passion in a leader is contagious to morale of men, higher is the passion in the leader high will be the morale. Passion makes the leaders commit to accomplish the task. Passion in leader gives boost to the adrenaline of the men under command and there is buoyancy in commitments, helps in building audacity, take challenge, face up to odds and reversals and spirit to bounce back or reverse the reversal. When the team finds the leader passionate about his command responsibility, about the mission, decisions taken and in execution of the plans, the morale of the men will be high. Morale and passion are complementary.

Basic Cardinals of Morale

Morale is leader dependent and it is command responsibility to ensure that men under command are with high morale. Officers are considered as the role model and their attitude and behaviour have a big say in the morale of the men, the officers having high morale will ensure that the men under him also have higher morale, the said cardinals are attitude and behavior based and does influence morale of the men:

- *Have an aim and establish attainable standards to meet the aim:* A leader must have a definite vision or aim and conviction that the planned task can be achieved. Over ambitiousness in aim and calling for standards beyond the capability must be avoided this is detrimental to morale of the troops.

- *Give out clear missions and tasking:* As a leader, you have to make people want to follow you, and nobody wants to follow someone who doesn't know where he is going.
- *Train your men and improve proficiency:* Leadership is all about identifying potentials of the men under command, giving them the opportunity to develop, making them proficient and develop the spirit to continue to be a professional.
- *Take responsibilities:* Leadership consists of nothing but taking responsibility for everything that goes wrong and sharing credit for everything that goes well with the subordinates/men.
- *Freedom to exercise initiative:* Leaders have to inspire their men to take initiative. Maintain a hopeful attitude, even in the face of discouraging setbacks. Men follow those who persist with hope, are creative, provide opportunity to excel, are ready to take calculated risks and encourage freedom of action/initiatives.
- *Show confidence in subordinates:* Leaders must trust their men, delegate responsibility and authority to them and encourage them to exercise decisions within the framework of the intent.
- *Recognise and award excellence:* Leadership is built on honesty, integrity and character. Honesty and integrity builds trust and credibility. Rightfully deserving and the true performer must be acknowledged.
- *Involve your men:* Leaders must carry their team; this is possible when leaders proves that they are worthy of the trust.
- *Demonstrate concern about the welfare of subordinates:* A leaders must have compassion and take care of their command, must be able to understand the concern of the men Quote Sun Tzu "*Regard your soldiers as your children,*

and they will follow you into the deepest valleys; look upon them as your own beloved sons, and they will stand by you even unto death".

- *Practice what you preach:* Leaders must practice what they preach, men will be more than willing to entrust their life.

The above selected cardinals are part of command personality and had very positive impact on the men, I have seen their effects thus I consider these as the most potent ones. Men with high morale swear by their leader. Morale is such a factor without it the organisation cannot survive, it is more than motivation. You can wait for some time to motivate but if morale is nonexistent nothing is going to move. It will be appropriate to say Morale is the initiator and motivation is the generator of positive human responses. Ingenuity and earnestness on the part of leader are two aspects which give the leader to think out ways to boost the morale and there are no end to methods and techniques.

"The best morale exists when you never hear the word mentioned. When you hear a lot of talk about it, it's usually lousy".

—Dwight D. Eisenhower

8 Personality

"The first act of leadership is coming to grips with yourself, who you are, where you are, and what is of value to you, and shaping yourself by acts of conscious will, into what you want to become."

—Fenwick .W. English

The 'personality' is the distinctive patterns of traits, outlook, temperament and behaviours that make a person exclusive. The personality is the set of trait and pattern of comportments that each person possesses which influences behaviour, outlook, temperament and the approach towards life. Leaders' personality is always under scrutiny of the men/team and any false projection from the perceived, expected and the established personality creates doubt in the creditability factor of the leader in the ranks and files which in turn generate fuzziness. Personality is thus an individualistic distinctive persona of the leader which creates an impact on the men; no two leaders can have the same personality. Personality must be adaptable and this brings dynamics in projecting the personality to meet the requirement of the situation as it must be obtainable at the given point of time. Versatility in personality meet the demand of situation but pseudo personality does not stand the test of ground realities.

A collation of natural personal traits which occur consistently, especially as determined by a certain pattern of responses in any given environment builds certain characteristics which are distinctive; this distinctiveness builds up and sets a matrix for the personality. There is a difference between traits and personality, where as traits are the natural elements which a man is born with or acquires and develops during his/her life time, on the other hand, personality is the projected image of the traits and characters of an individual in the social and vocational fields. Personality, therefore, is to be build and can vary with situations and ground actualities. I have seen a successful leader with a set of personalities in one particular unit, when moved to another unit could not establish himself with the same set of personality matrix. Personality must be oriented to the profession, group dynamics, work culture and the functional environments. Adaptability of leaders to mould the personality based on the requirement and demand of their assignments is a significant factor, personality matrixes therefore have to be suitably adjusted to meet the said demand and the requirements.

Each platform or strata of work demands different set of personalities and the leaders have to mould themselves and develop those personalities which will influence the outlook and efficiency of the men under command. Usually character and personality is considered same and interchangeably used in expressions. Traits and their disposition are not permanent, these keep changing with level of maturity and experience, and they can be developed and moulded based on the environment in which the leader is functional. Whereas in personality projection the leader is to decide the image that one wants to presents in front of others to create an impression, thus in building of the personality series of demonstrative traits which a leader is required to project need to be exclusively developed to lead and make men follow. Experience and exposure makes a leader to shape personality and gainfully employ it to achieve the desired goal.

"A man is but the product of his thoughts what he thinks, he becomes." quote by *Mahatma Gandhi* and *"Always be yourself, express yourself, have faith in yourself, do not go out and look for a successful personality and duplicate it"* quote by actor/kung fu exponent Bruce Lee, the said two quotes unequivocally brings out the aspect of self and originality in personality, a leader must perceive one's own personality to get established and recognized by the men. The individual qualities, character and born traits combine to give shape to the personality which an individual wants to project. One can say that trait and their character is one's soul - the real you, while personality is how you want others to perceive your real you. In corporate language the same connotation is applicable to personality and it is "how well one can get endorsed".

Another aspect about personality which I think is a misnomer *"bearing and the look of the leaders"*. Most of the successful leaders have not been handsome by look or demeanour, what matters the most is the person parse and how effective is the projection of the qualities of leadership to make people follow. There is a common saying *"An ugly personality destroys a pretty face. Beauty doesn't last forever, but a beautiful personality does"*, leaders may not be good looking but may be having a personality to impress the men and carry the team. Therefore, persona of an individual is arrangement of temperament, attitude and outlook and what is important is how these are projected. Another aspect which is related to personality is the performance and how the opposite party perceives the same. Leader's performance and the way he/she carries his/her personality do matter in getting things done. When the leader is among the men the personality must be the prime mover of commitment, involvement and spirit to achieve.

Leadership and personality go in hand in hand, leaders have to establish their personality to fit well with the group and make people follow the orders without questioning the authority of the leader. Leaders have to learn the art of adapting personality in various situations depending on the circumstances and the path selected to achieve the desired goal. Now the question arises - is personality the 'mask' which the leaders have to keep changing to meet the objective or it is to hide some of the weaknesses of the leader which can be counterproductive or detrimental in leading the team? The facade of personality can be used to mould the perception of the group or the team to achieve the objective or prove the authority of leadership and this does help. But still personality is the actual face of the leader and it can be used to achieve the set objective, the leader who uses personality in the spectrum of natural ability and the developed persona in projecting original self, the leader is said to be authentic. As the leaders' moves up the ladder and the level of the stratum changes, the personality quotients have certain amount of consistency. Higher the appointment and position, the leader is recognized by the established personality and which at this stage gets standardized, however by this time the personality has matured and self identity is well established , it is desirable at this stage that versatility in the personality continues to exist.

Personality Types

During my career in the Armed Forces I had experienced varied type of personalities in leadership both in the face of bullets and in routine affairs. The functional behaviour of the team/group and the impetus, drive and momentum of the work is dependent on the personality of the leaders. In indecisive leadership practises the actual behavioural traits gets camouflaged in the process of personality projection. Personality is a combination of human behaviours influenced by environmental factors, outlook and temperament matching up to the leadership traits, thus in spite of being individualistic by nature is very much mouldable, adaptable, concealable and imitable depending on situations and demand of the environment. This is best explained by the said quote

"Personality is logical arrangement of all your attributes, thoughts, feelings, attitudes, behaviours and ability. It is the distinctive pattern of yours heart and mind functioning—the way you think, feel, and behave—that makes you distinctively separate." The types of personalities as I have fathomed out from my observations I have listed them down, each has certain strong points which a young leader can incorporate to develop his/her personality, these are:

- *Conventional:* This type of personality believes in standard operating procedures, manuals, tradition and rules & regulations. Such leaders are stickler of orders and procedures, extremely thorough in their work, responsible and thus dependable. They have a strongly-felt internal sense of duty, which lends them a serious image. They're not comfortable with breaking laws or going against the rules, often tend to believe that things should be done within the gambit of law, in accordance to the procedures and within the approved plans. Have an excellent ability to take any task and define it, organise it, plan it, and implement it thoroughly till completion. They are very hard workers and industrious. As they go 'by the books' in all activities and they are hesitant to take any risk. They are impatient when things do not move as per their plans and tend to lose sense of direction. They take additional responsibilities and strive to accomplish the task in an efficient manner. By nature they are humane and compassionate. Orderly and organised, believes in tidiness and well laid out arrangements.
- *Risk-Taker and Enterprising:* Excellent in their skill, experimental by nature and not overly concerned with respecting laws and rules if these get in the way of getting something done. Detached but very analytical, they excel at finding solutions to practical problems. Adaptable and spontaneous, they respond to what is immediately before them. They focus on details and practical things. They have

an excellent sense of expediency and grasp of the details which enables them to make quick and effective decisions. They are loyal and faithful to their followers, believes in equity and fairness. They are impatient and cannot sit idle and seek engagement. Their self-beliefs are very strong, have strong principles and respect the organizational values. At times they suffer from rashness when meeting timelines, if not successful they tend to get angry however shoulders the responsibility. They are optimistic, full of good cheer, loyal, uncomplicated, generous, trusting and receptive.

- *Conscientious:* They are truly warm and kind-hearted, sensitive to other people's feelings. They are industrious, meticulous, diligent and methodical. They possess a strong sense of responsibility and duty, take their responsibilities very seriously and can be counted on to follow through, therefore reliable. They are knowledgeable and have good acumen of their profession. They believe that the organization is running because of them. They feel safe in secured environment, do not want to venture out to unknown territory, in crises situation tend to confine themselves in tried out solutions. Makes lot of deliberations in decision making to come to a perfect decision, not very optimistic by nature thus works on various contingencies to resolve any issues. Characterized by goodness, humility, sense of service, keen observations about people and extremely perceptive to other people's feelings.
- *Responsive:* Flexible, open-minded, original and creative by nature. Not proactive and does not like to do things which generate conflict. Analytical and observant, they weigh the pro and cons before deciding action. Play safe by nature and takes very calculated risk. They live from day to day and do not plan beyond a limit. They are creative and imaginative; highly reflexive and convincing. They are "doers", and are usually uncomfortable with theorizing concepts and ideas. Good in communication and vehemently project

their point of view. They are extremely perceptive and aware of others problem, warm and sympathetic. They vehemently pursue points raised by their command and where required stand by the commitment given.

- *Intuitive:* They are gentle, caring, complex and highly intuitive. They put a lot of energy into identifying the best system for getting things done, and constantly define and re-define the priorities in their lives, puts tremendous amount of faith into their instincts and intuitions. Optimistic and depends on natural course of action to tide over the problems and hopes for the best. This category is rare but does exist.
- *Idealist:* Possess strong value system, very principled and disciplined. Firm believers of ethos, values and traditions. They are perfectionists, who drive themselves hard in their quest for achieving the goals. They go by the books and strict followers of orders. Generally thoughtful and considerate, they are good listeners and put people at ease. Believes in honesty and integrity, very upright and have legal bent of mind. Considerate and helpful in nature, maintains transparency in their dealings. They are cause oriented and aggressively defensive and passionate about their cause. In an ideal environment they are comfortable, have tendency to avoid conflict situation and hesitant to work in field as they do not like to deal with hard facts and logic. They have controlled emotion and do not want to project their weaknesses. They do not take credit but passes the same to the subordinates/team. They are good managers and can convince people easily. They set example and follow their values to true letter and spirit. Popular with their team/group.
- *Methodologist:* Scientific and explorer bent of mind, investigative by nature. Independent, original, analytical, and determined, possesses good professional knowledge, competent and believes in structured approach. Very

observant and possess fast uptake capabilities, they grasp the essentials and are not time wasters. They are good strategists, carryout methodological appreciation of ideas, concepts and weighing them against their current strategy, they plan for every conceivable contingency. As leaders they are quite effective and are able to objectively see the reality of a situation, pragmatic by nature and very candid of their opinion. They easily don't take risk and are very deliberate; they take time to arrive at a decision. Ambitious, self-confident, deliberate and have vision, they dislike messiness and inefficiency, they value clarity and efficiency and will put enormous amounts of energy and time into consolidating their point of view into structured patterns/matrixes. They are individualistic and very reserved, not overly demonstrative of their affections. They are very rigid and do not accept changes to their plans, usually quite open to hearing an alternative way of doing something but unless it is not validated by them they are not confident of its incorporation. They tend to become absorbed with minutest of details, delays are acceptable to them. If things do not move as per plan they tend to lose their nerves and tolerance level depreciates. Sets very high standards for themselves and expects that others will be able to meet the same.

- *Go-getter:* Friendly, adaptable, action-oriented they are focused on immediate results. They are risk-takers and live fast-paced lifestyles, they are gambler by nature. Practical and down to earth, does not believe in wasting time and are impatient to complete the task at hand, posses ability to quickly improvise an innovative solution to a problem. They have good people skill. They are outgoing, straight forward, very enthusiastic, place little importance on introspection or theory. They have knack of looking through situation, quickly decide what should be done, execute the action, and move on to the next task.

They are people friendly and possess uncanny ability to perceive people's attitudes and motivate. Have strong self-belief and doggedly sticks to their principles, rules hold little value, but they will not under any circumstances do something which they feel to be wrong. They make decisions based on facts and logic, does not involve taking people's feelings into account. Have abundance of energy, are action-oriented and enthusiastic, they get very excited about their assigned task. They possess good convincing power and can sell anything to anyone and their own idea. They are not usually so good at following up, and might leave these tasks to others. They are good team man.

- *Ingenious:* They are intelligent, logical, original and creative thinkers. They have ability to analyze difficult problems, identify patterns, and come up with logical explanations. They are found to be constantly working to generate new theories, strategies and plans. They're usually extremely bright, and able to be objectively critical in their analysis. They hate to work on routine things, prefer to build complex theoretical solutions; however, when it comes to implementation they tend to leave it to others. They are very tolerant and flexible, strive constantly to achieve logical conclusions to problems and do not believe in emotional considerations in decisions making. They are overly critical and sarcastic with others, if their plans/ ideas are not taken at its face value they tend to become negative and cynical, forcibly prove their view points and disprove existing theories or others point of view. They usually have complex characters, and may tend to be restless and temperamental. Sensitive to failure and comes under pressure easily, have tendency of experimenting and using permutations and combinations to come to a workable solution during such circumstances.
- *Popular:* They are lively and enjoy being the centre of attention, have very strong inter-personnel skills. They

relish excitement and drama, usually very sympathetic and concerned for other people's well-being. Spontaneous and optimistic individual, they tend to become over-indulgent and place more importance on immediate action without looking at long-term consequences. They like to 'go with the flow' and trusting in their ability to improvise in any situation presented to them. Well-developed common sense and practical, very loyal and industrious, like to be in charge and exceptionally capable in organizing or running activities.

- *Imaginative:* Focused, logical, rationale and individualistic by nature. Posses' extroverted intuition, sense of visualization and sagacity of grasping things. Quickly absorbs and precisely understands a situation to resolve the issues, is logical in his approach and acts objectively. They are flexible and adaptable, usually extremely quick and accurate in their ability to size up to any given situation. Under stress, they may lose their ability to generate possibilities and become obsessed with minor details. They live in the world of possibilities and become excited about concepts, challenges and difficulties. When presented with a problem, they're good at improvising and quickly coming up with a creative solution. Creative, intellectual, curious, and theoretical, they are very optimistic. They are good in making strategies and grand plans but when it comes to grass root application or tactics they tend to leave it to others. Utopian in their imagination they have tendency to be unreasonable and unrealistic at times.
- *Supervisory:* They are 'responsible' type and take charge of the situation, focused, logical and rationale in their approach, they are called 'executives' also. They have ability to grasp complexities, absorb a large amount of information and are quick in decision making/judgments. They are very career focused and are not naturally tuned into people's feelings, has little patience with people who

do not see things the same way as they perceive. They love to interact with people, very forceful and have dynamic presence, have a tremendous amount of self-confidence and excellent communication skills. They are assertive, innovative, long-range thinkers with an excellent ability to translate theories and possibilities into solid plans of action. They are usually tremendously forceful and have the 'GO' to accomplish whatever goals they set out for. They're tireless in their efforts on the job, can read the intentions of their superiors and accordingly strive to accomplish the assigned tasks. They have tremendous amount of personal command and presence which works for them as a force towards achieving their goals, however this quality gets them alienated from the others. They work within limits and rarely ventures out.

- *Flamboyant:* They have outstanding people skill. They have very good bearing, smart and impressive outlook, their dress sense is immaculate and they carry themselves well. They have well developed sense of studying any situation and can mould themselves accordingly. Have excellent communication skills. They are warm hearted, conscientious, courageous, possess strong sense of conviction and takes their responsibility and duty very seriously. Have ability to carry their team and very possessive of their men. Likes to be the center of attention in social/official functions, very practical and have well-developed common sense. Have clear visions of the way things should be, loyal and hard working and likes to be in charge. Flexible and open-minded, believes in originality and creativeness, risk-takers who lives for the moment.

Personality and consistency are related components. Consistency should be in the ways of perceiving, thinking, acting and reacting as a person and this would be giving shape to the personality. Too frequent change in projection of personality does not hold well in influencing the people's perception. It is the consistency in individuals' thought, behaviour and emotional patterns which to a large extent gives out a definitive personality. I for one feel that image of personality is developed over a period of time and it gets identified with the leader, this I call certified personality. Certified personality and the inherent personality are two different facets of the leader's personality, certain tenable incorporations in both with changing situations and an environment within the scope of projection is always possible.

What is important that leaders must identify his/her personality and try to adapt the persona which the situation demands? The instinctive and responsive behavioural patterns in a given environment, attributes, thoughts, feelings, attitudes, manners and credibility over the time gets identified and accepted, and gives a recognisable individual entity to a leader. Leaders have to be versatile and highly imaginative in adapting styles from various types of personalities, and at the same time maintain the individual entity. The leader must have the ability to improve, develop or integrate any trait which deems fit and agreeable to a given situation. However, one has to be cautious; 'A wolf in sheep's clothing' attempt will not last very long in the perception front of the men whom the leader is commanding.

Personality Cognizant

One has to be aware of his/her personality which includes the complete scope from inherited to adapted personality. "It is not you who creates what type of personality you have, it the observers who through their observation gives a shape and type of personality", leaders have to be conscious of not only the projected personality but also the personality in which he/she has been positioned by the men. Personality consciousness enhances the scope of optimizing those components of the personality which have impact on the response and commitment from the team. Pragmatism in the personality both original and projected helps in shaping the level of acceptance of the leader by the team and is an important deciding factor in maintaining the consistency in the personality. Fickle personality creates gap in inter personal relationship and adversely effects the command of troops.

Another factor is carrying out self-retrospection/ monitoring of the defined personality, those who are apt at it show considerable adaptability in adjusting, keeping public persona and private self separate and have high behavioural consistency. Personality consciousness makes one to displays true dispositions and attitude consistently in every situation. To give the flip to your personality projection as perceived by the environment and be noticeable, I have few tips which I feel are basic fundamentals:-

- Immaculate conduct.
- Know when to speak up. Develop your own communication skills.
- Be loud but not obnoxious.
- Do not be afraid to talk to people, make conversation.
- Follow manners.
- Always remember that you represent your team/group/ unit.
- Do not be afraid to be different.
- Create a brand persona for yourself.

Personality Enhancers

Personality enhancement is proportionate to degree of self-confidence, success of adaption and consistency; ultimately it is a person's personality that determines whether people are impressed or otherwise. Importance of the enhancer is related to the question why do we require personality at all? The answer is very simple personality is projected to influence and sway the people under command towards you There are certain acts which makes the personality attractive and people tend to develop trust and belief, these are the enhancers:

- *Have Positive outlook and right attitude*: Maintain a good demeanor, smile warmly and project positivity in your body language. People must turn around to see you, be formal in your dressing sense and be smartly turned out. Do not be sarcastic or complain about others, avoid being self eulogizer. Must demonstrate earnestness and seriousness in listening to people's problems, ideas, suggestions and recommendations. Make yourself cheerful, your presence should bring good cheers, try to get the environment enlivened. Be approachable and mix freely with people.
- *Be true to what you commit:* Commitment once given must be honoured at any cost. The trust and faith depends on this factor, thus leaders have to weigh their commitments which are within their power and capability. None fulfillment of given commitment, is regressive and has negative impact on the personality, people tend to avoid such person. Leaders have to be very prudent and sure before giving commitment. Similarly promises must be weighed within the capability to fulfill before committing, backtracking from a promise make people lose faith in you.
- *Be a good listener:* Have patience to listen to people without showing irritation. Look in the eyes, hang on every word, and make people feel important. There is nothing more appealing than having someone listen to you intently making people feel like they are the only person in the world. Your body language must show the earnestness in your approach, purpose and sagacity in the interest towards the dialogue with the person. To be a good listener, one has to be very approachable and amicable. Developing faith is also dependent on this art, people approach only when they know that they will be heard.
- *Enlarge your horizon and Cultivate interest:* Leaders have

to be knowledgeable, having awareness and capable to converse. Leaders in order to keep themselves in focus, must be updated, cultivate new interests and be good conversationalist. When meeting people the leaders must use the opportunity to share and exchange their views, this generates interest and enhances personality.

- *Learn to make conversation:* This is an art, but to be good at it one has to have detailed knowledge of the subject, understanding of the issues and awareness of the prevailing situation. Once you have back up knowledge and data it is only then you can contribute, talk about it with others and be able to convince. Through conversation one is able to fathom the gravity and seriousness of the situation, concerns and obtain honest feedback. Good conversationalist is popular and people feel free to approach. This art also helps you to learn from others, for it is not possible to know everything. Conversation makes the personality more amicable and people friendly.
- *Meet people and enlarge acquaintances:* Make the effort to meet people, it not only exposes you but also broadens your horizons. This opens up fronts of acquaintances, familiarity, contacts, friendship and relationship. This reduces the gap in relationship with the command; approachability is enhanced and trust and faith develops. Developing interest in the personality is best achieved by knowing the people, understanding them and awareness of their concerns. Meeting and knowing people are most important aspect of leadership and personality development. Shyness and reticence approach towards establishing acquaintances is counterproductive in personality projection. Demeanor of 'people friendly' in personality projection is dependent on the openness and approachability of the leaders; it is not only leaders approaching their command but command wanting to meet and develop closeness with the leaders which also matters.
- *Look for lighter moments:* Everyone enjoys the company

of someone who possess ability to make them smile, leaders therefore must look for the humour and lighter side in a situation – there is always one in every situation. Humourist relief is much welcomed and at times helps in diverting tenseness. Lightheartedness to an otherwise dull or gloomy setting will attract people to the leaders. This ability enhances the personality. However the leaders must guard against sarcasm in humour, people like lighter moment but not leg pulling. Never target any one in particular, humour must be general. In reversals or facing odds or in a critical situation a simple lighter moment makes things easier.

- *Have an Opinion:* People like to talk to a person who has opinion, person without opinion is considered as dead wood and people tend to avoid. There should never be a situation when people feel that they are talking to a wall. Opinion can be negative and not to the liking of the person who is in conversation but still the said person has scope to project oneself to explain things. There is nothing more tiresome than trying to talk to someone who has no opinion on anything. Conversations have nowhere to go if there is nothing to expound on. In leadership it is the issue of decision making, people will approach only when they know that a decision will be derived and their view point will be taken seriously. People avoid leaders who fail to take any type of decision. Being honest and true to your word will bring admiration, respect and gratitude of others.
- *Be yourself:* The next most irritating thing is trying to be someone when one is not! Moulding oneself in order to just fit in someone's shoes, or to make oneself ape someone else, usually backfires. Attempting to be a carbon copy of someone else not only fails to fool, but reveals lack of authenticity. Originality of personality should not be camouflaged with a false front which cannot be or is difficult to be kept alive for very long. People are averse

to personality which lacks originality, as the perception of being fooled becomes an irritant factor. Whatever be the type of personality the leader might possess, what matters to the people is the transparency and visibility of the said personality. People have tendency to adjust to the type of personality, any attempt to superimpose or copy or to hide the negativity of the personality creates mistrust and lack of faith, and this distances the leader.

- *Be Accommodating:* Being supportive, accommodative and sporty is probably the most endearing quality one can integrate into the personality. Understanding the people and giving the justified support, being accommodative to resolve issues and giving fair deal to everyone without any prejudice, will make people approach the leader. People love someone who is encouraging, believes in them and helps them when they are down.
- *Treat people with respect:* Nothing improves a person's personality more than value and respect for others 'He who gives respect gets respect', understanding the people, giving credit to their values and respecting their entity is an important aspect of any personality. Compassion, being considerate and respectful is three important facets which make people attracted towards the personality. Honesty in approach and paying due respect are the factors which creates an everlasting impression on the people.

"We as humans have the power and ability to shape our personalities. When we develop ourselves to be all that we can be, we contribute to our own development, as well as make the environment better in which we are functional" Swami Vivekananda words brings out one important fact that building a positive personality is within reach of any individual. Enhancers are facilitator towards personality building and these give positive shape to the personality. *"The first act of leadership is coming to grips with yourself, who you are, where you are, and what is of value to you, and shaping yourself by acts of conscious will into*

what you want to become" a quote by Fenwick. W. English which enunciates the creation of personality and toning it with the functional environment. Personality is to be build and it is an ongoing process of development of character.

Toning your personality

Leaders have to tone up their personality to meet the expected demand of the men. Human-being is a 'social animal' he possesses behavioural attributes and personification which recognizes his/her standing. The attributes of social and workplace which need to be recognized for building personality are - social affiliations - recognition in the society and work place - association with the organization/team/group – self-esteem of the status granted - honour of being part of the organization - power bestowed by the organization - status of the appointment bestowed and its recognition - obligations towards the organization/society/team. It is when the leader feels that he/she is special it is then that maximum is derived toward accomplishment of desired personality. Therefore, personality is tunable and the art of doing this is called toning or harmonizing of personality. For doing so there are few suggested techniques which the leaders have to master and make it a habit, these are:

- *Extroversion vis-à-vis Introversion:* Personality is situation and environment dependent. Personality gets projected based on degree of demand within a situation and the expected outcome from the said situation or the environmental requirement. Fallouts of personality behaviourals depend on how long the situation extends or the environment wants it to last. Positive outcome results in personality enhancement whereas negative outcome results in reconciliation with the scope of personality imposition. Best combination of human behaviour is when there is low balance of introversion and high extroversion.

Balance tilt of either or both is situation and propensity of event based, proportionate ratio will vary from time to time. Some element of introversion will always be there in high extroversion. One who can maintain the required proportion will be a better manager and a good leader.

- *Tolerance:* There are traits, qualities, methods and techniques which a leaders adapts to influence their team, leaders require skill to create combination of conceptual and personal skill to lead their team. However what makes a difference in style of leadership and degree of success, when rests of the traits remain unchanged is the degree of tolerance. Tolerance towards behavioural idiosyncrasy of individuals coming in contact, uncontrollable situation, highly variable environment, adversity, ambiguity and lastly stress and strain are some of the important facets which the leaders have to master to give appropriate projection of the personality and leadership excellence. This brings confidence of men on the leader. To be very frank these can make or break a leader. A very apt quote of Rudyard Kipling sums up this aspect of tolerance *"If you can keep your head when all about you are losing theirs and blaming it on you; If you can trust yourself when all men doubt you, But make allowance for their doubting too; If you can wait and not be tired by waiting, Or being lied about, don't deal in lies, Or being hated, don't give away to hating and yet don't look too good nor talk too wise; If you can dream - and not make dreams your master; If you can think - and not make thoughts your aim, If you can meet with Triumph and Disaster, and treat those two imposters just the same, If you can make one heap of all your winnings and risk it on one turn of pitch-and-toss, and lose, and start again at your beginnings and never breathe a word about your loss . . . If you can talk with crowds and keep your virtue, Or walk with Kings nor lose the common touch, If neither foes nor loving friends can hurt you, If all men count with you, but none too much; If you can fill the unforgiving minute with sixty seconds' worth of distance run, Yours is the Earth and everything that's in it, And - which is more - you'll be a Man my son!"*

- *Adaptability:* Dogmatism and authoritarianism are two factors which is unacceptable to people and make them distance from the leaders. Moreover these make leaders rigid and inadaptable. Adaptability brings closeness of people towards the leaders. The leader who is apt in adapting is more acceptable as compared to leaders with dogmatic attitude. Leaders must learn to adapt as things change, circumstances change and people change. What the leader must do is adjust efforts to what is presented and respond accordingly. Never see change as a threat but make use of the opportunity presented to learn, to grow, to evolve and to be a better person. One cannot change our past, cannot change the fact that people will act in a certain way, cannot change the inevitable, the only thing leaders can do is to adapt and work their ways out. People follow leaders willingly when they have faith/believe that leader will not leave them in the lurch. Great leadership is not running away from reality, at times the hard truths, sharing difficulties and adapting with the situation at hand can inspire people to take action that will make the situation better.
- *Machiavellianism:* Manipulation of others as a way of achieving ones goal is Machiavellianism, ambition is good only till such time when there is fairness in approach and intent, using single means, honesty and hard work. When several dishonest means are made use of and manipulation is predominant to achieve desired goal and there is a motive behind such application, it is being 'Machiavellian' which is not good for the organizational environment. If leaders believes in 'scoring brownie points' for his/her self progression, he/she may fool few all the time but not all the people at all times. Sustaining manipulation and

opportunism over a long period is difficult; men under command dislike and distrust such leaders. Personality must be devoid of such characteristics.

- *Behaviour at Work:* Each personality have its uniqueness and style but certain basics which are applicable to all personalities are:
    - Be optimistic, attitude of 'Today is not that bad. It will look better tomorrow'.
    - Control your temper; do get mad only when warranted but then get over it!
    - Avoid having ego of your position. Be approachable.
    - Be positive, every attempt is possible! Do not give up easily.
    - Be prudent in selecting your men, once done, do not differentiate.
    - Don't let adverse facts stand in the way of a good decision.
    - Be original.
    - Get into details.
    - Share credit.
    - Check before putting your endorsement.
    - Have a vision.
    - Be demanding but know the limits of your men.
    - Do not show your fear.
    - Incessant optimism is a force multiplier.
    - Have courage to face, do not sly.

Personality of a leader is the kaleidoscope of temperament and character, learning about our Personality Type helps us to understand why certain things come easily and why we have to struggle to cope with certain other things. Learning about other people's Personality Type helps in understanding the most effective way to communicate and employ them to an advantage/positive outcome. Leaders have to keep grooming themselves so as to polish his/her personality; it is a never ending process. One has to guard against copying personality without understanding the repercussion. Always be yourself, express yourself the way you feel comfortable, have faith in your own personality and only take that from other personalities which you can confidently maintain, because false front cannot be held for long. Personality grooming is hardly taken seriously, what I have observed is that personality is being taken in the normal stride of existence in the organization without trying or attempting to develop it and neither the organization takes it as an special obligation. This is applicable to both the Armed Forces and the corporate.

> *"A man is but the product of his thoughts what he thinks, he becomes."*
>
> —Mahatma Gandhi

9 Attitude

"Attitude is a little thing that makes a big difference."
—Sir Winston Churchill

Attitude is defined as "A settled way of thinking or feeling about something" or "a feeling or opinion about something or someone, or a way of behaving". Attitudes are feelings and beliefs that largely determine how people perceive their environment and it is one's attitude that will eventually make the behaviour and contemplation of actions. Attitude is the 'bent of mind' of an individual which to a great extent is influenced by the thoughts and outlook towards life, personal observations, personal perception of feelings and sensitivity, prevailing surroundings and conditions which influence the environment. In totality, the attitude is the way of looking at things. It is an important component of leadership and man management. Attitudes reflect the quality of the leadership, it does have an effect on the team and it determines how well those who are being lead accept and epitomizes their response towards their leader. "Leadership is practiced not so much in words as in attitudes" very common phrase in Forces, in the military philosophy of leadership attitudes has a very special place.

What we think and how we feel are the two facets that makes the attitudes, it reflects to the way we react to a situation emotionally, psychologically and physically. The corresponding outcome of all of these is the behaviour. Whatever be the personality and the demonstrative traits of the leader, what ultimately matters is the attitudes. Albert Einstein quotes *"The attitudes of the leaders make the ultimate difference in accomplishment of the mission. Weakness of attitude becomes weakness of character"*. The attitudes are influenced by born attributes, expression of personal character and perceived views based on personal understanding. Attitudes can be developed and with experience and exposure it gets refined. As the leader gets associated with the team, *first,* he tries to adjust with the team, *second,* in order to make the team responsive to the command the leader brings refinement/ change in the attitudes of both self and the team and *finally,* depending on the functional environment keeps moderating the attitudes to optimise the potential to meet the objective. Attitudes creates an impression on the minds of the men, if there is positivity then belief in the leader is optimal and this in turn gives recognition to the relationship of the leader and the men. Attitudes in its right prospective are a great motivator and morale booster. Depending on the extent of the positivity in the attitudes possessed in a leader, it generates positive vibes of hope and realisation. Men give their best when the attitudes of the leader are right.

As per Epictetus Greek philosopher, any attitude is situational/environment governed and controllable, he said *"It is our attitude toward events, not events themselves, which we can control."* Therefore, attitudes are not a fixed behaviour or practice. What the leader believes will have a definite impact on his/her temperament and outlook and this in turn will make the leader behave in a particular way. The factors of values, ethics, ideologies, prejudices, creditability and self-esteem are factors which have direct bearing on attitude build up; any changes in one of the factor will have proportionate change in the said attitude. In my initial days in the battalion my commanding officer described attitude in a very lucid manner, "Thoughts come out in words and deeds. Words and deeds shape behaviour, behaviour reflects your thinking, and your thinking is your attitude".

"All that we are is the result of what we have thought. The mind is everything. What we think, we become", discourse by Lord Gautam Buddha, here attitude is associated with thinking, even in *Bhagwad Geeta* the attitude is related with the way of thinking. Thus attitudes gets their origin from the thoughts and beliefs of a person. The other important aspect is the way the leader perceives the realities of the events and the situations and his/her reactions thereof, here it is the mental appreciation process or way of thinking which determines the action and/or behaviour, attitude gets displayed by the action/behaviour. The personality aspects which do influence the attitude are personal desire, conflict of interests, importance of needs and the personal outlook.

There are two types of attitudinal orders in any human-being, positive attitudinal order and negative attitudinal order. Positive attitudinal order is positivity aligned to the approach, way of thinking and level of commitment to meet the desired goal, in doing so maintaining/sustaining the morale and motivation of self and the team. There is unison of purpose and commitment in the team in positive attitudinal order; it creates 'we all' syndrome. Negative attitudinal order on the other hand is aligned to conflict of purpose and negativity in belief and approach; this creates the 'me only' syndrome. Attitudes are an intangible attribute but very much a part of personality wherein both have tendency to modify/adapt with the environment and requirement of task/event. Positivity of one will correspondingly influence positivity of the other and same equation is applicable to negative attitudes.

There are two type of decision makers/leaders, one who identifies themselves with and works for the institution, is source of strength of their men, have belief in the system and not self-centered or self-promoter and on the other hand there are leaders who are keen, competent, ambitious, industrious, self-centered, self-promoter and uses the institution as tool for self-progression, the attitude of both are positive scale but are different. Former will have pragmatic attitude and the later is manipulative by nature. In both type of leaders what actually matters is the belief adopted in their respective attitudinal approach, both the leaders will give result.

The attitudinal spectrum comprises spread from highly positive, sliding downwards to neutrality and culminating to highly negative. Attitudes are an intangible attribute and part of personality wherein both have tendency to modify to/with the approach and performance. Positivity of one will correspondingly influence positivity of the other. Mahatma Gandhi had linked attitude with thoughts and actions flowing out of the thoughts *"Keep your thoughts positive because your thoughts become your words. Keep your words positive because your words become your behaviour. Keep your behaviour positive because your behaviour becomes your habits. Keep your habits positive because your habits become your values. Keep your values positive because your values become your destiny."* Arrogance, self-importance, egotism, bigheadedness, pompousness, snobbery, fixed mindset, argumentative and selfishness I consider these as attitudinal habits of individual's behaviour, these are the negative attitudinal traits but most of the people associate these in their parlance as "having an attitude" with negative connotation, thus attitude is mostly considered as negative of personality by most of the people. Positive attitudes are/have been considered as part of good character, thus mostly addressed as "having good character". This confusion will always exist, till such time we realize that attitude as such is a personal quality, therefore the positive attitudinal qualities are the one which makes the individual correct the negative attitudinal tendencies. In this chapter I am discussing only the attitudes which create positive impact and are congenial in making the leadership a driving force.

Positivity is contagious, it equally affects the others, and this must be part of the composite spectrum of the leader's personality. Leader's positivity is a vibe; it is absorbed by the men and equally reflects in their approach towards the task and commitment towards accomplishment of the mission. Always positivity need not succeed but it gives tangible alternatives to make attempts which do ultimately succeed. The positivity can be best described by a quote of Abraham Lincoln, *"We can complain because rose bushes have thorns, or rejoice because thorn bushes have roses."* Attitude universally has been scaled as positive and negative, positive attitude has always been the desired attitude.

There are certain attitudes which I think a leader must possess, in my combat experience I have seen leaders who have attitude are usually successful in leading their men in battle with confidence and purpose. The team/men work with commitment and are found performing when the attitude of the leader matches the feelings of the team and the men. The leadership attitudes which I found to be effective in command of troops are:

- *Attitude of Enduring:* Enduring is an attitude, it keeps you going, gives impetus to the spirit to continue to give fight and not to give up easily, enhances the capability to bear the stress and pain and improves perseverance against reversals/odds. This attitude must not be confused with trait or personality as the action of enduring is dependent on the prevalent/ground situation and the mental frame of mind to address the problem depending on the gravity of the situation. The spirit to not to give up without a fight and persistence in efforts are important attributes of this attitude. Leaders with the attitude of enduring bring fortitude and determination among the men under command. This attitude is very different from rigidity; here the leader seeks ways to overcome the odds, whereas rigidity is inflexibility like *"banging the head against the wall time and again"*. There is a saying *"A pessimist sees the difficulty in every opportunity; an optimist sees the opportunity in every difficulty"* and attitude of enduring is optimistic as till hope exists the persistency will continue, the will to fight, therefore, is a predominant factor and enduring leader will carry his/her team till the steam runs. General George Patton's aptly describes the quality of enduring and persistency in leader *"By perseverance, and study, and eternal desire of enduring and persistence, any man can become great"*, this attitude in leadership have been a battle winning factor, what is important is getting into the habit of this attitude with sense of purpose and maintaining the steadfastness in the approach.

- *Attitude of Perfection:* It is a way of looking at things, perfectionism is an attitude. Leader who is a perfectionist have attributes of organized approach, streamlining of procedures,systematicarrangementofactions,optimization of resources and being prepared for the unforeseen. Leader with this attitude will like to have intimate control, going into details, giving value to the ground realities and prudent in conceptualization of plans. In an operational environment leader with perfectionist attitude will not take chance, his actions will be well researched and in detail. A perfectionist believes that all planned outcomes are not always the expected, if it is expected then the propensity and inertia may not be as per the expectation or it can be the unexpected, therefore knowing yourself, the team and the variables influencing the ground situation is a must for the leader, therefore this attitude makes the leader to look into the issue in a methodical manner with logical reasoning. The ability to take challenges and bringing it to logical end is best achieved through this attitude. Thus the attitude of perfectionism has three basic attributes i.e. clear understanding, logical application of mind and to be in command of the situation.
- *Attitude of Continued Existence:* It is an instinct of survival i.e. not giving up easily; this is an attitude which builds the

fighting spirit. The attitude seems similar to perseverance but is very different. The attitude encompasses risk taking, creativity in approach, ingenuity to meet the challenges, resourcefulness and highly inspired spirits. The attitude brings determination and the spirit of 'last man last round' in the team. When things do not move as per plans due to certain changes in the path which are beyond the planned scope of task, the attitude of survival gives the team to work the way out. This attitude is more pertinent to task which are very difficult and risky or when handling reversals it gives impetus to the will to succeed and/or gives hope to survive. When odds are against, uncertainty is prevalent, probability of failure is high, morale is vulnerable to collapse and in spite of reverses hope to survive and succeed is always there then this attitude is at the top of its positive spectrum. Will to survive is a tendency and a leader with the attitude of continued existence will make the best of the situation.

- *Attitude of Daring*: It is an attitude to take risk, have stomach to face the odd/reverses, have courage of conviction and forthrightness. This attitude is adrenaline of confidence. Degree of willpower and determination to persevere in face of odds and resolve towards the goal is an important attribute of this attitude. Audacity has two facets of occurrences *firstly* while in process of meeting the challenge in the field and in face of reversals, taking risks for accomplishing a given task and *secondly* audacity of taking the decision with probability to exploit the opportunity. In face of the situation, decision outcome is affirmative and resolve to succeed at all cost is predominant aspect of the attitude and it is positive in the former case; and for later case to take decision is definitive but certain degree of contemplated acceptable reversals or unpredictable negative outcome is in the possibility, but taking the stand of going through with the decision, in this case the attitude is of self confidence. In both the cases, the attitude has positive connotation. The attitude of audaciousness thus have attributes of spontaneity, diehard resoluteness, confidence on self and the beliefs, positive temperament and is based on gravity of situation, therefore the attitude does not have any fixed disposition or scale. Gambling must not be considered as an attributes of this attitude, there is difference between audacity and taking chance without knowing the outcome. Audacious leaders must be competent enough to know the difference between risk and gamble, risk is always calculated whereas gambling is taking an unknown chance. What actually matters is the controlled application of this attitude, I have seen many operations when this attitude having iota of rashness or taking the gamble have resulted in reverses. The success depends on judicious daring at the right time, with logic and speed in decision and action. Confidence of the leader and that of the team on the leader does matter; attitude of both has to be positive and matching. A quote by General George S Patton is also applicable to this attitude, *"One continues to learn about war by practicing war"*, the attitude of daring is developed in a leader by giving exposure to decision making in no go situations and encouragement to take risk. Daring leader with the attitude of audaciousness will make the unwilling to follow, two quotes I would like to give out *"I do not fear an army of lions, if they are led by a lamb. I do fear an army of sheep, if they are led by a lion"*, these are the words of Alexander the Great, and on similar lines Napoleon Bonaparte said *"If you build an army of 100 lions and their leader is a dog, in any fight the lions will die like a dog. But if you build an army of 100 dogs and their leader is a lion, all dogs will fight like the lion"*. It is only the lion hearted audacious leader who have the attitude of daring will lead by example and from the front.

- *Attitude of Play Safe:* This attitude has both the positive and negative spectrums. The negativity is very obvious, it contains hold back and retarding influence. In certain job and profession this attitude has positive and effectual impact but in others such an attitude is considered as lack of courage to try out something more than the standard or new. This attitude is dependent on the belief 'why only me or why should I' or 'let it be as it is' or 'someone else is there', *secondly,* the attitude is based on type of job demand like bomb disposal where the safety of self is more important. Generally the attitude of play safe in Armed Forces other than the demand of the job is considered as negative attitude as the killer and survival instincts are lacking , no one in Forces are ever happy with a tie rather than going in for an outright victory. I admit all human-being have certain degree/amount of this attitude, the prominence of the attitude is in the outlook and the basic character of 'self first'. The degree of this attitude will depend on the ratio of how much the leader gives to 'self' and what importance is given in making a mission successful or the interest of the organization. Another aspect which this attitude basically gets demonstrated is in the proportion of commitment vis-à-vis the concern for the self in relation to the desire for achievement of the target. When the concern for self is on the higher side and does not commensurate with the commitment, attitude of play safe is on higher pedestal whereas it is at lower pedestal when commitment is higher. Play safe attitudinal prominence is thus the ratio of the concern 'self' in a profession/job and credence given to accomplishment of the mission.

- *Attitude of Optimism:* Let us not confuse this with positive attitude. This is an independent attitude related to hope. Expectation and probability of something positive/good. This attitude in its real perspective counters the scale of negativity 'all is lost'. In an adverse circumstance or situation or things not moving as per plans, this attitude generates the spirit of pro-activeness to bring the situation to a positive inclination. A leader with this attitude is considered as positive and this increases the scope/gives an impetus to forward thinking. Person with this attitude is a non quitter and continues to strive to manage the situation to a positive decisive end. The attitude does not allow a person to stagnate or reach a plateau; he keeps learning, keeps improving and is open to change. Sanguinity, buoyancy, resilience and strength of character are outcome of this attitude.

- *Attitude of Righteousness:* Ethics and belief in organizational values are the attributes of this attitude. This attitude builds a leader and brings confidence of the men in the command. The attitude and its proportion are directly reflective to uprightness in command of troops and the respect of the command. The attitude is proportionate to the degree of courage of conviction and the moral character/fiber of the leader. It is considered as an attitude for it projects the personality of 'fair in dealings' which in turn makes men follow their leader or stand by his side. It is a very demonstrative attitude which builds the personality of the leader, determines the approach and degree of interpersonal relations. "*Morality is the basis of all things and righteousness is the substance of all morality*" quote by Mahatma Gandhi elucidates that this attitude demands transparency and straightforwardness. Leader having this attitude has to be the role model and practise what he preaches.
- *Go-Getter Attitude:* 'Can Do it...!' types. When taken in its right perspective, leader with this attitude is enterprising; aggressive, a dynamo and a live wire. Leader with this attitude acts as a role model and believes in *'Leading by Example'*. Why I consider this as an attitude - it is a behaviour related to confidence and mental makeup of the leaders that affects the outlook - creates belief and trust. Person having this attitude is cheerful, eager to take on challenging tasks, will go beyond the call of duty to

accomplish the mission and to prove his competency will leads from the front. Leaders with this attitude show the way to the men under command and rally up to the trust entrusted. Traits of professionalism, competence and self-belief are the force multipliers of this attitude. Such leaders do not care about the rank, position and status but remains always responsive to shoulder responsibilities and carry the team. This attitude generates energy and motivation among the men. Such leaders out of hundred are ninety-nine times successful. This attitude is an initiator of motion in the team/group, when applied in execution of task it generates positive vibes in men.

- *Attitude of Easy Going:* Leader with this attitude is carefree, enjoys life, makes acquaintances, keeps pleasing company and brings cheerfulness in the environment. Live life attitude improves the demeanour of the leader and same gets reflected in the behaviour, it helps in bringing closeness in interpersonal relationship. The attitude possesses behavioural attributes of personification of taking things in stride, or 'as it comes' open approach, approachability, optimism, accommodating, compassion and obliging. Leaders with this attitude are practical, social and good manager of human resources. Living-life attitude have proportionate impact on the team behaviour and the output. The team spirit gets heighten due to the said attitude of the leader. This attitude in a leader gives inclusivity with the environment and enhances functional compatibility with the team.
- *Attitude of Matter-of-fact:* Practical and down-to-earth attitude of a leader makes him/her sensible and rational. Knowledge of self, the men under command and the situation as on ground are the mainstay of this attitude. Leaders with this attitude are best in exploiting the potential and optimization of the means and resources. They are very adaptable, approachable and understanding. They look out for windows of opportunity and know how

to optimally exploit such situations. Professionalism and use of common sense are two important features of this attitude. Practicality and understanding of strategies/tactics, application of the lawful procedures in execution and economy in employment of resources are the essential attributes of this attitude. Leaders with this attitude have high order of tenacity. Simplicity and sanguinity are important face of this attitude. This can also be called the constructive attitude.

- *Attitude of Zeal:* This attitude encompasses the attributes of fervour, passion, devotion and enthusiasm. Leaders with this attitude will be able to influence the team to give selfless dedication and willing participation. Person with this attitude is always a front runner and will be leading from the front. Leaders with this attitude work for the interest of the organisation and are very loyal. The attitude makes a leader rather popular among the men, the gap in the interpersonal relationship is very well bridged, the realization by a group and every member of the said group that the organization is above the personal 'self' does get predominance in the relationship spectrum, and the conflict of interpersonal interest is at minimum level. This attitude is demonstrative by nature; however 'action speaks louder than the words' must be kept in mind by the leaders as all the attributes are closely watched by the team/men under command.
- *You're Right so am I:* Person with this attitude is an egalitarian, accommodating and adaptable by nature. Not argumentative but are assertive, such leaders are the one who carry their teams and make adjustments to make things happen. Person with this attitude is very approachable and compassionate. This attitude is most beneficial when team/collective decision is to be taken. Such leaders use democratic methods to arrive to a decision, thus are very acceptable. Degree of assertiveness is dependent on the

degree of shouldering of responsibility of the decision taken by the leader. Leaders with this attitude must be highly committed and with impeccable integrity. Person with this attitude does not want to get involved with controversies and wants to stay clean.

Personality gets determined through compulsive attitude and attributes of characters of an individual. There is a very thin line between the attitudes and the character attributes, most of the times both get inter mixed in interpretation and perception. The highlighted attitudes are the one which I consider are the essentials of leadership attributes which make the command/men to respond positively to the leaders' behaviours and actions. Attitude is the mirror of one's personality, it is the feelings and beliefs that largely determine how people will perceive their leader and it is one's attitude that will eventually lead to behaviour patterns and reaction of team/group/men under command towards the leader.

Attitude of a leader are an essential facet of leading men in all type of job/work environment. All human-being have attitudes of their own which are distinctive from the acquired or developed attitude. The inherent attitudes do influence the acquired/developed attitudes. Attitudes are environment dependent, which have direct bearing on the perception build up. Any abrupt attempted change in one of the attitude due to personal prejudice will have proportionate change in perception spectrum created by the leader. The attitudes on which the leader does not have belief, however the same is being used to serve a purpose will eventually become evident as the behaviour pattern will not be compatible with the attitude and in doing so the whole attempt becomes 'dramatics'. One has to guard against such perception among the men under command. A good leader is the one who does adjustments in the attributes of his/her attitudes and in doing so introspectively and with ingenuity tries to make his/her acceptability factor with the environment more pronounced.

Carrying one's Attitudes

What really matters is the way the leaders carries their attitudes, just possessing of attitudes is not end all of good leadership techniques but making the attitudes matter which is of paramount importance. A leader who is able to carry his/her attitudes well will have good backup from the team/ men under command. The question is how a leader carries the attitudes when the attitudes itself are abstract and intangible in nature. Any attitude is dependent on three basic factors Trust, Commitment and Involvement of both the leader and the team. When levels of all three are balanced, faith in the leadership becomes more dominant. When the leader is able to develop the faith of their men under command, leader is said to be carrying his/her attitude appropriately. Leaders are admired most for honest conviction, forward-looking approach, inspiring demeanour and having high competency level. If men are willing to follow the leader they first want to assure themselves that the person is worthy of their trust. Leader is only as good as long as the words are followed by deeds and commitment on ground, this must be visible to the command. Without the credibility and genuineness of the attitudes the leaders will never be successful. The leaders therefore must:

- *Indentify the Attitudes:* A proper selection of attitudes and establishing the creditability of the applied attitudes for furtherance of the selected aim must be gauged appropriately by the leader. Combination of proportionate degree of applicable attitudes will create an environment of belief in the men under command with reference to the intent and rightfulness of the path chosen by the leader. In identifying the potential of attitudes and deciding the application of the chosen attitudes to maximize the returns from the team/men under command, is an art which the leader must know and master. All human-beings have combinations of attitudes in different proportion and magnitude. Rightful use of the attitudes to create sense of trust and belief is an important facet of leadership skills. Understanding of one's attitudes and its effect on leadership command, therefore, is an important perquisite of personality development and personality is directly linked with the attitudes which one possesses.

- *Never Force an Attitude:* There will always be situations when all the facets of the natural, acquired and developed attitudes can be applied in one given task. Environment also demands only certain type of attitudes and anything which is forced upon is rejected thereby reducing the creditability of the leader. A leader is a very transparent entity, whenever it tries to give a false perception it is detected, it is always better to be original self. Very few leaders are there who can dramatize their personality over a long sustained period. Men under command can see through their leaders, thus it would always be prudent to be genuine and forthright in approach. Never force your attitudes on to the team/group, instead try to make it acceptable.
- *Never Create False Perception of an Attitude:* What you don't have do not try to show to create a false perception. Attitude is a behaviour and gets reflected in all the actions, never can a false image be shaped to mislead the command. Lack of an attitude can always be made up through the team/group attitudes or alternate course can always be worked out. Leaders must not ever be called a 'show off' by the men, this amount to unwilling following or men take advantage to create the sense of false ego in the leader which can subsequently lead to failure of purpose.
- *Attitude must match with Personality:* Attitude must go side by side with the personality. Personality must not be confused with the physical appearance. Small or thin physical stature does not mean that they cannot be having

attitude of audaciousness. Personality is the projected image of character, thinking, communication, soft skills, self-belief and the competence. When attitudes are in the matching frequency with the personality it creates an aura of impact on the team/men under command. This develops the confidence and the trust. When the attitude is commensurate with the personality it is easy to carry the attitude and mould it to the required dynamics of the team, the task and the objective.

- *Attitude and Approach:* "No one ever finds life worth living—he has to make it worth living", same is applicable to attitude, and it is how the leaders approach their attitudes. Just having the attitudes is not end-all of leading men; it has to be aptly applied in accomplishment of the task. Attitude of any person is not only understanding the suitability, but also identifying capability with demand of assignment and sustainability of performance which matters, thus the approach has to be pragmatic, down-to-earth and realistic depending on the demand of the situation. Too much and too less of an attitude can be detrimental towards accomplishment of the task. The right quantum of positivity, expression of appropriateness and connecting the attitude with the task makes the approach positive. All attitudes have certain pro's and con's, to maximize the pro's and negate the con's which matters, when the approach towards the task commensurates with the intensity of the attitude, it is only then the leader is said to be totally committed towards the team and the objective of the task.

'Carrying one's attitude' for a leader is very important facet of leadership. Attitudes must be guarded so that the perception of the men/team is not influenced and negativity creeps into the working environment. The degree of flamboyancy and show off of one's attitudes has to be controlled. Leaders' attitudes must be such that it must not overwhelm the attitudes of the others in the team, if this happens the initiative gets killed and complex starts developing. More over authority bestowed must not be used to force upon the attitudes which may not be acceptable to the team/men under command. Attitude is a personalized behaviour and is associated with individualistic characteristics, thus same attitude will not be applicable with all. Degree of variance and intensity of attributes will be different in each individual. "The attitude you have will affect your ability to rule and it will determine how well those you lead will respect you. It will also reflect in their behavior towards their leader and in a team", thus attitudes does matter in leadership.

Attitude Builders

The factors which determine attitudes are experience, environment and culture. These factors provide an avenue to introspect the existing attitude and adopting the acquired attitudes. Experience is the developer of attitudes, whereas environment and culture are arbitrators of the adaptation of attitudes. There are certain areas which are obligatory to build the natural, acquired and adapted attitudes, the listing of the attitude builders are based on my observations of officer's action and demonstrated attitudinal dynamics in various combat situations:

- *Self-Belief and Attitude.* The leaders must have self-belief on their attitudes. It gives confidence in application of the attitude. The attitude is proportional to the degree of self-belief; leaders with better and sound self-belief will maximize the output of the attitude. Attitude in itself has the characteristic of adjusting to the personality; the merit thus is associated to the degree of the self-belief one possess. The self-belief makes the leaders responsible of their attitudes and this increases the scope of adjustment with the environmental/team parameters of functioning.

Attitude is environment dependent and environmental imperatives of values, beliefs, ethics, ideologies, ethos, culture and customs have direct bearing on attitude build up. The buildup of attitude in the positive scale requires support of self-belief.

- *Career and Attitude Enlargement*: The attitudes require boost, stagnation have detrimental effect on the attitude and the performance. Job enrichment and enlargement as career progression/promotions provides motivation which reinforces the attitudes. The attitudes must adapt to the changes. Changes on the other hand are boosters of attitudes. Opportunity rejuvenates the attitudes; this in turn gives impetus to the personality and scope for adjustment with the environment. The opportunity for personal progression resuscitates the personality and correspondingly influences the functional attitudes. Potential of any person is not only suitability and capability, but also the attitude of leadership.
- *Relationship and Attitude*: Interpersonal relations directly influence the attitudes. Relationship with peers, superior and subordinate is directly proportional to buildup of attitudes. When the functional and informal relationship is accustomed to the attitudes, the relationship is said to be positive. Relationship does play a major role in building attitudes; it brings finesse, mellowness and vibrancy in the attitudes. The attitudes on the other hand develop the trust and belief in the relationship. Synergy in relationship actually means more than meeting, it is art of understanding the other party's not only point of view but also the mind and attitudes, this in turn helps in establishing the relationship. Attitudes influence the behaviours which in turn influence one's aptitude in maintaining relationship. Making a person react in a certain way in a given situation depends on the positivity of the relationship. Relationship is one of the most important factors in building the attitudes.

- *Recognition and Attitude*: This has two very important facets, credit of the work and acknowledgment of the leader by the team. In the first case it is a motivational perspective of progression and in the second case, it amounts to creating credibility within the team and establishing an identity of the personality by the leaders. In both the cases, the consequential attitude reciprocations comes to play. The confidence of the attitude is based on the positivity of the degree of recognition. A leader who has been recognized for his contribution in the field of operations will not only make endeavours to maintain the same attitudinal application but also try to develop attitudes which are consequentially at secondary level and give impetus to the involvement. The recognition of the team on the other hand boosts the confidence of the leader's attitudes.
- *Mentoring and Attitude*: The attitudes are dependent on the level of supervision, lesser the supervision greater is the responsibility and more positivity in the attitudes. Greater is the supervision the attitudes get dominated by the supervisors' attitudes. The attitude application is possible when the leaders have freedom of action and room to apply their ideas/vision. Trust of the seniors will determine the degree of reduction in supervision and more reliance will be on directives. Freedom of action is most desired for it facilitates speed in execution, provides initiative to exploit the opportunities and gives impetus to level based decision making. Attitudes are most important factor without which freedom of action gets restricted; positivity of attitudes gives confidence to both the leader and the men under command. This factor also helps in fine tuning of the attitudes in relation to the task and its execution.
- *Position and Attitude:* Leaders and his position in the decision making process determine the effect on the attitude. Leaders in the decision making spectrum will

have their place earmarked/dedicated and in relation to the importance of the position decision making will be their command responsibility. Degree of responsibility will determine the value of the position. Depending on the functional position the attitudes would get affected, this in turn will make the leaders deploy their attitudes to justify their position. Another aspect which plays an important role in the leadership attitudes is the acceptability of the position of the leader by the command. Leadership is through process and/or by designation or appointment, in all cases the suitability factor of position of the leader and correlation of the leader and the team is equally important to make the attitudes effective, a very common phrase in Forces 'no man is a leader until his appointment is ratified in the minds and hearts of his men' explains the relationship equation. The attitudes and resolve thereof are based on the position of the leader.

- *Trust and Attitude:* Attitude is productive when the level of trust and dependability of the team/men under command is high. Trust is professional competency and commitment dependent, when levels of both are balanced trust and faith are dominant. Attitudes in this regard will have an essential role to play as to get the best out of the men, they must feel that you are their real leader and must be assured that they can depend upon you; attitudes thus reinforce this trust and belief of the men. Basic factor in any sphere of operations is the human relations and attitude is linked to this relation, if the equation of relationship is not strong or non-existent then having or effecting attitudes is not relevant. Success of attitude depends on how the attitudes are regulated and synergized with the relationship and the trust bestowed by the men under command.
- *Opportunity and Attitude.* It provides scope to self-development and career progression. The attitude is proportionate to the scope of opportunity. One have to

look into both sides of opportunity, one is the opportunity to the leader i.e. scope of self-progression and second is the opportunity to the team/men under command i.e. scope and latitude to perform. In both cases, the attitude adjustments are mandatory. Opportunity is good only till such time there is fairness in approach and intent. When several means are made use of or its combination to achieve self-desired goal and there is a motive behind such application, it is being over ambitious which is not good for the organizational environment and gives a negative flip to the applied attitudes. Opportunities give good impetus to attitudes and development of the attributes to improve the attitudes. Similarly giving opportunity to men under command authenticates the belief which the leaders confer in the men. Decentralization, freedom of action and delegation is dependent on the attitude and the trust developed. The confidence in subordinates and the team makes the leader to reinforce the positivity of the attitudes.

- *Knowledge and Attitude:* 'The knowledge broadens horizon', eagerness to know, learn and to cultivate new interests improves the awareness level and builds confidence. Knowledge improves the scope and provides opportunity to share and exchange views, enhances the level of competency, improves the working relationship and understanding of organizational environment. The attitudes gets developed and nurtured with knowledge. The attitudes gets pronounced when the degree of competency, proficiency and awareness builds confidence, trust and reliance of the men on the leadership, when this is on the higher side the leaders is said to be having useful attitudes. Knowledge enhances expertise and professional acumen, if the level of competency of the leader is higher the attitudes is said to be having positive impact. Competency gives value to the attitudes and these values give recognition to the personality. Excellence is said to be prevailing attitude by General Colin Powell ,US Army, *"If you are going to achieve excellence in big things, you develop the habit. Excellence is not an exception, it is a prevailing attitude"*, the knowledge increases the value of competency and proficiency which gives impetus to the spirit of attainment of excellence, this is an important component of leadership.

- *Participation and Attitude:* Leaders' participation in the assigned task, being part of the team during the execution of the task and connecting with the vibes of the men, gives the leader's attitudes a big boost. The attitude depends on degree of sincerity in participation of the leader, a very conservative leader will have a different set of attitudes as compared to forward thinking leader, and similarly avant-garde leaders will be having different set of attitudes in comparison to 'in-the-shell' and introvert leaders. The leaders' positive vibes and vibrancy gets radiated within the team and this is possible only when the leaders' participation is intense and intimate. It is like a tug-of-war, when all hands are there the tug is stronger but if leader is only a cheer leader there is shortfall of two hands. When sweating bodies touch each other and leader is part of the team the vibes adds to the team spirit. Attitudes in such a scenario do make an impact. Participation provides opportunity to introspect the attitudes.

The attitude is an important facet of leadership, greater is the positivity of attitudes more pronounced are the leadership qualities and the personalities associated with attitudes. In actual terms the attitudes are mirror to the personality of the leaders. What I have observed in the corporate and Forces that attitude is defined and is considered as a dual dynamic of 'good/bad and positive/negative attitude'. The various components and variety of attitudes which a human-being posses and which have bearing on the personality of the leader cannot be ignored or lack of it taken in its literary meaning, all actions of the leaders are governed by the leadership attitudes and the dynamics of the functional environment. Attitudes are temperament and outlook dependent thus it will have various scale, degree and intensity which can be gauged from bad to good or negative to positive.

In this chapter, I have covered the 'Attitude' which is an important facet of the personality of a leader; it plays a very important part in the process of application of leadership qualities and command of troops/men. Isolated and fixed mind approach towards 'Attitude' is detrimental towards absorption of leadership attitudes and training of the leaders in management of their command. To conclude this chapter, I want to quote Dennis Waitley, *"The winner's edge is not in a gifted birth, a high IQ, or in talent. The winner's edge is all in the attitudes, not aptitudes. Attitude is the criterion for success."*

More than attitude the ego is more prevalent in both Forces and the Indian Corporate. Attitude is more linked to the position of ego and it is for this reason that there are many fault lines in interpersonal relationships and work management, ask any common man his inference of attitude is related to the degree/level of ego. This is one of the neglected field of personality development both in Forces and outside forces and it is for this very reason aspect of negativity is more associated to the word 'attitude'. Every human-being is born with attitudes and how these are developed to create a positive impact on the others and the environment is a matter of concern, to make this happen the attitudes have to be enriched and aptly applied to achieve successes both in personal life and professional fields. Attitudes are adaptable thus repertoire can always be enlarged.

> *"Leadership is practiced not so much in words as in attitudes and in actions".*
>
> —Harold S. Geneen

10 Risk Taking

"Actions speak louder than words. In the days to come the Goddess of Victory will bestow her laurels only on those who prepared to act with daring."

—Heinz Guderian, Achtung-Panzer

An exceptionally important facet of leadership is the risk taking ability. Capability to take decision on 'risk' is an integral part of command/management. There is no task which is not without risk. Tasks factored predominantly with changing variables have direct risk applicability, where propensity of changes are higher the risk taking is more frequent. Whereas the tasks which have less variables or more stable factors the elements of risks is less. The equation of risk is dependent basically on the degree of fluidity in situational forces and volatility of variables on which the said situation is dependent. Risk will always be inherent to the content of any task and courses to any action. In actuality where the outcome is uncertain or whenever anyone venture into the unknown or where possibilities and probabilities cannot be determined to an exact degree, then one is bound to take risk. Another aspect of taking risk is associated with the need of the job, to quote Mark Twain, *"Necessity is the mother of taking chances"* and this phrase very aptly makes it clear that risk is part of performance and result.

The attitude to play safe and perceived outlook of "where it is, as it is" have become very prevalent both in the corporate and Armed Forces. The dependency and remaining within the proved and tested operating procedures/systems and applying of set matrixes has become tools for play safe. For example in automated and mechanised industry this factor is somewhat relevant as the variables are constant and fixed with very restricted influence of human behavior/changing environmental factors. But in case of industries/organizations where variables are not fixed, fluidity in operations exists with changing ground factors at functional levels; the factor of risk is coexistent. Thus risk taking is an important facet of leadership qualities and cannot be ignored.

Leadership in itself is having certain quotient of risk element, thus the factor of risk taking in the decision making and execution is part of the nuances of command and its responsibilities. Inert leadership is always counterproductive and adversely affects the faith, belief and dependency of the men under command. Life as such is full of risk, then how can there be leadership without risk. Risk in itself is a word which puts caution and it is this mental hypothesis which makes human-being avoid risks and irony is that same human-being inadvertently takes the unknown risk in day to day activities. The basic instinct of survival compels human-being in taking chances; it is a matter of interpretation of this instinct to develop the attitude of taking risk. Fear of risk thus is a prevalent factor due to perceived uncertainty of the outcome.

The aspect of gamble and risk must be clear in the mind of the leaders. Mostly people confuse between the two, in gamble outcomes are based on supposition where as in risk the outcome is known or anticipated. In gamble the individual believes in the factor of providence and destiny, the complete processes from planning to execution is based on assumptions, the hypothesis is never on sound footing. Whereas the risk is process based, it involves deliberations, analysis and planning for contingency. Taking decision to go through with the risk is the most difficult part of leadership, it is not only the leader who is involved but the men under command who have to execute the task also get affected by the decision and thus their willingness to go with the decision of risk taking must be the part of risk consideration.

Changingsituations,fluidityinoperationsandinconsistency in combat variables/factors make risk taking compulsive in Armed Forces. This involves the complete spectrum from decision making of the commanders to the operators on the field. In a combat environment the windows of opportunities are of fleeting in nature and very constricted in time and space, apt exploitation of these opportunities demand certain amount of risk taking. Windows of opportunity are never constant, neither sequential nor part of any planning and does not have any contingencies. Timing is the crucial factor and leaders are expected to first identify and then exploit it, therefore taking risk has only two options, take advantage of the opportunity or fore going of the opportunity, ultimately the question is of consequences or gains vis-à-vis loss. Spontaneity is the very essence if one decides to take risk.

I have been witness to the leadership from the lowest level to the senior officer/management level, I found that there is lot of hesitation in risk taking and this is mostly in the cases which are beyond the scope of fixed matrix/assembly line concept of tasking. The aspects which were predominant are the issues of self vis-à-vis organization, responsibility vis-à-vis accountability, clarity vis-à-vis ambiguity in the vision, compartmentalized working environment vis-à-vis freedom of action, domain sensitive responsiveness, nervousness of operating on new turf and fixation to "fixed/shift or timed work culture" when the employee thinks let someone else do it "my time now is over". These create a sense of hesitancy. Junior leaders thus become senior dependent and looking back over the shoulders syndrome is prevalent in a big way and the seniors on the other hand do not want to disturb the calm "where it is, as it is". At senior command/management level the tendency of deliberations to hold on to decisions at times makes risk taking tentative.

Risk taking is a knack and it requires mastery, thus one has to study, analyze and accustom oneself with risk taking. To quote T S Eliot, "Only those who risk going too far can possibly find out how far they can go." Unless one ventures into it one cannot gauge the positivity of risk taking. Courage to take risk creates the trust, belief and willingness of men to follow the leader. Here I want to highlight three idioms which makes it clear why risk taking is necessary:

- *"Pearls don't lie on the seashore. If you want one, you must dive for it."* —Chinese proverb. Nothing comes on the platter, when one strives, takes the risk and bears the pain it is then a person is able to achieve. The best is beyond the reach and risk is part of the challenge.
- *"Take calculated risks. That is quite different from being rash."* —General George Patton. Risk is not gamble; it is known and exists in the task, one has to be prepared to accept risk.
- *"Necessity is the mother of taking chances."*—Mark Twain. All tasks/jobs have inherent risk factors; the decision to take risk is therefore a necessity. Doing the job/task in itself involves taking risk.

Risk and Their Types

There are two type of risk taker, one who is not involved in the decision making of taking risk but is an active participant in the event and other is the one who is making the decision of taking risk and is responsible/accountable of the outcome of the decision. In both the scenario the leaders are involved, therefore the leader cannot be absolved from taking decision or participate in the conduct of/or be part of the operations. Risks basically is part component of any task, some risks are inherent and hidden, or risk is the part of the process, or risk cannot be ruled out in totality in any of the planned task or there cannot be any task which does not have scope for opportunity and windows to improve/accelerate. Therefore risk taking will always be there *"One cannot refuse to eat just because there is a chance of being choked"* —Chinese Proverb explicitly explains that risk is a necessity.

The risk can be categorized depending on the degree of involvement of the leaders and the type of task, in other words it is involvement and outcome ratio which is an important element of risk in decision making or taking the risk. I have categorized types of risks as:

- *Calculated Risk*: Here the leaders analyzes the task and the risk involved, detailed input of the task and associated parameters of risk are available , appropriate appreciation of the risk and the associated factors are carried out to derive at logical deductions with contingent/alternate courses of actions. The risk and it likely fallouts are worked out and contingencies prepared. This type of risk is termed as intelligent or calculated risk. Question now is how to take intelligent calculated risk? It is when leaders clearly identifies the risk involved and plans and prepares to maximize the prospect which would enhance the scope of successful accomplishment of the task/mission but minimizing those risks which are detrimental. The confidence to take such risk depends on availability of accurate inputs and dependability of the systems. In intelligent or calculated risk the uncertainty and certainty of the opportunity is taken into consideration and proportionate anticipatory precautions are catered to minimize the risks; accordingly the plans are worked out. Probability and risk ratio in such type of risk is low as the leader is prepared for taking the call on risk; the extent of risk and success is maximum in this case. You can also call this type as 'measured risk'.
- *Inherent Risk*: This is a known risk and is inherent in the task/job. All parameters of the risk are defined and to negate the

risk men are trained and equipped. The complete process has inherent component of risk at varying degree and stages. Decision to take risk does not exist but participation in the task itself is risky. Here the certainties of risks are known factor. Mentally all participants are prepared to accept the risk, like 'neutralizing of ticking IED' or 'leading the troops across the enemy mine field'. Here one is compelled to take risk; there is no backing out once the leader and the team have venture into the operation. The degree of risk taking ranging from moderate to high is proportionate to the task, target and the dynamics of field of operations. However, this type of risk is best handled once the level of discipline is high and obedience to command is definitive.

- *Unwarranted Risk*: When the leaders acts precipitously, without sufficient information or without taking time to think or thoroughly understanding the consequences or not carefully going into the analysis of the presented situation he/she is said to be taking unwarranted risk. Unwarranted risk is more of a gamble and dependency on the providence is predominant. The lack of preparation and detailed analysis of the task makes/compels the leader to become unnecessarily cautious/conscious of the uncertainty as all actions are based on anticipation. In this scenario the leaders acts without taking the time to minimize the risk involved. The degree of risk is high vis-à-vis chance of success in such a scenario is low.
- *Impromptu Risk*: This risk is not part of the course of action but is impromptu by nature which crops up due to unanticipated changes. Can also be termed as unprepared risk. In the planning and execution process the factor of uncertainty is very restricted due to the standardized procedures and actions. The risk is impromptu due to abrupt changes in situation, corrections/modification to plans or certain uncertainties creeps into the set objective during the process which had not been catered. The fault line in the process in such a scenario will compel the leader

to take the decision to initiate certain actions to bring back the process onto the track. Leaders in such a scenario have to intimately monitor the process and keep contemplating the likely occurrences of events. The risk and event components of the process are interrelated factors, these runs simultaneously till the target is achieved. Another aspect is the fluidity in the operational situation which creates impromptu space and time, which have to be compulsorily addressed to keep the plans on the tracks to reach the desired objective. The ratio of certainty to uncertainty of risk correspondingly decides the frequency of pop up of impromptu risk factors in standard or contemplated operating procedures

- *Progressive Risk*: It can be further divided as start course risk, mid course risk and end course risk, as the course progresses, the risk aspect keeps progressing. The risk taken at the start course provides the momentum, whereas the mid course risks provide stability and sustainment, and end course risk guarantees maintenance of speed to ensure success. This type of risk is usually taken to carry out the start, mid and end course corrections or when evaluating the progress of the courses in retrospection, certain risk have to be incorporated to achieve the planned target. The factor of anticipation of risk is constant, calculative and certain. The involvement of the leader is very intimate in the process of planning and execution.
- *Opportunity Risk*: Risk taken to create a window of opportunity to be exploited to achieve the desired objective or meet contingencies which have retarding effects. Here the leadership quality of courage and boldness plays an important role. The leader is aware of the risk and the consequences. When an opportunity is being created with an option of risk, the decision is deliberate and well planned. This type of risk attributes more when the leader is striving for success or there is holdup in the operations. The aspect which the leader must master are patience to

lookout for opportunity, take initiative to initiate actions which can create opportunity and when presented with a opportunity to take decision to exploit it, in all these risk will always be predominant factor.

- *No Risk:* Play safe syndrome is predominant. There are leaders who are so career conscious that they want to 'toe the line' of least resistance, there is a saying "If your life is free of failures, you're not taking enough risks", thus the question of risk by such leaders does not arise. For such leaders I would like to quote Dr APJ Abdul Kalam, President of India, *"My message, especially to the young people, is to have courage to think differently, courage to invent, to travel the unexplored path, courage to discover the impossible and to conquer the problems and succeed. These are great qualities that they must work towards"*, to succeed risk has to be experimented. I have been very allergic to such leaders they are the biggest irritant but other thing is such leaders also do well in life and career as they believe in 'smile up and kick down' philosophy to please their seniors, a piece of advice to such leaders and I think the quote of Theodore Roosevelt, 26th President of the U.S. is very apt and relevant *"Far better is it to dare mighty things, to win glorious triumphs, even though checkered by failure than to rank with those poor spirits who neither enjoy much nor suffer much, because they live in a gray twilight that knows not victory nor defeat"*.
- *Experimental Risk:* This type of risk one can afford to take. Experimenting with the new prospect, putting in play new ideas and exploring new opportunities are the risks that one can afford to take. In experimental risk the degree of cautiousness is more predominant. Moreover the aspect of trail method of risk management does exist in this category of risk taking. In such cases, the percentage of failure is very low, while the rewards of taking risk and success are greater. A risk is an event that might happen at some point,

once it happens; it is no longer a risk, but a problem, which is required to be managed. If the leader is able to master this then experimenting with risk will not remain taking chance with the risk.

- *Non-affordable Risk:* This type of risk one cannot afford to take. In this case, the consequences of making a mistake while taking a risk would be too enormous. Taking risk in such a scenario becomes detrimental or counterproductive. There is a difference between non affordable risk and no risk. Irrespective of the demand of the task no risk is taken, whereas in non affordable risk one is willing to take risk but the project does not permit risk taking. In such circumstances it is better not to interfere in the process e.g. defusing an activated bomb/IED. The risk in such a scenario is inherent, however the contingencies are very well worked out, alternatives are well planned and persons handling are well trained and equipped. In such process the parameters are well defined and precision in execution is the only terms of reference.

However risk taking in decision making, execution of tasks and taking responsibility on its fallout is not a very common phenomenon when it comes under the ambit of professional employability. Here I would like to again quote Dr APJ Abdul Kalam, President of India *"Thinking is progress. Non-thinking is stagnation of the individual, organization and the country. Thinking leads to action. Knowledge without action is useless and irrelevant. Knowledge with action converts adversity into prosperity"*, thus risk taking is a necessity if one is desirous of success. Effective leadership requires sound judgments and the ability to make the correct decisions. A leader must use judgment to bridge the gap between knowledge of the known and the appreciation of the unknown to arrive at valid conclusions. During this process a leader must weigh the risks against the odds to determine his or her decisions. Common sense also plays an important part in risk taking, it is said use of risk requires the common sense without it there is no sense in taking risk and then repenting. Risk taking is a process of judgment and depends on the character of the leader, thus risk takers can be categorized as rash, high, calculative, moderate, low, play safe and no risk taker. If we juxtapose the type of risks and the category of risk taker, we would find varied characters and trait combinations in a leader and certain aspects which are dormant can be developed during the process of leadership practice.

In my opinion, one cannot standardize the quantum or quality of risk takers. Risk taking is not an instinct but mental appreciation of the options depending on the ground realities and situation, where the factor of applying one of the contemplated options to resolve the problem is examined and which has the maximum possibility of success is applied based on the level of perception of the leader. Thus risk taking is always calculative but the degree may vary. Experience of the success ratio in comparison to the risk which had earlier been experimented also plays an important part in risk taking; this can have both positive effect of self-belief and negative effect of tentativeness. No human-being is a blind risk taker, thus risk taking is an ability and can be very much be developed. In some cases it is extrovertly visible and in some cases it is introvert and dormant and gets activated depending on the situational considerations at the time of decision making. What actually matters is the timely appreciation and the indulgence in application of the decision to take risk.

Why Risk Taking?

This is very academic, still I am covering to bring out/highlight certain issues which I felt that a young leader must understand the significance of human psyche and associated factors of aspirations to achieve. The question is why one should take risk, there are number of theories and explanations. However, I feel the basic human instinct to survive makes a human-being to experiment with risk and all other factors/reasons are secondary. The will to survive and to prove the leadership competency, the leaders have to develop all the requisites of risk taking ability. The reason why one gets into taking risk is attributed to:

- *Desire for Achievement*: This is very common behaviour for any human-being; the desire to achieve makes an individual to attempt risk. This attitude gives drive to the intension of achieving success, determination and capability to bounce back in the event of reversals/ risk not paying the anticipated dividends. Besides being personally or professionally beneficial, taking risks at times may be a necessary step towards pursuing success. The yearning of achievement in itself makes people think of taking risks. In order to assure success a person may try out something new or probe the unknown and in doing so take advantage of the presented opportunities by taking risk. To accomplish the task or attempt to use the opportunity provided in reaching a desired objective or the desire to stand out when others have failed compels a person to take risk. Desire to achieve makes the person to try out ideas and fathom or test his/her reach; this in turn creates resolve which gives boost to the self-belief and motivates the leader in taking risk. Change and growth is part of desire, if one is not growing then correspondingly the desire is absent, I am of the view that "nothing in this world will ever stay the same, change is bound to happen", thus desire will likewise has to change and to make this change to meet the desire one has to venture into taking risk. Desire to achieve has to have certain limits and must be ethical, should be within the capability and at no point it should be over ambitious. Over ambition creates tendency to gamble and result in rashness.
- *Meet the Target:* When a person has set a target then to meet the date lines he/she may have to take risk and/

or in the case when operations do not move as per plans and the desired target is likely to get out of reach then the person has to experiment with risk to achieve the target. Thus in the contingency of the target not getting fulfilled, the said person in order to maintain the self-esteem or keep the commitment made will take certain amount of risk. Risk to meet the targets may be in form of opening an new avenue, opportunity to explore the new ideas, acquire benefits of new machine and live up to the credentials and creditability of meeting date and timelines. In combat environment time to address the target is also dependent on natural phenomenon's which directly influences the combat planning e.g. phases of moon or high tide or weather conditions etc and in order to exploit the opportunities provided by such factors taking certain amount of risk gets automatically factored in the planning and execution.

- *Factored Risk:* In the conceptual thinking and planning, the leader within the framework of the functional responsibility has to factor risk or the risk on its own gets factored depending on the operational parameters. This can be said to be the nontangible risk and the individual does not have any choice other than to go through the motion and indulge in the risk as warranted by the plans. The conceptualizations of plans depend on two aspects visualization and appreciation of the fallout. The conceptual planning and application/conceptualization of the plans in itself will have certain elements of inbuilt inescapable risk; such risks are mostly addressed as part of logical application of the overall concept. This can be termed as compulsory risks and has to be indulged.
- *Accountability:* This is one of the factors which in its entirety gives impetus to accepting risk to accomplish the set target. Taking risk provides opportunity to stand out and to present oneself as a true leader. Taking risks may be a necessary step in actively pursuing success for which

the leader is solely responsible and accountable. When it comes to taking risk one cannot ignore the fact that in order to achieve a conclusive and guaranteed accomplishment of the assigned task, he/she in the process of decision making has to visualize prospective risk factors. The accountability factors make the person work out contingencies to address the fallouts if any and in doing so underwrite risk.

- *Passion Driven:* The passion to achieve, to prove oneself, set records or accomplish a task as challenge which has been a failure earlier and/or take the task as a personal challenge, such undertakings does create adrenaline in risk taking to make the success more than an achievable phenomenon. Risk taking may not only benefit the career-path where one is already on, it may actually open up avenues and possibilities to the passion driven person. Passion makes people experiment with risk.
- *Appetite for Risk:* Some people are born to take risk; they are adventurous by nature and are willing to experience risk. The person believes in taking chances. While risk taking without doubt is very personal, it doesn't occur in a vacuum either. One has to prepare oneself to take risk and be aware of the possible fall-outs. In this scenario one just cannot throw out a plan without seeing the whole process and visualize what the end can be or look like. However, taking a chance is very much a part of decision making which is by habit becomes compulsive in this category of persons. Such people believe in adventure and experimenting with risk.
- *Rising Adrenaline:* The level of adrenaline in a human-being keeps varying; confronting situations gives an impetus by boosting the level and when it is at higher level it compels a person to take risk. Adrenaline prepares the body to react to danger, it plays a very large role in the will to fight or flight reaction. The situation may be such that an adrenaline reaction compels one to experiment with risk. In combat situations the sudden burst of adrenaline does

make the officers and their teams to take risk to achieve a held up task or exploit the windows of opportunity or taking advantage of the fleeting moment.

- *Developments:* No two situation can be same, thus application of template in fluid situations is never possible. In undertaking a task, the process of execution passes through a defined path but as the volatility is never constant certain changes and non factored variable developments keep taking place. These series of developments creates number of windows with varying speeds and provide opportunity to exploit and/or gain an advantage. Thus risk taking becomes compulsive in such an environment. Non willing person in such a scenario cannot avoid the risk and has to take the decision either to go through the process or move out of the task. There is no other way out here; one has to try out the risk.
- *Reputation:* Certain personality has a fixed reputation of compulsive risk taker; such individuals will keep taking both calculative and reasonable risk to prove their credentials. Leaders with this quality are always bold in their approach. When a person's reputation is based on past successful endeavours/achievement and is at stake, he/she tries to follow the same parameters of risk taking to achieve the present desired target. Making risk an 'opportunity' to succeed is one of the ways of projecting the personality or meeting the expectation of the men under command/team, more so as the team has developed certain faith and trust on the leader based on his/her past performances. Both reputation and personality in this case is dependent to the extent how often the leader has given the opportunity to risk and the success ratio thereof. An important factor in leadership is how the leader takes the challenge of the risk, leaders differ in their perception and willingness to take risk thus the tendency to assume or avoid risk does have an impact on the process of risk taking. Risk and its application is effective in two ways

firstly how long it takes the leader to make a decision and secondly how much is the confidence level in taking the right risk. Therefore the reputation of the leader as daring and successful makes risk taking compulsive and these calls for adjustments in the personality projection of living up to the perception of the observers/team. Risk taking has three dynamic variants these are high, low and no risk. The approach and personality of leaders in risk taking is directly related to degree of proactive tendency and the level of confidence. When both the ratio are high then it is high risk taking aptitude, if both are same it is calculative risk taking , when either one is low and the other is moderate it is low risk aptitude and when both are low it is no risk aptitude . There can never be any permutation or combination in type of aptitude, as risk is a single factor. In conclusion I would like to quote a Japanese Proverb *"Fear is only as deep as the mind allows"*, thus perception of risk is how we perceive fear.

- *Loyalty:* Commitment to the organizational interest, honour, ethos and values makes risk taking an obligation to loyalty. The obligation to loyalty is one of the factor wherein order to meet the aspirations certain quantum of risk inherent to the organization's risk appetite have to be undertaken. Here the likes/dislikes to risk are not an issue and there is no scope for such considerations. In order to live up to the set expectations and to be successful the leader is compelled to take risk, it is this element which makes the men to risk life to achieve the desired target.
- *Experimentations:* The urge to experiment makes a leader to try out the 'risk'. The basic issue in this type of scenario is that the objective is known but one does not know exactly how to get to the desired results. Thus experimentation with risk is one of the ways to meet the desired objective. The person here has to be positive and firm with his/her resolution of 'I want to be successful'. Another dimension of experimentation is trying out new ideas and equipments

and both are used as force multipliers to achieve the positive results. This human tendency of experiments compels one to take risk.

Why Leaders Should Take Risk

So far in general I have discussed why one has to take risk and what the associated factors are. Now, the question arises why should the leadership take risk? The circumstances/conditions which make an individual to take risk or create the need to take risk have direct bearing on the technique of leadership practice. Basically, risk taking is the associated factor in distinguishing and making a distinction between the leaders and their type. A leader who runs from risk taking or remove himself/herself from the associated accountability thereof will lose credibility and create a divide in the trust and belief of the team. A leader has to understand the necessity of taking risk and till such time he/she does not move out of the safe and comfort zones, will never be comfortable with volatility of operations or handling of contingencies or taking mid course corrections on the fault lines and managing success. Leaders cannot be happy with stalemate or being a drag or being a pushover. "Only those who risk going too far can possibly find out how far they can go." is equally applicable here, this is an often said phrase in Forces and in 'approach to life' the Indian proverb which is very commonly quoted "until one does not enter the water the depth cannot be fathomed", these aptly elucidates the spirit of risk taking. There is a definite imperative of risk and I believe that it is the survival instinct which makes the leader to venture in risk taking. Why must the leaders take risk? Some of the reasons which I attribute are:

- *Creates Opportunities:* Taking risk creates opportunities; this in turn increases the prospects to take on bigger role/responsibilities and opens up new avenues. Faith of the management/superior officer on the leader gets reinforced and the opportunity provides the space thus opening up the scope for job enlargement/professional enhancement. Risks give a leader an opportunity in trying out new strategies, carryout process refinement and enlarge the spirit of ingenuity. Professionalism comes from opportunity and risk provides exposure. General Douglas MacArthur very aptly described the value of risk and opportunity *"There is no security in this life. There is only opportunity"*, taking risk to exploit opportunity guarantees security to life, professionalism, enhancement and success.

- *Confidence Building:* Risk breaks barriers and increases the confidence level. Risk generates confidences which makes a leader innovative, try out ideas, experiment with options, creates new benchmarks, gives impetus to forward thinking and boosts the level of motivation. A confident leader will venture into the unknown areas to find out better solutions to any problem. Risk is a mentor; it helps the leader in making aware of his/her limitations, reach, latent potentials and provides the scope to improve and develop the leadership skills.
- *Stand out:* Taking risks provides opportunity to stand out and to present oneself as a leader. Risk takers always stand out among the crowd of contemporaries; successful outcome of an assignment brings admiration and trust. A good risk taker has leadership standing and men under command develop confidence, this in turn makes commitments and involvement reciprocal to the generated confidence level on the leader's credibility, faith and trust.
- *Learning:* Risk taking brings growth. One learns from risks, the lessons brings confidence, builds courage to try out new ideas, and gives a boost to self-belief and confidence. The habit of risk taking makes one demanding professionally; this attitude compels the leader to acquire better knowledge to understand the dynamics of the assignments. Prudent risk takers will always be personally accountable of their decision and its outcomes – feeling the

glow when it goes right and the pains when it fails – but what matters the most is to learn from the risk, improve and indulge again; this is a continuous cycle of developing the acumen of taking risk. Learning during the profession plays an important part, and with regard to risk 'How much one learns from taking risk depends on how often one takes risk', as each risk has something new to teach.

- *Overcome fear of failure:* The fear of failure is a major roadblock to success. Fear of failure is the single biggest obstacle that prevents the leader in venturing into risk, to quote Winston Churchill *"Play the game for more than you can afford to lose... only then will you learn the game"*, till we do not venture in taking risk one cannot realize the value or learn to take risk. Failure is only failure to the extent one see's it in that way; failure can be made stepping stone to venture into risk. Leaders have to consider the failure as relative nuance of experience to overcome the fear. The desire to achieve has to be backed up by taking risk. Fear of failure and not taking risk actually in itself amounts to taking risk of foregoing or exploiting the opportunity which would have had a definite positive impact. Thus the misconception of avoiding risk need to be first eliminated, 'Failure is not the opposite of success but a stepping stone to success' so is 'risk is not a path to failure but a way to exploit opportunity'. *"The time to take counsel of your fears is before you make an important battle decision. That's the time to listen to every fear you can imagine! When you have collected all the facts and fears and made your decision, turn off all your fears and go ahead!"* General George S. Patton rightfully elucidated the fear factor, fear is there till such time you are not into the risk, once you are in it one has to forget fear and for fear any leader cannot waste opportunities. In war right opportunity seldom comes and is very rare.
- *Force Multiplier*: "Success won't fall in your lap - you have to pursue it". Besides being professionally beneficial, taking risks is a necessary step when actively pursuing success or

meeting the goal or where others have failed risk provides opportunity to achieve success. Risk opens up avenues, gives impetus to adrenaline of adventurism, develops the sixth sense of anticipation and improves the sense of alertness to exploit opportunities. However the risk must be based on logic, common sense, judgment, capability of absorbing the fallouts/results, professional competency to handle the presented opportunities and anticipation. As I have earlier said, risk is not a gamble, one has to prepare for risk; it is an impetus to professional growth. It is a force multiplier.

Effective Risk Takers Attributes

The effective risk takers have certain attributes and characteristics, these can be developed. Risk is unavoidable and one has to live with it, one thing is certain that is if you want to reach your true potential without risk it is not possible. In the range of the leadership techniques, risk taking is an integral part of success management. Risk taking is not taking a chance; but a matter of understanding, practice and discipline. Risk involves coming out from the comfort zone and doing something differently. The risk taker is not a total greenhorn in the field of profession, but with experiencing and experimenting risk acquires certain level of professional common sense or acumen and the attitude of daring. Risk taking is not necessarily a knee jerk action – it combines understanding of the professional imperatives, strengths to bear reversals, ability to bounce back and compatibility with the team/group dynamics. Risk taking must go hand in hand with the relationship matrix of 'work, machine and the people'. Risk taking is a behaviour/attitude, a process and which has no set matrix; one can learn to get better at it. I am listing certain attributes which I feel a leader can develop, these attributes are felicitators in taking decisions on risk:

- *Stable Emotions:* A person who can face the reality is said to be emotionally stable. The degree of maturity is higher in emotionally stable person; person with this attribute possesses capability to understand the nuances of the task and its related outcome. Stable emotion makes risk takers to control annoyance and anger, these facets are not very common in emotionally sensitive man. Self-control and cool composure is important aspects of emotional stable risk taker and this can be developed as a personality trait. This attribute makes risk takers have control over their nerves and before venturing into the realm of risk taking weigh all the consequences. The art of self-control must be mastered by emotionally sensitive risk takers who at times are very impulsive by nature. The negative factor which must be guarded by emotionally sensitive person is that they usually breakdown on setback and in the process lose control over the situation, more than one contingency must be planned by such person to maintain the momentum of the confidence level in risk taking and maintain stable emotions.
- *Common Sense:* Understanding the situation, timely initiation of action of immediate response without waiting for orders, using self-retrospection of logic in consonance to the professional knowledge or acumen gained and keeping the actions within the purview of regulations or established norms and practices, the person is said to be using common sense. Persons possessing this attribute are ideal risk taker, they knows how to use the situation, are calculative, logical and exploits the windows of opportunity in the interest of the task. Sound common sense is based on degree of awareness, level of professional competence and being aware of nuances of the task. Person with common sense does not gamble with the risk. Shrewdness is must for common sense, as this makes the risk taking more pragmatic and sensible. Common sense therefore is:

- o Knowing of what, why and how
- o Knowing of limits
- o Knowing the rules and laws
- o Knowing the likely outcome
- o Knowing where do you stand
- o Knowing where to look for support
- o Knowing the team
- o Knowing yourself and your reach

- *Orthodoxy:* Leader with this attribute is conforming, hard working, diligent, conscientious and serious. He/she follows the rule book and is moralistic by nature. Good part of such person with this attributes is persistency, they do not give up easily, and this makes them a calculative risk taker. Attribute builds belief in values, ethos and regimentation, and the desire to up hold these gives impetus to self-esteem and pride, which in turn compels him/her to take risk to obtain the desired target/goal. Risk takers with this attribute are thorough and meticulous by nature. Rigidity must be avoided as it makes the risk taker speculative.
- *Boldness:* The person is said to be bold when he/she is adventurous by nature, is enterprising, can take on sustained stress, is experimental by character and is unrelenting. Person with this attribute does not wait for opportunity to present itself but makes use of the presented circumstances to meet the goal/objective. He is raring to take risk and does not waste any time when presented with an opportunity. Person with this attribute leads from the front and shoulder responsibilities. Does not sulk nor passes the buck when it comes to taking the decision to accept the risk. This attribute can be developed by sustained exposure to nuances of the job, practicing prudency in decision making and take the challenge of risk as integral part of the assignments/task.
- *Self-discipline:* Leaders with this attribute are controlled; understand responsibilities and works within limits,

well aware of their capability, very ethical and enduring by nature. Person with this attribute is not impulsive nor is in a hurry, very deliberate and weighs pros and cons pragmatically. Follows rule book but takes chances within the purview of their capabilities when situation so demands. Interest of the organization is paramount and is very dedicated to the assigned task. Does take risk when convinced that it is in interest for the accomplishment of the task. All actions leading to the risk taking are kept well under control and are regulated. Contingencies are beforehand worked out. In another word one can say it is an orderly risk taking. Person with this attribute does not give up easily and in case of success believes in proactive pursuit with the aim to exploit the maximum gains of the risk.

- *Self-Determining:* This attribute makes leaders resourceful, prefers their own decisions and are self-sufficient. Such persons have confidence, belief in the capability of the team and self and takes responsibility of their decision. They are self-assured and independent, very self-reliant, no-nonsense type and realistic. Quick thinker and never lets an opportunity go waste. To achieve and confirm the trust bestowed on them, such leaders are ready to take risk. While taking risk will weigh the outcome in its positivity, they are not rash but experimental by nature. Are in a habit of probing, thus deliberately weigh the pros and cons before coming to decision. They are very bold once they decide they will go through with the risk.
- *Passion:* Leader with passion is outgoing, committed; possess self-belief and dynamic by nature. Is full of enthusiasm and very dedicated. Obsessed with the task and carries out the task with vigour and élan. Readily accepts challenges and leads from the front. Passion for profession makes the leader with this attribute serious and highly committed; such person believes in personal involvement and the associated self-esteem. Risk taking

is considered as part of the job and taken in the stride as professional requirement/perquisite. Person with this attribute is willing risk taker in the interest of the organizational benefits.

Risk taking involves self-introspections at each level of task execution. The effective risk taker while getting into a decision loop of taking risk must ask certain questions and search for the answers to these questions. The answers will determine the degree of willingness/commitment towards risk. List can be exhaustive but there are certain rudimentary questions which in my opinion gives the leader the affirmation in determining the scope of risk to be taken:

- What am I afraid of? What is stopping me?
- What will I gain?
- What kind of information will help me to make calculated assessments before considering and/or going through it?
- What is the worst case scenario that can occur?
- What contingencies I have to plan or how will I handle the fallout?
- What are the possible opportunities that I will miss, if I do not react?
- Outcome of lost opportunities vis-à-vis worst case scenario?
- What is my experience telling me about this particular risk?
- What are the possible options available to me?
- What is my reach?
- How much further I have to plan?
- In case things do not move as anticipated on whom should I depend for any advise/help?

Once the leader gets the answer to the above questions, definite course of action will emerge which will facilitate in making decision to take the risk. When decision has been taken then there must not be any ambiguity in the mind or fear prevailing, as these will have retrograde effect. *"In war, you win or lose, live or die - and the difference is a flick of an eyelash"* quote by General Douglas MacArthur, opportunity gives you very limited space and time, that is why no windows of opportunity must be missed, a leader in Armed Forces have to take decision within the gamut of risk and its outcome to ensure victory, any indecisiveness and fear can be fatal. Risk taking is an attitude, one can learn to get better at it as one gains experience, develop the sense of understanding the dynamics of risk and apply it with common sense and ingenuity.

One thing I can say that risk taking becomes easier when the degree of security of job/service is high, this makes the person to experiment with risk therefore the fear of failure is relatively low. Where there is insecurity/risk of losing the job, people tend to play safe and avoid risk. The organization which has appetite for risk the aspect of security or insecurity of job does not arise. Risk taking must be accepted as perquisite of successful leadership and need to be encouraged. Where the failure/mistake is taken cognizance and gets reflected towards the credential of an individual, the experimentation with risk is impinged. I found very few players who are ready to take risk, and most toe the line of status-quo syndrome, follow the safe matrixes/templates and/or depend on the senior's attribution or directives. The culture of the organization in accepting risk as productive essential is also an important driving force towards proactive and bold leadership. The enlarged scope and latitude given to experiments with risk to the young managers is a very important aspect of increasing the confidence level in risk taking. The developments of the leaders and risk taking have to be endorsed as an important personality buildup by all levels of command/leadership positions.

Tips for Building Risk Taking Habits

- Come out of the comfort zone to do anything differently.
- Risk-taking is an attitude and one can learn to get better at it.

- Develop appetite to take risk.
- Disassociate the perception of the worst from actual probabilities.
- Failure is relative to the extent one sees it that way; it is one step towards success.
- Life as such is full of experiments; do not fear to give risk a chance.
- The perceptiveness of success must be positive, avoid ambiguity.
- Once decided do not hesitate, go through - all out.

The risk taking is a mind game and as the level of professional competence, exposure, experience and confidence grows risk taking ability alongside also grows, as one starts taking right risk then venturing into risk becomes easier. What is of importance is - getting into the habit of timely and proper initiation of risk taking decision/practice. One thing is very definite that is success is never at the arms reach one has to pursue it and risk taking is part of this pursuit. In conclusion I would like to quote Dr APJ Abdul Kalam, *"Difficulties in your life do not come to destroy you, but to help you realize your hidden potential and power. Let difficulties know that you too are difficult"*. Till such time the problems are going to be encountered in the process of execution of tasks, situations are going to crop up with varied options to resolve the problems and this would give number of choices to the leadership to resolve, in doing so the leader has to take the call and this is what I call is the risk, thus risk must not be feared as it will be co existing with the hope to achieve and survive.

> *"It seems to be a law of nature, inflexible and inexorable, that those who will not risk cannot win"*
>
> —John Paul Jones

11 Leadership Mannerism

"Those who command themselves, command others".
—William Hazlitt

To behave in a manner conformable to what is right, proper, or appropriate is said to be mannerism. The behaviour and mannerism are important facets in establishing the leader in the environment. The leadership mannerism and the related comportments are the basic foundation on which the trust between the group and the leader is established. In this chapter, I want to bring out certain qualities which are the basics of leadership mannerism and contain both personal behaviourals and demonstrative comportments which have direct influence on the perception of the leader by their men under command.

Leaders have to decide on what standard code of mannerisms' to build their behavioural comportments; this is to a large extent will depend on the functional environment and its dynamics or the work place culture. Indifference on the part of the leader in defining the approach towards commanding of the men and the unit will definitely reflect on the outlook and the personality, this in turn will get reflected in the mannerism and behavioural comportments. Indifference creates negativity in the environment and when the same gets reflected in the leader's mannerism there is loss of confidence, conviction and belief between the team and the leader, in

Armed Forces such leaders are termed as snobs, here I would quote Dr APJ Abdul Kalam, President of India which reinforces my opinion, *"Those who cannot work with their hearts achieve but a hollow, half-hearted success that breeds bitterness all around"*. While genetically certain predispositions of character and manners will be existent, their impact will depend upon an individual's interactions with the surroundings and what has been imbibed from the environment to enhance the personality. Personality reflects the genuine nature of character and mannerism brings acceptability to the personality.

Therefore, a leader has to make a place by way of conduct and personal values. *"What a man is, depends on his character; but what he does, and what we think of what he does, depends on his circumstances"* said George Bernard Shaw, thus the leader adapting to or in the process of making place has to project the character in its right perspective to make the environment conducive to the acceptability factor, this helps in establishing the reputation and defining the credibility of the character of the leader. Basic factor in any sphere of operations is the 'Human factor' and most important aspect of this factor is establishing functional compatibility, the leadership mannerisms and comportments does influence the development of faith, trust and dependability equation. Successful command of the team will depend how the said mannerism and comportment are regulated and synergized within ones personality and projected in its right perspective so as to have positive impact on the discernment of character of the leader among the men under command. It is a matter of application to build certain mannerisms and comportments to reinforce the attributes of the recognizable character. The aptitude of interpersonal relationships is much dependent on the mannerism. Officer who identifies this and makes it as an approach to command will be the best manager of human resources. There are traits, qualities, methods and techniques which a leader adapts to influence the team, but the most effective skill is the use of functional comportments and personal mannerism to lead the team. Thus what really makes the difference in style of leadership and degree of success is manners and the behavioural conduct.

The personality of the officer to a large extent is manner and comportment dependent and gets determined through certain compulsive vis-à-vis controlled attributes of characters which are dependent on the demand of the environment and attunement equation between the leader and the team, the mannerisms and comportments are very much part of the conduct which makes the equation tenable . Thus forced personality or giving a false persona of behaviour and manners will be misleading, counterproductive and corrupting the perception of the men under command, such persona often masks the true nature of an individual. Such endeavours do not stand for long as dramatization of personality cannot be sustained over a long period and at the same time maintain the same consistently. Behavioural patterns and the consistency is one of the important factors which give a definite shape to the mannerism and comportment. Positive outcome results in personality enhancement whereas negative outcome results in widening of the gap in the relationship equation between the leader and the command.

The leaders have to respect values, beliefs, ideologies and ethos of the organization in which he/she is serving; mannerism does have to uphold these without any personal prejudices. Acceptability of leaders' manners and associated demonstrative behavioural comportments within the gambits of environmental/organizational demand, are important factors which the leader must consider. Therefore, what are the mannerism and comportments which impact the maximum when leading the men into the battle/combat? I have tried to list out few of them which in my opinion have positive impact on the motivation and morale of the men.

Basic Comportments for a Leader

Ethics: The leadership projection is character dominant and which in turn is directly influenced by ethics which the leader upholds. One of the primary tasks of the leader is to inspire and lead from the front; this is possible only when the leader possesses high order of ethical standards. Leaders are bestowed certain responsibilities which are personal, professional and social , all these responsibilities are guided by ethics and depends on the standard of the imbibed and groomed mannerism and comportments of the leader. The leader must be adaptable and understand the organizational ethics, which must get reflected in his/her behavioural comportments; this is an add-on to the personal ethics and must reinforce the ethical principles of the leader. Organizational ethics in my opinion is always the bench mark on which the personal ethics must be juxtaposed; this will give definite direction to the mannerism and comportments depending on the leader's conviction. Thus ethics is a fundamental component of leadership practices and leaders are the one who have to set the expected standards. It is compulsive on the part of the leader to maintain the ethical standards so that he/she can set an example as well as provide creditability to the personality. The perception of the men under command is positive about the leader when ethical credibility gets established and reinforced by mannerism. The ethics play an important role in building the trust and faith of the team/unit. Some observations on effective ethics which are battle winning factors are:

- *Personal Ethics:* The leaders is gauged by ethics which he/she displays, if one gets into listing the personal ethics it is a long one. The leaders when confronted with testing situations and the degree of tentativeness in their attitude, behaviour and temperament during the execution of the task is on higher side in such situations the ethics becomes vulnerable, what matters is how does the leader muster his/

her conviction, live up to the troops confidence and carry the team into the assigned mission. In combat situation, the most important primary component is the willing participation and selfless commitment of the team/group. The ethics which matters the most in obtaining this type of support from the team/group and must be projected as the leaders ethical characters are:

- *True to oneself:* Personal integrity and honesty are two important facets on which the leadership stands. Leaders have to be transparent when it comes to projecting personality and character. Dramatics does not stand too long as the same is gauged by the men under command and creates distrust. Originality and being true to oneself bonds the personality, meet the expectation of the team and sincerity towards the purpose.
- *Close to reality:* Appreciating the reality and 'down to earth' approach brings the leaders close to the team/group. It makes the leaders and men relationship stronger. Participative leadership is predominant when this ethics is stronger. Transparency during dealings and personal interaction bridges the gap between the team and the leaders and builds the confidence levels.
- *Egalitarianism:* Not being parochial when dealing with people and giving equal opportunity to each member of the team/group. Cohesiveness of the team is largely dependent on this facet. Taking the team into confidence and fairness in the dealings creates conducive work environment where willing participation is the hallmark. Men expect their leader to be fair and understanding, single act of glaring injustice, error of judgment or prejudicial inclination will be detrimental to the influence. Men must trust their leader in order to follow him
- *Show of Authority:* Leadership cannot be forced upon or thrust down upon the men. No man is a leader until

his appointment is ratified in the minds and hearts of the men. Authority must always be used rightfully and within the purview of the appointment. Misuse of authority and blatant use of service privileges of the appointment makes the link with the team weaker. Men under command tend to exploit the leader's ego for wrong reasons.

- *Treat with Dignity:* Leaders must treat men under command in the same way as they want to be treated by their men. Ethics of respecting the self-respect and the self-esteem of each man is important comportment which enhances approachability, bonding of relationship, belief in the leadership and the acceptability factor.
- *Fairness and Compassion:* A leader must have compassion and take care of his or her people. Leaders must display empathy "put themselves in the other person's shoes". An awareness and responsiveness to the feelings is crucial for fairness. It is not that a tough and hard task master cannot be fair and compassionate, what is important is not being prejudicial and biased.
- *Reverence:* Blatant criticism, sarcastic remarks, insulting or any action to cause disrespect to seniors or contemporaries or colleagues or subordinates is not ethical. Reverence is giving value to each individuals self-respect, feelings, sentiments and loyalty and it is the leader's ethical responsibility to give credence to each team member's right to dignity. Disagreements or contentions are part of professional nuance and must be taken as leadership responsibility to get these settled and in doing so self-control predominantly within the expected ethical standards must be ensured; here the leadership comportment demands sensibility and giving appropriate credence to the self-esteem of each member of the team. Self-respect of each man must be valued and respected.

• Professional Ethics

This aspect is as important as the personal ethics. Integrity, selflessness, credibility and courage are very much part of this, which the team/group expects from their leaders. Respect and commitment to the organizational principles, vision, values and the ethos does give an impetus to the personality of the leaders. This in turn makes the ethics of the team/group stronger. Ensuring compatibility and establishing matching frequency with that of the team is wholly dependent on the professional ethics. Thus professional ethics basically amounts to how does a leader command and sustains the integrity, commitment and cohesiveness of the team/group:

- *Professional code of conduct:* Ability to take timely decision, during adverse situations standing by the side of the men/team setting personal example, not breaking under prolonged stress and roughing it out with the men, 'mess-tin sharing' attitude, never grumbling or getting grumpy when odds are against and understanding towards the feelings of the team/group are some of the expectations men have from their leader. Ethics binds the leaders and the men. Stand alone leaders can never motivate the team/group. Professional commitment, involvement and integrity are the elements of code of conduct to which the men under command look for and accordingly gauge their leaders. Willing participation and commitment of the men under command depends on this ethic.
- *Honesty towards the Profession:* Being honest towards the profession is an important element of ethics. Casualness and non committal of purpose have diminishing affects on the faith/trust imposed on the leader. Potential of any person is not gauged by competency, suitability and capability in relation to demand of assignment and sustainability of performance, but also the honesty towards the profession. Honesty to profession is

synonymous to truthfulness, uprightness, candour, commitment and selflessness. These all combine to make the ethical standard of the leaders in honesty and it matters the most in battle.

- *Exemplars of the Profession:* The leaders not only have to lead by example but also demonstrate certain actions which make the people follow. *Firstly,* such demonstrative action which creates confidence in the men under command. *Secondly,* consistency in approach, decision making and involvement, inconsistency and adhocism must be avoided as this creates reluctance in the team/group. *Thirdly,* examples of commitment should always subsist in all actions and must be persisted; any deviation will break the trust of the team/group. *Fourthly,* leader's originality, initiative to exploit opportunities and shouldering responsibility of the initiative/decision irrespective of the outcome are great binder of trust and faith. *Fifthly,* level of tolerance is indicative of level of stress bearing capability, breaking down at any point will be retrogressive and break the momentum, and thus leader has to ensure that level of self tolerance and that of the team is optimum. *Sixthly,* underwriting the genuine/honest mistake encourages initiative and induces commitment in the ranks but what is of importance is leader's prudency in recognizing genuine/honest mistake. *Lastly,* lack of orders is no excuse for inaction, leaders have to take initiative and make a call, and this is one of the important aspects of leadership ethics which must not be relegated at any cost as it will create an impression of ambiguity in the character of the leader. "*The willingness to put oneself at risk and seeing the possibilities in a situation while others are seeing the limitations develops trust of subordinates*" the leaders must exemplify this ethics to the command.
- *Tolerance:* Degree of willpower, determination to persevere in face of odds and the physical stamina to

sustain hardship determine the tolerance level, when it is same as that of the team or better, it creates positivity in the working relation of the leader. Positivity of approach, acceptance of risk, responsiveness towards the cause and sensitivity to the interest of the organization is largely dependent on the tolerance level. Leaders having a positive mindset and are willingness to persist, gives confidence to the team. Tolerance improves the aptitude of adaptability, leaders must learn to get used to and adjust during adverse situations. Keeping cool and being patient in face of the odds brings spirit to bounce back and improves fighting spirit in the team.

- *Knowing the Team:* When the leader knows the individuals those who make up his/her group or team the level of trust, confidence and closeness increases. On the other hand, individuals who make up the team/ group if they understand their leader, the trust on the leader increase. When the leaders identifies themselves with the group in every possible way the group cohesion is said to be high and the team/group associates itself with the leader, the solidarity and esprit- de- corps in the team is proportionately higher. When the whole group/team becomes a single entity with a high level of solidarity and esprit-de-corps, and is inspired by the enthusiasm of the leader it is then that optimal relationship equation is said to be existing, in such an environment team/group and the leader jointly take initiatives. When the team/group is briefed properly, are well-instructed, well-trained and has high level of proficiency, the leader finds confidence in achieving the targets/overcome hurdles effortlessly. Calling men under command by their name, knowing them and giving due regards to their profession gives boost to their morale and creditability to the leader's concern towards his/her command, this age old leadership practice is now slowly waning out.

• Courage of Conviction

This is the righteous behaviour of a leader which has a direct influence on the team/group performance. Leaders must have courage of conviction to follow the paths based on spirit of righteousness and morale courage in achieving the desired goal. Courage of conviction is nothing but the morality to do/say what one thinks is right even when others may disagree. Here I would like to quote General Douglas MacArthur *"Last, but by no means least, courage - moral courage, the courage of one's convictions, the courage to see things through. The world is in a constant conspiracy against the brave. It's the age-old struggle - the roar of the crowd on one side and the voice of your conscience on the other"*. The right conviction must be supported by three fundamental perquisites and these are transparency, fairness and honesty. Calling 'spade a spade' is very difficult and it requires lots of guts, it looks simple but takes lot of courage to do so. When the men under command are aware that they are going to get a fair deal from their leader, the trust and faith level sees corresponding increase. At the level of decision making this comportment in a leader is a must have quality in carrying out right deductions, inferences and arriving at selecting the right courses of action. The considerations in arriving at the right decision making gets confirmed to the appreciation of the actual ground situations by the leader and truthful reporting by the command, the courage of conviction thus is at both ends. General William Slim (Viscount Slim) said, *"If you want to talk to men, it doesn't matter whether they are private soldiers or staff officers, if you want to talk to them as a soldier, and not as a politician, there are only two things necessary. The first is to have something to say that is worth saying, to know what you want to say: and the second, and terribly important thing, is to believe in yourself. Don't go and tell men something you don't believe yourself, because they'll spot it and if they don't spot it at the time, they'll find out."* Thus I feel the fundamental perquisites of courage of conviction are:

- *Transparency:* Every member in the team has great expectation from the leader that is they want their leader to be transparent in all dealings. Favouritism and notion of 'only selected few' in dealings are very retrograde factors and making it obvious is totally counterproductive as it adversely affects the spirit of existence in the team. Transparency is not only related to dealing with men under command alone, it also equally applicable to the capability of the leader in handling of the team, leader's behavioural comportments and maintaining 'open book' approach. Transparency permits group and the leader to carry out right retrospection of each other thus facilitating in increase dependency and the resultant mutual faith and trust. The transparency increases the scope of rightful approach with no baggage of conscience at both ends.
- *Fairness:* This has some similarity with transparency but is different when engaged as a behaviour, the basic fiber of this comportment is being just, practical and reasonable. The courage of conviction and its application in man management is correspondingly proportionate to the degree of fairness demonstrated by the leaders in handling of men under command. Justified selection/appointments of men, ensuring the need of equal opportunity and openness in expression of views are the key elements in ensuring success in any operation; this brings willing participation and respect for leadership decisions. Evenhandedness and impartiality in approach/dealings gives standing to the faith and trust of the men on the leader. Fairness in thoughts, actions, processes, results and approach is directly linked to the morale fiber of the leader. In essence, the virtue of fairness establishes moral standards for the unit/group and the leaders. Fairness requires that the leaders:

- Handle all similar situations similarly and with consistency.
- Handle each member of the team each and every time without undue favouritism or fixed prejudice.
- Do not spare defaulters. All should be handled in the similar manner with same intensity.
- Conscientiously gather and verify facts, provide an opportunity to explain or clarify and give chance to amend. Follow up with corrective measures.
- Not take unfair advantage of mistakes. Educate the team so that mistake is not repeated.
- Understand the rights, interests, and perception of all team members and carefully evaluate. Keep everyone on the same plinth and approach each with an open mind.
- Assert that everyone will receive an equal opportunity and be honest in implementation.

o *Honesty*: The honesty in the leader's mannerism and comportments basically are the sincerity of intention and honesty of purpose. One thing is very certain, that is men under command can easily see through any pseudoism or artificiality in the factor of honesty. Honesty in itself can proportionately increase or deteriorate/dilute the level of faith and trust. Men prefer an open minded leader who is able to mould well with the team/unit and who in turn carries the team. The values, ethos and principles of the organization plays an important role in fixing the relationship quotient between the leader and the men but honesty on the part of the leaders gives the impetus to building the relationship. The acceptability of the leaders depends on the factor of sincerity of intention and honesty of purpose.

- *Sincerity of Intension*: First thing which all men under command gauge is the intension of the leader.

What does the leader want and in the process what will he/she likely to achieve? When this becomes clear then tasking of the team and willing participation becomes easier. In Armed Forces this may not be fully applicable as 'order and obey' is more predominant factor but in corporate sector this is an essential aspect of establishing leadership. Intension must be well defined, transparent and in all its fairness without any hidden agenda; it also must be ensured that it is in consonance to the organizational objective and within the purview of the task. Any kind of doubt or ambiguity is going to create an environment of suspicion between the leader and the group/unit. Intention must be crystal clear and should be known to the men under command, any mala fide or duplicity or deceit or sham in intensions and subsequently the same getting exposed during the course of action or accomplishment of the task will definitely bring down the level of faith and trust of men. Good faith of a leader is reciprocal to the degree of honesty of intention and same is also applicable in officer – men relationship. It is an important aspect of confidence building measure between the leader and the men.

- *Honesty of Purpose*: Very important aspect of leadership is to convince the men the purpose. When the purpose is corresponding and aligned to organizational goal/common team objectives, the leader's trust and faith is higher. Selfish ulterior motives in purpose are counterproductive. Leaders have to stand up for what he/she believes; honesty starts with being original, authentic and true to the command responsibility. Honesty of purpose is about communication, making men under command to know the facts and the purpose of the assignment/task. Endeavour should be to never give half story or try to hide the story; the level of confidence on the leader is higher when actual is shared.

- *Uprightness:* Conscience is central to the leadership. Uprightness in belief and in performance of duties gives value to the leadership in terms of reputation and creditability. To be conscience, one must be willing to do the right thing even when it is difficult, have desire to do what is right within the law and for the best interest of the organization. The leaders with conscience will always be sure of what he/she is doing and ensure that the organization's name is never tarnished by any act contrary to the ethos and values. Conscience does make a difference in style of leadership and degree of success. Conscience as a trait is a guide to leader's behavior and mannerism , this in turn helps in:
  - *Developing Bond:* Trust and faith, between the leaders and the team/group is the bonding elements. Conscience of the leaders brings men under command closer, as the level of confidence increases. Fairness in approach, going by the rules and ensuring the rightful dealings makes the bond stronger.
  - *'Practice what you Preach Attitude':* Consistency in the conscience by the leader makes the team/group believe in the virtues and values of the leader. Virtues and values correspondingly add to the degree of conscience, the leader with virtues and value will always have adherent followers. "If leaders practice what they preach, men are more willing to entrust them with their career, security, and sometimes with even their life", the values and virtues add up to create principles of life and

the leaders have to exemplify the same in words and action every time, that too consistently. Self-discipline is another aspect of this attitude; leaders have to be very mindful of his/her acts and must be within the gambit of the assigned duty and in consonance to the values of the organization in vouge. Spontaneous manners and behavioural comportment rather than displaying disguised self is generally appreciated and this increases the creditability of the leader.

- *Constructive Interactions:* Communication is the best source of interaction. It is the best bridge of gaps. Consistent and constructive communication creates bond and beliefs, a simple gesture of calling a worker by his name and asking 'I hope everything is fine at your end' makes a world of difference in the inter personnel relationship. The second aspect is the participation of the leaders – compulsive participation is part of the task whereas the preferred and associated participation is expected from the leaders by the team/group, this improves the interaction levels. Leaders have to keep themselves associated with both the task and the team/group expectations. Leading by example is another every effective measure of constructive interaction. Under such circumstances the team/group likes to be associated with the leaders.
- *Professionalism in Approach:* Competency of the leaders is directly proportionate to the professionalism in approach. Leadership is a profession, how well can a leader project self as a professional that matters. Men under command respect a leader who is professional and demonstrate professionalism in all dealings. Proficiency and professionalism brings trust and belief in men and builds confidence,

the commitment gets an impetus due to the trust and confidence. Leaders have to keep themselves updated with the latest in the profession, improve the level of competency and maintain sound proficiencies; here I would like to quote Field Marshal Sam Manekshaw, Indian Army *"What are the attributes of leadership? The first, the primary, indeed the cardinal attribute of leadership is professional knowledge and professional competence. Now you will agree with me that you cannot be born with professional knowledge and professional competence even if you are a child of Prime Minister, or the son of an industrialist, or the progeny of a Field Marshal. Professional knowledge and professional competence have to be acquired by hard work and by constant study."*

- *Morale Courage:* The courage of convictions and courage to see things in their right and ethical perspective is termed as moral courage by General Douglas MacArthur. Moral courage constitute three rudiments i.e. being honest and true to oneself and the command, willingness to meet danger or adversities in spite of fear and risk to life, ethical in attitude to distinguish between what is right and wrong and be able to always stand for what is right. Most important facet of moral courage is to take responsibility of the decision taken and not to pass the buck. Standing for the righteousness, committing self without any prejudice to get your men through the adverse situation created due to leader's own fault, never leaving the men in face of danger and never palming off the blame for failure or getting involved in the blame game also tantamount to having high degree of moral courage. Higher is the degree of moral courage more will be the faith and trust on the leader. The ultimate of moral courage is - when cornered at the last point of desperation still being ethical - then you are the leader with guts.

- *Rationale in Approach:* Leaders whose actions are based on reasons rather than emotions/beliefs, is practical, who understands the ground realities and believes in logical course of action, is said to be rationale. A leader who is down to earth is more preferred by men. High talks and flashy leader may create an impression but when it comes to following the leader into battle, faith and trust of the men is more on a rationale leader. Conscientiousness in behaviour and mannerism of a leader is important to give authenticity to the endeavour of rationality in approach.
- *Attitude of Resilient:* The ability to bounce back, recoil and recuperate and capability of withstanding shock are some of the qualities which the men under command look for in their leaders. Resilience is the capacity to withstand stress and strain especially in an adverse situation, regaining the lost ground, adapting to the situation to exploit the given opportunity and spirit to rebuild/reconstruct again after a reversal. These qualities in a leader motivate the team/unit and make it stronger and it requires lot of moral courage to be a resilient leader. Faith and trust also to a large extent is dependent on the quality of resilience in the leader. Team/unit resilience on the other hand also builds up the capacity of resilience of the leader, thus it is the proportionate level of confidence on each other which optimises this attribute. The quality of resilience keeps improving and can be developed with the experience and type of relationship existing between the team/unit and the leader. Factors that contribute to resilience are:

- Self-belief and positivity, understanding your strength, abilities and weakness helps in resilience building. Considering oneself as resilient (rather than as a victim).
- Close relationships with the team/unit. Understanding each member of the team/ unit and knowing their pulse, this builds confidence, develops trust/faith levels and helps in rightful employment of men.
- The ability to manage strong feelings and impulses. Self-discipline, control over the reactions and positive personal example gives impetus to the resilience of the team and improves the leader's confidence.
- Leaders must display enthusiasm and be expressive and energetic. Enthusiasm is infectious and influential; it develops the spirit to fight back.
- Good communication skills and officer - men relationships.
- 'I am in control' attitude and demonstrating confidence to recoup - are two very important factors which boost the resilience quotient between the team and the leader.
- Logical and effective problem solving aptitude builds confidence level and trust. The will to resolve and to fight back is predominantly dependent on the ability of problem solving.
- Leader's competency/professional efficiency and professional acumen are the factors which improves the quality and degree of resilience. This also in turn enhances the team/unit resilience.
- Seeking advice, help and resources does improve the level of resilience. Assured

support from the organisation, seniors and command improves the degree of resilience.

- Finding optimistic meaning in life despite difficulties or adversity.
- Build incredible stamina and sustaining power to accomplish difficult missions. Habit to fight at all cost.
- Remain alert and stay focused. Anticipate contingencies.

Personal Mannerism

Leadership ability doesn't automatically come with the title of the appointment; the title only bestows authority and power. Thus leadership has certain defined responsibilities towards the task/job, men under command and the organization. The responsible mannerism is one of the focal point among the leadership qualities. Leaders thus have to be ethically disciplined and well mannered to make acceptance viable and authority effective. It is not only the competency of the leader which matters, what is of importance is how does the leader behave and the manner in which the behaviour is projected. It is not necessary that a competent leader will always be good and acceptable. Manners and etiquettes thus correspondingly get projected from the attitude and the outlook of the leader. The importance given to the mannerism by the leader gets reflected in the command of the unit/team and responsiveness of the men to the orders. Etiquette helps the leader to value other human-beings where as manners are important as it is associated with character and the behaviour of the leader. Good mannerism gives contentment to the men of being associated with the leader. Certain manners which have impact on the thinking of the team/group and closeness in working relationship are:

- Return back compliments appropriately.

- Reply when someone speaks to you.
- While speaking have eye contact.
- Appreciate others.
- Listen to people.
- Speak explicitly and clearly; do not mumble.
- Be punctual and do not keep people waiting.
- Have neat, tidy and organised work place.
- Do not keep people standing, always offer seat.
- Avoid dressing down of individual in front of others. Do not embarrass and humiliate with intentions.
- Avoid fidgeting with phones, texting and emailing, etc. while men are trying to carry on a conversation or waiting for audience.

Professional Mannerism

Professional mannerism is another important aspect which the leaders must practice and follow this helps in gaining confidence of the team/group and project leadership personality in the right perspective. Leaders have to ensure that the manner and conduct are value based and demonstrate true professionalism in management of operations, to do so foremost the leader has to be aware of professional responsibilities, understand the nuances of the task/mission, plan the professional commitments, apprehend the values of people skills and maintain a high degree of professional integrity and honesty. Developing of charismatic personality and special talents to inspire people to follow is directly linked to good professional mannerism. The issues on which the leaders must pay attention are:

- Control tempers, demonstrate self-control and convince people with rightful projection of arguments.
- Apt and good decision must not be clouded with ambiguity/doubts.

- 'Buck stops here' attitude must be prevalent but give opportunity to discussion and introspection.
- Check small things and go into details.
- Share credit openly.
- Remain calm, cool and patient. Keep personal problems away from the team/group.
- Be demanding but also understand the capability and capacity of each man under command.
- Optimism is a force multiplier, be cheerful in adversity. Give hopes but never break aspirations.
- Communicate with all, do not side track anyone. Be approachable.
- Maintain a proper focus in all activities.
- Set standards and ensure these are attainable.
- Do not exploit others weakness or be cynical.
- Encourage competition against standards rather than each other.
- Allow subordinates the freedom to exercise initiative.
- Establish accountability but remember your responsibility.
- Show confidence in subordinates, encourage participation.
- Encourage, motivate and reward.
- Underwrite honest mistakes and give opportunity to improve.
- Follow 'need to know' notion, must share decision making with subordinates.
- Be prudent while tasking and be clear with 'must do' and 'should do' of the directives.
- Listen to your subordinates and seek ideas.
- Demonstrate concern about the welfare of subordinates.
- Practice what you preach.
- Avoid self-boasting.
- Do not undermine the seniors or their decision, reflects poorly on the personality and integrity.

In this chapter my endeavour was to bring out behaviour patterns called mannerism, the conduct what we expect from our leaders. There are certain repetitions of characters/traits/ behaviours/attitudes in this chapter which I felt has optimal influence on the mannerism and comportments of the leader. Leader is always a role model and his/her manners are under scrutiny. When good manners are practiced it has impact on the psyche of the team or group in particular and the work environment in general. In Armed Forces manners of leaders is part of grooming. Basically good manners help in:

- Putting people at ease
- Creates a favourable impression.
- Makes one's personality attractive.
- Encourages relationship and professional engagement.
- Builds self-esteem.
- Creates positive vibes in the body language.
- Makes others and self feel good.
- Good Manners do not cost anything but gives good returns.

In the corporate sector, the aspect of leadership mannerism is very provisional even though stress is given on development of leadership mannerisms and behavioural comportments but leadership practise is restrictive by its very nature of compartmentalized concept of application of leadership and interpersonal relationships. Acquiring of leaders gets predominance instead of nurturing leaders and we find ample number of instances especially among the junior leadership cadres who have risen to leadership position by rapidly changing assignments by job hopping without developing the leadership skills or aptly adapting to leading the team/ group, the scope of unfit leader thus always exists in the corporate sectors. Till such time continuity is ensured in the leadership, there is going to be the tendency of adjusting/ accepting mediocre leaders. Thus the leadership mannerism will be a casualty. Armed Forces have lot to offer here in terms of grooming and development of etiquettes, very many may argue that manners are forced; yes I agree it is forced that is how it gets imbibed and the conduciveness in the environment is created. Manners and etiquette cannot be dependent on personal wimps and fancies; it has to be uniformly applied discounting ego, seniority syndrome and the position.

"If a man has any greatness in him, it comes to light, not in one flamboyant hour, but in the ledger of his daily work."

—Beryl Markham

12 Communication

"Developing excellent communication skills is absolutely essential to effective leadership. The leader must be able to share knowledge and ideas to transmit a sense of urgency and enthusiasm to others. If a leader can't get a message across clearly and motivate others to act on it, then having a message doesn't even matter."

—Gilbert Amelio
(President and CEO of National Semiconductor Corp)

"The basic building block of good communications is the feeling that every human-being is unique and of value." Being able to communicate effectively is the most important of all life skills. Initially I was avoiding this chapter as so many write up and views exists on communication, but during an interaction session in the management meeting I found that communication is very well understood at all levels but when it comes to actually communicating, there is lot of inhibition in the ways and method of communication and getting the point across for the desired effect/purpose. The problem is that 'good communication skills' is a word so overused yet many of us do not fathom the meaning and behavioural aptness involved in doing so.

Good language need not necessarily mean that one is a good communicator or oratorical skills makes a person a better communicator what actually matters is being a confident and amiable communicator, capable of establishing trust and maintaining a strong contact at all levels of interactions. Communication is not only verbal or written; it also encompasses physical gesticulation or the body language and the behavioural attributes. Effective communication is much more than being able to talk; it is also the ability to listen and understand others, to "read" and interpret body language and to know the best ways to get the points across. What actually matters in communication is quotient of influence and ability to connect.

With latest tools and methods of presentations of views and ideas being available yet we find that people fail to communicate, influence the listener and put the point across. Developing individual communication style, expressions, gesticulations and listening skills are essential if you want to communicate successfully and have a direct impact. In the Armed Forces the interpersonal communication is an essential element of command, day the young officer enters the barracks he/she starts learning the communication techniques. Communication is considered so vital that without which any commander cannot think of going into any operation. In the Armed Forces group cohesion is a very important element of operations and this is totally dependent on the degree of rapport built between commander and the men under command. Rapport, on the other hand, is a function of inter-personal communication in a group. Soldiers willing response is proportionate to the unflinching faith which he has on his commander, thus it is the morale responsibility of the commander to establish an altruistic relationship and this is possible when contact and communication is absolute. From the grooming days the officer is trained in communication, it may be the simple form of delivery of orders or complex issue of motivating the team to the spirit of 'Charge of the Light Brigade'. Thus in my opinion process of communication includes involvement, passion, association, compassion, empathy, statesmanship, oratory, understanding, intelligence and connecting with people.

Holdbacks in Communication

Barriers/impediments to communication can be many and classified under organisational, physical, cultural, linguistic, and interpersonal. The internet is full of illustrated examples of communication barriers, I am not discussing these. What I feel is the greatest impediment or holdback is the inhibition and hesitancy, this is what makes communication restrictive. In the Indian Armed Forces especially Army on commissioning an officer as per the tradition of the regiment is made to stay in the barracks with the men, secondly where the troops are region based an officer is made to study and learn their language and culture and lastly where there are mixed troops the national language is used and troops are made to undergo cadres to learn the language. This is basically done to clear the communication gaps and holdbacks. The barriers have been vividly explained in various books and articles, experiencing the Armed Forces and Corporate functioning I am describing certain actual holdbacks and barriers in communication which I found deserve a mention:

- *Intelligence*: The very first basic understanding of communication is to know which conversation/talk is going to trigger what reaction and this requires intelligence. The lack of basic common sense of what to speak or what not to speak or when to speak is one of the predominant factors of successful or unsuccessful communication. Clarifying own position, being confusingly diverse in outlook and opinion, excessive verbalization, shyness and being reactive are some of the facets of conversation which adversely effects the basic human conversation techniques. In communication, intelligence is directly related to accuracy, lucidity, precision and appropriateness to the purpose of communiqué.

- *Connectivity*: Establishing connectivity is related to influencing the other party, in case the party is not influenced then the connectivity is said to be not established. The connectivity is the quotient of conversational intelligence (C-IQ) and how the same is applied to determine the receptiveness in the spectrum of positivity, this is based on the content of the communiqué and assimilation of the content. C-IQ brings prudency in the approach to communication and facilitates the assessment of the sensitivity of the addressee. The connectivity is thus based on the high/low C-IQ and engagement between the communicator and the addressees. The other way of looking at it is how the communicator establishes the rapport with the addressee's/team. Till such time the matching frequency between the communicator and the addressee is recognized connectivity cannot be established in the communiqué. The other aspect is establishing the interpersonal connectivity, communication equation between the team and the leader plays an important role in establishing the relationship quotient and this is very much dependent on the degree of established mutual trust and compatibility equation.
- *Uncertainty:* The basic cause of uncertainty is vagueness in the thought (C-IQ), insecurity in the communicator, ambiguity and indecisiveness. An uncertain communicator will have gaps in communication and this will affect the interpretation factors of what is being said and what is being inferred. The degree of preparedness of the communicator is an important facet which determines the level of uncertainty. The personality and the associated body language to a large extent are greatly influenced by this factor.
- *Ego:* This is predominant in most of the human personalities and a great inhibitor in communication.

Maximum cause of gaps in communication is due to this factor. Communication is always a two way process thus ego has to exist at both ends. Communication is not about winning, it's about getting things done and one has to compromise. To be an effective communicator one must also be conscious of own bias, then the ego can be moderated. The complex of superiority and advantage of authority are two issues which are primary facet of ego, if this get influenced with bias then communication becomes a dictate and in communication this does not hold ground when human outlook/apprehensions matters.

- *Expression:* Most of the time we default when our expression and body language does not match the tempo and content of the communiqué. Mismatch in expression gives way to perception dodging and tends to lead in faulty interpretations. Many nonverbal signals that can easily be misinterpreted when the expression is mismatching e.g. aggressive attitude that may be intended by the communicator to display confidence can be interpreted as arrogance. On the other hand excessive gesticulation is seen as an attempt to hide lack of knowledge or a purposeful distraction from the principle purpose of the communication. Expression, body language or tone of voice should be aimed at giving stress on the importance of the point, to gain control over people/situations and in circumstances where there is a need to regain control of the conversation to create a more positive/effective environment. Expression must be considered as an aid to enhance the method of passing on the desired message.
- *Wisdom to Listen:* Communication cannot be a total monologue; it being a two way process certain space has to be given to the addressee. Thus patience and fortitude to listen is an important aspect of communication. One has to be very clear about aspects of interjections, interruptions, clarifications and projection; each has different listening and regulating/handling approach. To make the

communication effective the respondent quotient must be proportionate to the applied wisdom to listen. Most of us in the position of authority in the leadership gambit tend to dominate communication as one way process.

- *Identification of Communication Blind Spots:* The blind spots are psychological and behavioural, both are unique and unpredictable, thus quotient of compatibility, building relationship , acceptability of the communicator, behavioural reactions, acuteness of mindset, creditability and/or faith and trust factors of both the communicator and the addressees are the unknown areas and in reality are the blind spots. Thus the important issue is to fathom the actual depth of these before venturing into planning of the content of communiqué and the desired objective to be achieved/impact to be created. Attitudinal barriers to communication thus result from personality conflicts due to the inadequacy of capability to identify the blind spots. The human interest and awareness profile of the communicator therefore assumes importance in the identification process. Another aspect which I consider is equally important is the outlook and temperament; these are great blind spot fillers and can be modified to suit the situation.

The important arena in communication is the working communication. As leaders in Armed Forces, the proficiency in working/operative communication is given importance, it is often said who is good at it then leading the men into the battle is never an issue. I was always in agreement with this thinking. I have seen very many generals who were very good in paper work, when it came to applying it on ground and where the troops are active participants, these generals failed and on the other hand there are generals who could make the dead rise out of nothing through effective communication. Reading off the script is the easiest communication but not an effective one. Till the time the leader is not committed into the communication, it cannot become effective.

Must Have In the Leader

- *Ability to carry out Assessments and Appreciation:* The leader must be capable in carrying out the assessment of the emotion, mood, sensitivity and the impact effect of the conversation on the party. To do so leader has to carry out the appreciation of the content, objective and the desired assimilation. The assessment and appreciation will determine the scope of the communication and the method to be adopted to make the communication meaningful, assimilative and absorptive. This will facilitate in scripting the communication as per the requirement.
- *Personal Touch:* Leader has to be very particular when it comes to giving a personal touch to communication especially interpersonal communication. A distant or unconnected communication cannot build the communication bond, establishing bond is essential in all communication and this is possible only when the men have faith and trust on the leader and when personal touch is added it increases the creditability. Accepting the leader as 'one of their own' does makes a difference in the scope and acceptance of communication.
- *Positivity:* In all communication, the positivity factor must be predominant. The voice, body language, posture, gesticulation and eye contact with the audience must be creating positive vibes in the atmosphere. What I have seen is the first word utterance itself gives out the degree of positivity in the leader. Sarcasm, taunt, cynicism or mockery is a big NO, this makes the audience/addressee hostile, uncooperative, obstinate and stubborn and the worst part of it is the lack of trust and faith in the leader.

- *Communication Style:* Leader has to adapt to the language, communication culture and habits, communication emotions of the audience/addressee, this brings closeness and sentimental attachments. Leader must have his own communication style, the men when they are familiar with the leader they will accept the style, in this case the leader is expected to be honest with the communication and at no point of time should try to make fool of the faith and trust bestowed by the men. In my young days I have seen generals addressing troops with very strong accent of British 'Hinglish' and yet were very well understood and the language aptly assimilated by the regional troops. The style must cater for appropriateness of language in different contexts as crucial reference point. Effectiveness of style as a communicator is entirely contingent to adaption to different situations, different environments, different type of audiences and different objectives and purposes. Being a confident and amiable speaker set up trust with the audience/addressee and this helps in maintaining strong relationships. This is possible once the leader has a distinctive style which is different from the others.
- *Honest Communication:* This is one of the most important aspects of communication. Honesty in terms of purpose, intentions, objectives and meaning. At no point of time the communicator must underestimate the audience. Pseudo and artificial communication does not hold for long. The leader must not take any chance with bluff at the cost of losing the faith and trust. Here the leader has to ensure that neither fudged facts are put up, neither hidden agendas incorporated nor any ulterior motives be made part of the communication. The honesty encompasses both the personal and professional ones; this should be evident in the approach, emotions and conduct of the leader during the communication. No man is a leader until his/ her appointment gets ratified by the men and honesty in

communication relationship has a big role to play in this aspect.

- *Appropriateness of Language:* Control over the language is must, the language must be understandable, empathic, meet the context's requirement, convey to people clearly, simple but assertive and meet the personality of the leader. It must present the leader in the right prospective and in positive frame. Language must be such that the audience identifies themselves with the leader. In Indian Army, the leaders are trained to use the language of the troop which they are commanding, regional troops are used to set parochial pattern of language and until and unless they are addressed in the same tone and language the communication is said to be not complete. Thus context and type of audience does matter in use of appropriate language. Right phonetics gives the right meaning to the words used in the language, this can be region or state or area based.
- *Content of Communication:* Brief yet specific but the content must be simple, cover essentials and be useful. Long monologue must be avoided, communication is said to be effective till the time interest stands thereafter it is talking past each other. What is important is connecting with people. The contents of communications should not have gaps as fillers at times become counterproductive. The communication content is said to be more effective when it is 'We/Us' centric instead of much of 'I' centric. Another aspect is storytelling, this must be avoided no one is interested in listening to stories. Focused content is the best one.
- *Understanding Others' Point of Views:* Here we all go very wrong, as leaders we think that communication is mostly one way processes of passing orders, giving instructions, addressing men under command or reading out messages. But communication is one of the methods of establishing a

relationship, increasing the scope of approachability, assist people to find their place in ever changing environment or create collaborative environment of mutual functioning. Now to do this the leader must listen and understand others view points.

Communication is much more than initiating conservation, it is a gambit of creating a relationship and projection of the personality. In order to maintain contact quotient with the people, communication is a great filler of gaps that may exist in the relationship equation. From my observations I have highlighted certain issues which I felt makes the relationship responsive. If the men are clear of what, why, how and the leader bestows faith and trust on them, they would go more than half way to close the gap and establish bonding relationship. I used to always advice my juniors to clear off any biases, not to unnecessarily doubt people and never be sarcastic to make communication worthy. Once inter personal gap reduces the output proportionately increases that too more willingly at both ends.

Communication-Interpersonal Relations

This is the field which I want to deliberate upon, as I found people have lot to say but when it comes to implementation very few actually know about its efficacy and importance. I have found lot of gaps in both the corporate sector and the Armed Forces. Most of us in leadership are of the opinion that communication must be for the professional purpose, this is very much right but the human issue is the linked factor which cannot be sidelined or overlooked in totality. Thus communication must not be considered as mere conversation or passing on of thoughts or way of getting message across. The ability to communicate accurately, clearly and as intended, is a vital skill in interpersonal communication. The aspects which does influence the interpersonal communication relationship and which the leadership must consider to make these as part of their repertoire are:

- *Genuineness*: The genuineness of leader which influences the audience/addressee is the honesty of purpose, originality, concern, professional competency and the spirit of involvement/participation. Audience prefer total transparency in the communication and the communicator. Any communication which has iota of stratagem is fathomed very fast and this breaks the credibility of the communicator. Some dramatics in communication is acceptable as it creates interest but excessive is taken as sign of camouflaging the hidden agenda's this again makes the audience lose faith and trust. Genuineness is the personality and honesty is the founding character of this personality, genuine communicator actions are the indicators of genuineness. Therefore, the communicator must always keep themselves in the focus of the audience/addressee, this helps in building relationship.
- *Openness:* Communicator is said to be open when he/she is candid in expressing his/her opinions, sincere and straight forward. Alongside this the communicator must be approachable and can create compatibility quotient conveniently. Openness makes the leader creative, accepts new ideas and adapt to changes. The leader is forward thinking and well aware of responsibilities. The reticence brings closeness in the relationship and effectively fills the gaps both physical and psychological in the communication spectrum.
- *Credit and Encouragement:* Leader who shares and dedicates the credit of successes to the men under command and shoulder the blame of failure is highly regarded and adored. This makes the leader close to the command and encourages men to open up. The communication is facilitated with inspired acceptability of the trust and mutual faith, wilful obedience of command and

commitments towards the objective of the communication. Encouragements on the other hand make the audience's belief on the leader stronger and the communication dynamic. The communication in its entirety in this type of attitude is a filler of the gaps in the relationship and helps in creating the solidarity and *espirit-de-corps*.

- *Knowing People:* Knowing the person with whom communication is to be made is an important aspect of leadership. Leader who can effectively communicate thoughts, ideas, and feelings is better equipped for success both on the job and in personal relationships. Effective communication is much more than conversation; it is the ability to understand others, to read the reactions, interpret associated body language and to know the best ways to get the points across. Communication is said to be intimate when the communicator is closer in the relationship equation with the addressee. Best communication is when the addressee is addressed individually and to do this the communicator must know the addressee well and be able to make the communication adaptable to the discern frequency of the said addressee. Here, it will be prudent to quote Sun Tzu *"Regard your soldiers as your children and they will follow you into the deepest valleys; look upon them as your own beloved sons and they will stand by you even unto death"*, thus knowing the men under command makes communication effective and it develops a strong interpersonal relationship. "A good company commander will always call all his men by name", I always believed that, when men are addressed by their name the response level is very high, it is more better when the person is of knowledge that his boss just not only recognizes him but is aware of his family also - you call him by name and ask him how well his daughter did in her school exams - see the difference. Establishing the rapport is an important facet of communication.

- *Tact:* Knowing when to start and when to retreat is an art of communication. The art lies in appreciating the situation, tuning the communication technique, assessing the impact and the degree of absorption, knowing and understanding the physical and the psychological limits and the appropriateness of language in different contexts is crucial. Effectiveness as a communicator is entirely contingent on how one adapts to different situations, different environments, different audiences and different objectives. Little bit of common sense, lots of ingenuity and innovativeness pays good returns. The tact must encompass demonstrative assertiveness, judgement of emotions, situation based empathy, politeness mixed with aggressiveness, keeping the level of rapport at the positive level and awareness and respecting the feelings.
- *Confidence Building:* The amount of confidence the audience/addressee has on the leader and vice-versa does matter the most in any communication. The most effective confidence building measures are respecting of the self-esteem, mutual creditability, honesty in relationship, trust and faith and mutual supportiveness. When the proportion is proportionate to the desired perception of both the parties then the level of confidence is said to be high. The leader has to think of various confidence building measures like participative communication, recognition and credit to positive contribution, bestowing responsibilities, mutual trust and faith and boosting of the team solidarity , basically the aim must be to make the addressee realise his/her value and importance to the organisation. Basically what matters in the confidence building measures are the leader's imagination, common sense and ingenuity.
- *Mannerism:* Leadership comportment has a big role to play in the communication. From personal appearance to conduct the complete spectrum of mannerism does makes

an impact on the communication and the relationship equation. Everyone is eager to establish a relationship with a decent mannered person. Body language in communication is the part of mannerism; the leader must ensure no negative vibes gets transmitted due to negative gestures, facial expressions and attitudinal displays. Saying something and showing something will be interpreted in a varied manner and give rise to apprehensions in the minds of the audience, one has to guard against this.

- *Preparation*: Best communication is extempore, however for all to speak extempore is not easy. Extempore speaking is an art and one has to master it, it involves the sense of appropriateness; tailor the message as per the audience, good knowledge and suitability of the subject matter to meet the demand of the occasion, judiciousness in respect of use of words and expressions and lastly shrewdness in the approach. But for the rest it would be prudent to prepare for the communication, it is advisable to have the right script and rehearse the same, keeping a small note in the pocket can be helpful. Mental preparation is another important facet of communication, until one is not sure of what to communicate and visualize the temperament it would be creating among the people. A well prepared communication must cater fostering of interpersonal relationship as this will enhance the creditability of the leader and develop the faith and trust.
- *Be Brief Yet Specific:* No one is interested in story, what people expect is candid communication, straightforward, plain talking and specifics. Brief and yet specific communication gives a leader personality of man of words, this also bridges the gaps in the relationship. Knowing what interests the men under command is essential for the leadership and it is very important to hold the interest during the communication as this will facilitate the absorption of the contents. When the communication is brief and specific then the essentials get registered fast

in the mind. Communication is not gossip or chitchat and this must be clear to the leadership. When the audience is convinced of the purpose of the communication the bondage of interpersonal relationship automatically get proportionately enhanced.

- *Empathy*: Lastly it is the empathy which makes the communication meaningful. Understanding of the other person's feelings and emotions are essential of communication. Compassion and concern gives authenticity to the approach and is a great soothers in the communication, this brings bondage and acts as comfort. Developing empathy helps in better understanding and in effective responsiveness.

Communication is very personal and thus varies from person to person; it is an important facet of leadership soft skill. In an combat environment, the aspect of communication and the inter-personal relationship does gets arranged due to the very requirement of the operations, there are ample opportunities in combat which get created when both leader and men are found standing shoulder to shoulder in the same fox hole facing the bullets. Communication is an essential aspect of operations; the ambit includes, putting across of the essentials of the plans and maintaining of the cohesiveness of the unit/team to accomplish the mission. Lack of good communication is detrimental to the very cause. Thus communication is considered as an important element of Principles of War

In the Indian Corporate sector the situation is different, there is too much of compartmentalization and issues of multifold echeloned hierarchy, this dilutes the communication process thus creating the interpersonal gaps. Another aspect is the authority vested on the leaders at detachment/team/group levels, it is my personal observation and opinion that authority vested in corporate environment is very controlled one with little scope of initiative or experimentation. Leaders stick to their job, are confined to the work shift, are reluctant to venture out from the known turf and interpersonal relations are confined to the scope of the job. This makes the scope of communication restrictive. Professionalism is good but the personal touch to leadership is very restricted thus gets distanced from the grass root workers/technicians. Continuity of leadership is another factor, I feel this is more due to three facets of employments which are prevalent –lack of guaranteed continued retention vis-à-vis job hopping tendency, factor of continuity in employment and stiff promotional avenues and lastly frequent change in leadership cadres this is more so at the middle and junior management levels, in other word it is the stability factor and sustaining leadership. Therefore, the leadership in the Indian Corporate has to be more proactive in developing interpersonal relationship and good communication techniques.

In conclusion to this chapter few tip's some of which my senior's in Forces had given and some which I experienced, just jotting them down for consideration:

- Be confident of yourself and be well prepared. Must be very clear of the need of the situation/occasion.
- Be totally apolitical and do not display any biases
- Speak clearly. Don't mumble. Do plain and straightforward talking.
- Stay focused and be in eye contact. Don't do anything which can cause distraction or accept any distraction.
- Be brief. Don't over talk a point.
- Never allow the other person to lose interest.
- Never force yourself on the disinterested audience, wait for opportune moment or create conducive environment first.
- Never be in a hurry to conclude once into communiqué.
- Clarify and affirm yourself before committing, do not allow misunderstanding to crop in.
- Do not interrupt, be patient and listen, this will give you time to think.

- Arguments must be logical and fair, control your temper, never allow limits to be crossed and gracefully conclude without hurting anyone's sentiments.
- Stick to the issue at hand do not mix too many issues, tackle each issue separately.
- Speak and act with regard for the other person.

Communication has varied means and modes in today's world, the efficiency and usefulness is beyond doubt more effective as well as covers a very large spectrum. Yet personal and face to face communication has been found to be more effective when dealing with human resources. Communication is never complete until the feedback is personally received by the communicator and getting in situation feedback is the best way to know the effectiveness of the communiqué, here I would like to highlight an anonymous quote "What is the shortest word in the English language that contains the letters: abcdef? Answer: feedback. Don't forget that feedback is one of the essential elements of good communication".

> *"Leaders who make it a practice to draw out the thoughts and ideas of their subordinates and who are receptive even to bad news will be properly informed. Communicate downward to subordinates with at least the same care and attention as you communicate upward to superiors."*
>
> —L. B. Belke

Epilogue

Endeavour was to bring out certain observations on some of the important elements of leadership. The canvass of leadership is so large it is not possible to cover all the aspects, therefore decided to address the essentials which I felt the youngsters must master to establish themselves as leaders. The contents have been dealt in chapters with the aim of keeping them separate and independent. Leadership is a composite factor of humane elements therefore observations of various authors on the basic human psychic will be somewhat similar but differences will exist. I have shared my experiences so that the leaders reading this book can develop/enhance their skills and leadership instincts

The idea to make the attempt to jot down my thoughts came when I joined the Indian Corporate world after my retirement from the Armed Forces; I used to discuss with my son the difference in leadership in corporate and how managers/ junior manager took interest in establishing themselves as effective leader. My son was the one who suggested that I should pen down my observations and highlight issues which I have experienced during my command of troops or have observed during combat, this may help some of the budding leaders to develop their leadership instincts. Today he is not with me; publication of this book will be my gratitude to him and thus I have dedicated this book to him.

Writing this book I lived through my entire career in the Indian Army and my associations with command at various levels, visualizing incidents and episode of application of high quality of leadership, certain leaders those who really impressed me by their way of handling of leadership practice both during combat and in command of formation have been incorporated when discussing certain issues. I have time and again repeated certain qualities and traits in various chapters but these are relevant to the chapter in particular, the repeated qualities and traits are those which are 'must have' irrespective of the position and the practice of leadership. The quotations which I have used are from my personal collection which I had jotted down over the years from display boards, lectures and presentations during my service.

Another aspect which made me retrospect the leadership qualities when I compared the military leadership with that of the corporate leadership at the functional levels, I was of the opinion that touch of selflessness was lacking. Functioning in the environment of frequent shift in leadership cadre is a big challenge in the corporate sector; by default of job hopping the quality does get affected at the middle and junior management levels, this phenomenon does increases the scope of undesirable/unfit leadership getting into the system. Some of my corporate friends will vehemently counter my observations, for them I would like to quote a line from my collections "leaders are trained and neutered just exposure to the job or giving jumps in appointments does not make a leader". My endeavour therefore was to bring out the basic leadership qualities which get developed due to the consistency in the leadership cadres and the way it is neutered to make it effective. Identifying the potential leaders is a challenge for the management and developing the leader is their responsibility. Another aspect is that leadership cannot be without the 'reserve bench' otherwise there will be a void. The leaders, therefore have to develop leaders who can continue to maintain the momentum.

"Years may wrinkle the skin, but to give up interest wrinkles the soul. You are as young as your faith, as old as your doubt; as young as your self-confidence, as old as your fear; as young as your hope as old as your despair. In the central place of every heart there is a recording chamber. So long as it receives messages of beauty, hope, cheer and courage, so long are you young. When your heart is covered with the snows of pessimism and the ice of cynicism, then, and then only, are you grown old. And then, indeed as the ballad says, you just fade away."

—General Douglas MacArthur

Index